D1452802

Columns of Vengeance

Columns of Vengeance

Soldiers, Sioux, and
the Punitive Expeditions,
1863–1864

PAUL N. BECK

University of Oklahoma Press : Norman

Also by Paul N. Beck

The First Sioux War: The Grattan Fight and Blue Water Creek, 1854–1856 (Lanham, Md., 2004)

Inkpaduta: Dakota Leader (Norman, Okla., 2008)

Library of Congress Cataloging-in-Publication Data

Beck, Paul Norman, 1958–
    Columns of vengeance : soldiers, Sioux, and the Punitive Expeditions, 1863–1864 / Paul N. Beck.
        pages ; cm
    Includes bibliographical references and index.
    ISBN 978-0-8061-4344-6 (hardback)
    1. Dakota Indians—Wars, 1862–1865. 2. Dakota Indians—History.
3. Dakota Indians—Wars, 1862–1865—Personal narratives. 4. Indians of North America—Wars—1862–1865. 5. United States—History—Civil War, 1861–1865. I. Title.
    E83.86.B44 2013
    978.004'975243—dc23   2012046593

The paper in this book meets the guidelines for permanence and durability of the Committee on Production Guidelines for Book Longevity of the Council on Library Resources, Inc. ∞

1 2 3 4 5 6 7 8 9 10

To Hugh and Mary

Contents

Illustrations

FIGURES

MAPS

Preface and Acknowledgments

In the summer of 1862, Minnesotans found themselves engaged in fighting two wars. The first was an external war versus the rebellious southern states that had seceded from the Union to create the Confederate States of America, and the second an internal war against the Eastern Dakotas or Santee Sioux. Although the Civil War lasted longer and was vastly more important to the history of the United States, it was the Dakota War of 1862 that proved far more destructive to the people of Minnesota—both whites and American Indians.

Growing up in Minnesota, as I did, one learned early on of the Dakota War. As a child I visited many of the sites involved in the fighting and read numerous books dealing with the conflict. Later, while doing research for my dissertation, I encountered the diaries and letters of soldiers who had served on the Punitive Expeditions against the Sioux in 1863 and 1864. I found the information in these documents about the soldiers' experiences, family life, and views of the Dakotas to be fascinating, and I never forgot them.

It is because of those diaries and letters that I decided to write a book about the Punitive Expeditions. There are a number of sources that adequately discuss the expeditions. However, they all tend to approach the expeditions the same way, as a military campaign of the Indian wars: the army marched into the West, defeated the Sioux in battle, and then returned home. These sources were often from the top ranks, the official reports of the main officers and generals serving in the campaigns. While they provide an adequate coverage of the events, they leave key aspects of the campaigns untouched.

Although fought in the West against American Indians, the Punitive Expeditions were part of a larger conflict, the Civil War. The strategy and tactics of the campaigns were like those of the war back East. The officers and enlisted men, for the most part, had joined the army to fight against the Confederacy. Officers had seen their careers advanced, or in General John Pope's case damaged, by the eastern military campaigns of 1861 and 1862. Planning, supplies, reinforcements, and transportation for the operations in the West were all affected by events occurring in the Civil War back East.

Also not discussed in most sources is the massive impact the warfare had on all divisions of the Dakota people—Santees, Yanktonais, and Lakotas. For the Santees, the Dakota War and Punitive Expeditions brought them to the edge of national destruction, shattering and dividing them as a people and scattering them across the Great Plains from Canada to Nebraska. For the Yanktonais, one military engagement struck them as hard as Pearl Harbor and the events of 9/11 did the United States. The Lakotas, still smarting from their defeat in the First Sioux War, engaged the U.S. Army once more, growing in their knowledge of how to fight the whites and beginning a war that would eventually embrace much of the Northern Plains. Further, although the common view is that the expeditions were a complete victory for the military, this is not exactly accurate. The Sioux showed an ability to adapt to the artillery and small arms advantages of the army, fought a successful rearguard action to the Missouri River, made excellent use of terrain during the army's march through the Badlands, and scored numerous individual feats against the soldiers.

What also sets this study apart from early works on the Punitive Expeditions are the points of view of the common soldier and those Sioux caught up in the conflict. In doing research for this book, I read the books, articles, diaries, and letters of more than 120 soldiers who served in the campaigns. Often left untold is the Dakotas' view of these events. Personal narratives from the Sioux are more difficult to obtain, but those I have located, along with those of the soldiers, tell us much about the expeditions and add a human side to the conflict. By using a more "bottom up" approach, a richer, more complete understanding of the Punitive Expeditions of 1863 and 1864 and their impact on the participants emerges. For the soldiers, the campaigns remained a matter of revenge even after the generals and politicians claimed other reasons for the expeditions to continue. For the Sioux, the conflicts rained disaster down upon the Dakotas, many of whom had no desire for war; led to a devastating slaughter of the Yanktonais; and caused the Lakotas to be pulled into the fighting. Overall, the military offensives often struck the wrong targets among the Sioux, leaving one to wonder if the expeditions were necessary or just an opportunity for John Pope to use a military solution in order to redeem his career.

There are many people to thank for their support and assistance in the writing of this book: The staff of the Minnesota Historical Society, Greg Wysk and Jim Davis of the North Dakota History Society, and Ken Stewart of the South Dakota Historical Society for their help in obtaining the diaries and letters of the soldiers on the expeditions. Kristina Southwell, University of Oklahoma Library, and Starla Siegmund and Jenny

Baker, Wisconsin Lutheran College Library, for their assistance in finding much-needed materials. La Donna Brave Bull Allard for her help with the Yanktonais. Everyone associated with the University of Oklahoma Press, including Emily Jerman and free-lance copyeditor Margery Tippie, with particular thanks to acquisitions editor Alessandra Tamulevich for her guidance and support. My gratitude to Gary Kraft for his excellent maps. A very special thank-you to Bobby Reece, who encouraged me to start this project and got the ball rolling for me. Finally, as always, Pro Gloria Dei.

Columns of Vengeance

CHAPTER 1

The Coming of War

"WE . . . WERE IN A
STARVING CONDITION"

From the earliest settlements at Plymouth and James-
town, Americans had always been expansionists. Ever moving
westward, crossing the Appalachian Mountains into the interior
of the continent, they were driven by a desire for land ownership,
personal independence, and the idea of a better life. Independence from Great Britain only accelerated the expansion. The new
United States grew with more states joining the Union, a rising
population, and the continuing desire to push farther west, which
meant defeating those American Indian tribes that resisted the
encroachment.

In 1803 President Thomas Jefferson finalized the purchase of
Louisiana from the French, doubling the size of the United States.
Shortly thereafter, Jefferson sent a military expedition led by
Meriwether Lewis and William Clark to explore up the Missouri
River and report on what they discovered. As the Lewis and Clark
expedition made its way up the Missouri, they encountered the
Northern Plains leaders of the Dakota, or Sioux, nation. The
meeting was cordial, and the Americans continued their journey.

Two years later in 1805, farther to the east, another army officer, Lieutenant Zebulon M. Pike, also met with chieftains of the Sioux. Traveling up the Mississippi River, Pike held a conference with the Sioux near the mouth of the Minnesota River in present-day Minnesota. Pike's purpose for the conference was to purchase two sections of land from the Sioux for the establishment of two military posts in the area, one of which would be Fort Snelling.[1]

Pike's conference occurred hundreds of miles to the east from where Lewis and Clark met with the Sioux. Spreading from the woodlands of eastern Minnesota to the western prairies of present-day Nebraska, Wyoming, and Montana, the Sioux nation encompassed an extensive territory. It is unknown whether Lewis, Clark, or Pike realized they had encountered a people as expansionist as the Americans.

The origins of the Sioux are unclear. It is known that they migrated to the region that became Minnesota, but when and from where is not known. The Lakota Sioux believed that their people emerged from the Wind Cave in the Black Hills. The Mdewakantons of the Eastern Sioux felt their place of origin was the mouth of the Minnesota River.[2]

By the seventeenth century, the Sioux were firmly settled in Minnesota but soon began to move westward. The Sioux called themselves Dakotas, the "Da" meaning "considered" and the "kota" or sometimes "koda" meaning "united or allied." Sioux was the name given to them by neighboring tribes, meaning "snakes," and quickly picked up by the white Americans moving into the region. Initially, certain Sioux bands—the Lakotas, Yanktons, Yanktonais, Sissetons, Wahpekutes, Wahpetons, and Mdewakantons—comprised an alliance called the Seven Council Fires.[3] In turn, these seven bands were made up of smaller bands. The Lakotas consisted of seven—the Oglalas, Brules, Miniconjous, Hunkpapas, Sans Arcs, Two Kettles, and Blackfeet—and would push the farthest to the west. The Yanktonais had four bands—Hunkpatias, Wazikutas, Kiyuksas, and Cutheads—while the Yanktons consisted of seven. The Yanktons and Yanktonais, who saw themselves as one people, along with the Sissetons, Wahpekutes, Wahpetons, and Mdewakantons called themselves Dakotas. However, the Lakotas referred to the four latter bands as Santees and considered them the elder, or father, division of the tribe that remained in Minnesota when the Lakotas, Yanktons, and Yanktonais migrated farther to the west. The name Santee meant "camp at knife," a name whose origin is unclear but may refer to the pipestone region in southwestern Minnesota. The Santees, never a cohesive group but four independent bands, held high prestige among the Sioux, especially the Mdewakantons, as they were believed to be the descendants of Tohake, the first Sioux man to emerge from the Wind Cave.[4] As the various band and tribal names can be confusing, the term "Sioux" will be used to refer to the entirety of the Dakota nation, while "Santee" or "Dakota" will be used when discussing the four eastern bands.

Starting in the late seventeenth century, the Lakotas, Yanktons, and Yanktonais left Minnesota, expanding the Sioux territory westward. While the hunting of buffalo and trapping of beavers for trade with the British were the main motivators for the migration, a lesser factor was the increasing warfare with the better-armed Ojibwas pushing into Minnesota from the northeast.[5]

Although a militant nation, the Sioux never saw themselves as the aggressor. To them all warfare was defensive. Their expansion to the west was necessary to obtain the resources such as grass, water, and hunting they needed to survive. They believed that to obtain the lands they wanted, they had to fight those nations that currently held them. The first wave of this westward surge occurred from the late seventeenth century through the mid-eighteenth. The Lakotas, Yanktons, and Yanktonais, well armed with trade muskets and equally well mounted on horses, drove the Otos, Cheyennes, Missouris, and Iowas out of the lands east of the Missouri River in present-day North and South Dakota. They were then halted from crossing to the west banks of the Missouri River by three powerful tribes: the Hidatsas, Mandans, and Omahas.[6]

By 1775 the Lakotas felt the need to again expand their territory. Buffalo hides were in high demand for trade with the Spanish and French, yet the buffalo herds east of the Missouri River were becoming depleted. From 1779 to 1802 outbreaks of smallpox devastated the sedentary Hidatsas and Mandans, weakening them militarily and making possible a second wave of Sioux conquest, this time across the Missouri River. Moving rapidly, the Lakotas soon reached the Black Hills. They further expanded to the south with military victories over the Omahas and Poncas. By 1803 the Lakotas held new hunting grounds that ran as far west as the Yellowstone River in present-day Montana.[7]

Involved more with trapping beaver than hunting buffalo, the Yanktons and Yanktonais were content to remain behind in the lands east of the Missouri River. Numbering some five thousand, the Yanktons settled in the lower James River valley and the Yanktonais occupied the lands between the Missouri River and the James River south of Devil's Lake. Unlike the Lakotas, who were nomadic, the Yanktons and Yanktonais embraced a more seminomadic or even sedentary lifestyle. They settled into round earthen lodges, used bull boats, planted crops, and fished. Although not as dependent on the buffalo for survival, the Yanktons and Yanktonais still continued to hunt them for trade and meat.[8]

The Yanktons, and especially the Yanktonias, became the bridge between the Lakotas and Dakotas. Members from all three divisions intermixed and maintained a close alliance. Charles Eastman, a writer of Mdewakanton and Wahpeton descent, stated that the Sioux were "a patient and clannish people; their love for one another is stronger than that of any civilized people I know."

Living in the center of the Sioux nation, it was the Yanktonais who took on the important role of mediators for the various villages, bands, and divisions of the Sioux, easing tensions, working out problems, and keeping everyone united. They often preferred diplomacy to confrontation.[9]

Faced with a depleted buffalo herd and a rising population (Lakota numbers had increased to fifteen to twenty thousand people), the Sioux initiated one final burst of expansion, starting in the 1830s. Along with their allies the Cheyennes and Arapahos, the Lakotas pushed southward into present-day Nebraska and Kansas. By 1849 they had defeated the Pawnees along the Platte River and so badly crushed the Hidatsas, Mandans, and Arikaras as to make them nearly subjugated nations to the Sioux. Meanwhile, the Yanktons and Yanktonais pushed northward toward Canada, giving battle to the Crees and Assiniboines.[10]

At the midpoint of the nineteenth century, the Sioux were at the height of their power. They controlled an impressive amount of territory, encompassing parts or all of eight present-day states. They had decisively defeated a number of their enemies and neutralized many more. Soon, however, pressure from a larger, even more expansionist people put all their victories in jeopardy.

In 1820, after exploring the Platte River, Major Stephen Long wrote a report of his expedition that referred to the Great Plains as the "Great American Desert." Long deemed impossible the settlement of this vast, barren region by Americans. But although a daunting barrier, the Great Plains only briefly stopped the expansionist Americans.

Stephen Long may have believed that the Great Plains would prove an impassable barrier to further American expansion, but by the 1840s trails were being created across the prairie to the rich farmlands of Oregon beyond the Rocky Mountains. What started as a trickle of some 200 emigrants in 1842 became a flood by the end of the decade. Thousands of Americans fleeing economic hardships back East and encouraged by the success of the

Mexican-American War and the discovery of gold in California poured into the West. In 1849 30,000 miners heading for the mine camps in California passed through Fort Laramie, and the following year 50,000 people used the Oregon Trail. Between 1850 and 1854, another 145,000 travelers passed through Fort Laramie. These newcomers crossed over Sioux territory, putting increased pressure on the supplies of grass, water, and wood as well as making hunting more difficult.

In 1851, with tensions mounting on both sides, the federal government held a meeting with the various Northern Plains tribes at Fort Laramie. The resulting Fort Laramie Treaty was to keep the peace among the tribes as well as with the incoming emigrants. The treaty also allowed the United States Army to establish posts along the roads to better administer the peace, for which the tribes would receive annuities from the government.[11] Three years later, although stationed in the West to ensure peace, the army instead initiated a war with the Lakotas.

The First Sioux War began in August 1854 with the killing of a cow by a Miniconjou man after it had been left behind by a Mormon emigrant train heading for Utah. Upon reaching the nearby Fort Laramie, the owner of the cow demanded justice from the army. Eventually a small expedition of soldiers, led by inexperienced Second Lieutenant John Grattan and supported by a drunken interpreter, was sent to arrest the man responsible for the killing. The ensuing conflict, known as the Grattan Fight, left all twenty-nine men of the expedition dead and led the following year to a much larger punitive military expedition, commanded by General William S. Harney. Harney's victory at Blue Water Creek against a surprised Brule camp left many women and children dead and so shocked the Lakotas that they quickly requested a peace conference with Harney, ending the war.[12] Later, in 1857, a summer conference of the Lakotas was to take place at Bear Butte, near the Black Hills, where a consensus was reached by those who attended that the Lakotas would defend their lands

and not back down before the Americans again.[13] The 1850s
were also to find the Dakotas under increasing pressure from
white settlement.

In 1849 the Minnesota Territory was established, with Alexander Ramsey appointed the first territorial governor. Arriving in
St. Paul in May, Ramsey immediately advocated that a treaty be
signed with the Dakotas, placing them on a reservation and opening their lands to white settlers. Ramsey stayed at the home of
Henry H. Sibley, a local Indian trader, businessman and Democratic Party politician, who endorsed the idea of a treaty, using his
influence among the Santees to encourage their involvement.[14]

At the time, the white population of the new territory was small
but growing at a rapid rate. In 1849 there were 3,814 white settlers; by 1858, the year Minnesota became a state, the number
had jumped to 150,000. The demand that the approximately
6,000 Dakotas sell their vast land holdings was impossible to
deny. In the summer of 1851, two treaty conferences were held
with the four Dakota bands. The Upper Sioux bands of the Sissetons and Wahpetons met with government officials at Traverse
des Sioux and the Lower Sioux bands of the Mdewakanton and
Wahpekute at Mendota. What transpired at the conferences was
a disaster for the Santees.

The treaties sold some twenty-four million acres of land in
Minnesota, Iowa and the soon-to-be created Dakota Territory for
minimal amounts of money. The upper bands received $1,665,000
and the lower bands $1,410,000 in cash and annuities. Against
these totals, Indian traders such as Sibley put in claims and were
awarded cash payments by the government. Sibley asked for and
received $145,000. The corruption was obvious, with Indian trad-
ers, government officials, and Indian agents all working together
to steal from the Dakotas, who were quite aware of what was
being done to them. Even Ramsey profited by the treaties, accept-
ing $55,000 of the available money. In 1853 the U.S. Senate inves-
tigated the charges of fraud, finding that deceit and oppressive

actions had occurred, but did not punish anyone for the criminal and unethical behavior.[15]

The reservation awarded to the Dakotas consisted of a section of land running 150 miles along the north and south banks of the Minnesota River with a width of 10 miles on each side of the river. In 1858, with settlers still desiring more land, the Santees were pressured to sell off their lands on the north bank of the Minnesota. Joseph Brown, the current Indian agent, hoped to obtain $5.00 an acre for the land, but the Senate Committee on Indian Affairs lowered the price to $1.25. Even this was too high for the Senate, which further decreased the amount. Eventually the Treaty of 1858 paid the Dakotas 33 cents an acre for the one million acres of land sold to the government. Yet again, the corruption of the Indian traders robbed the Santees of most of the $266,880 they had been awarded. Sibley and thirty-four other claimants were granted $155,000 of the treaty money.[16]

Placed on a reservation where they did not want to live, the Dakotas soon saw the Minnesota River valley inundated by settlers who surrounded the reservation, making hunting increasingly difficult and causing the Santees to become ever more dependent on the annuity money and foodstuffs provided by the government. With growing hunger and social problems, the Dakotas began to divide over the issue of assimilation. Some Santees believed the only hope for their people was to convert to Christianity and take up farming, while others firmly insisted on retaining the traditional culture.

The Yanktons and Yanktonais were also under pressure to sell land to the federal government. In 1856 the government began talks with the Yanktons to sell a sizable section of land between the Big Sioux and Missouri Rivers. On April 19, 1857, Indian trader John B. S. Todd, who led the American delegation, finally achieved the signing of a treaty. The Yanktons sold 14 million acres of land for 12 cents an acre. They also received a 400,000-acre reservation, the Greenwood Agency, with annuities to be paid over the next fifty years. Within four years the new Dakota Territory would be established and the lands thrown open for white settlement.[17]

The government had less success with the Yanktonais, who refused to sign any treaty giving away tribal lands unless the entire Sioux nation, including the Lakotas and Dakotas, agreed to the sale. In the Dakota language, Yanktonais meant "little end dwellers." The Yanktonais lived from the western borders of Minnesota across the northern plains of what would soon be the Dakota Territory. A seminomadic people, they served as go-betweens for the Lakotas and Dakotas. They had close ties to the Hunkpapa band of the Lakotas and they also had a long history of peaceful relations with whites, having never harmed or fought against them. In fact, some Yanktonais had supported the Americans in the War of 1812. But as with the Lakotas and other Dakotas, their interactions with the Americans were changing. By the 1850s the Yanktonais were faced with declining food sources, disease, and pressures to sell their lands. Upset with the Yanktons and Santees for selling tribal lands, especially because certain areas sold belonged to them and thus were sold illegally, the Yanktonais were also unhappy over troops being stationed at Fort Pierre and newly established Fort Randall, built on Sioux lands.[18]

The Yanktonais were not alone in their feelings of betrayal over the signing of the various treaties. The Yanktons felt they too should receive part of the Santees' annuities for land sales in Minnesota, and the Lakotas were furious at the Yanktons for signing away their lands, lands they believed the Yanktons had no right to sell, as they had belonged to the Lakotas through earlier conquests.

The 1850s proved to be a time of growing problems and tumult for the entire Sioux nation. There were disagreements among the Lakotas and Dakotas over land sales and quarreling among bands and villages over whether to assimilate or resist the rising white encroachment and threats to the traditional way of life, including the ability to hunt and trade for a living. And always there were more roads, new forts, and constantly increasing numbers of white settlers. Violent acts were starting to occur between the Sioux and the Americans. In 1854 it had been the brief First Sioux War. Then, in 1857, came shocking massacres of white settlers at Spirit Lake, Iowa, and Springfield, Minnesota, led by a Wahpekute chieftain named Inkpaduta.

Inkpaduta and a small band of followers, numbering some forty to fifty people, had refused to sign the Mendota Treaty selling Wahpekute lands and declined to move onto the new reservations, preferring to continue to live on traditional Wahpekute lands in northern Iowa. These same lands soon attracted white settlers. In 1838 Iowa had become a territory and, eight and half years later, a state with a population of eighty thousand whites.[19] Most citizens of the new state lived in eastern Iowa along the Mississippi River, but more hardy souls pushed into northern Iowa.

For several years relations between Inkpaduta and the incoming settlers were sometimes tense, with Inkpaduta and other Sioux harassing whites, wanting them to leave the area, but overall interaction between the two groups was cordial. Inkpaduta even had several good friendships with whites. But in 1854 a kinsman of Inkpaduta was wantonly murdered and the murderer never apprehended by the white authorities. This embittered Inkpaduta, only fueling his frustrations over the influx of whites onto lands Inkpaduta still believed belonged to the Wahpekutes. Yet Inkpaduta's village continued to exist next to the emerging towns of the area until a devastating winter struck in 1856.

The winter was brutally cold, with massive amounts of snow that did not let up for months. Running low on food and facing starvation, the citizens of the town of Smithland took out their fears on the Sioux. A militia surrounded Inkpaduta's camp, took all their weapons, and exiled them from the area. Soon after leaving Smithland, a grandson of Inkpaduta died from the cold and hunger. Rearming themselves by robbing unsuspecting settlers, the Wahpekutes moved to Spirit Lake in northern Iowa, only to find this remote area had also been settled by a number of whites living in cabins spread along the three local lakes. From March 8 to 10, 1857, Inkpaduta's band proceeded to murder every man, woman, and child they found except for the four women they took prisoner. Leaving thirty-two people dead behind him, Inkpaduta moved into southern Minnesota and attacked the small frontier community of Springfield some two weeks later. Another seven people died in this assault.[20]

Inkpaduta's revenge raids threw the region into a panic. Thousands of settlers fled to escape the wrath of the Sioux, who, it was believed, were rising to massacre all the settlers. Several military expeditions failed to capture Inkpaduta. He escaped to the west, living among the Yanktons and Yanktonais. Unpunished, Inkpaduta became a frontier boogeyman constantly accused of committing further hostilities against the whites. Some Santees saw Inkpaduta as a renegade and aided the army in trying to apprehend him, but most respected him and quietly approved of his actions in defending his people—especially since the 1860s found conditions worsening for the Sioux.

In 1860, gold was discovered along the upper Missouri River in present-day Montana, and hundreds of hopeful miners started to make their way to the minefields. To reach the fields, they passed through lands held by the Lakotas and Yanktonais. Some traveled up the Missouri River, but many crossed overland to Montana. The Sioux objected to this overland travel, maintaining that the Fort Laramie Treaty allowed only for river travel up the Missouri River. Over the next five years, Congress authorized three wagon roads and established military posts at Forts Berthold, Union, Rice, and Wadsworth, while miners continued to reach the minefields by steamboat and road.[21] Frustrated, the Sioux became divided over how best to respond to this new challenge to their sovereignty.

On March 2, 1861, President James Buchanan signed legislation authorizing the establishment of the Dakota Territory. Prior to this, settlers had already been moving into the southern corner of present-day South Dakota, founding the town of Sioux City in 1855 and Sioux Falls the following year. By 1860 two thousand whites were living in the region, and within two years, when the new territory was officially opened to settlement, this number had risen to five thousand.[22] Also living in the territory were the Yanktons on their reservation and the still roaming Yanktonais, along with bands of Lakotas and Dakotas who hunted buffalo there.

In Minnesota, conditions on the Santee reservation were at poverty levels. With so many settlers in the Minnesota River valley, hunting was largely ineffectual. Traders on the reservation were charging high prices for food and taking more of the annuity monies when they arrived. Starving, with their culture and traditions under assault from Indian agents and Christian missionaries, and constantly facing the racism of local settlers, some Santees tried to escape by assimilating into the white culture, becoming Christians and taking up farming. Many Dakotas just tried to survive as their resentment toward the whites grew, and events took another turn for the worse with the coming of the Civil War.

It was the expansionist desires of Americans that led to the United States' most destructive war. Victory over Mexico in the Mexican-American War added nearly 500,000 square miles of territory to the growing nation. This victory came with a price, as the North and the South divided over the issue of slavery in the newly acquired region. After the presidential election of 1860, when the Republicans—opponents of slavery expansion—won the contest by electing Abraham Lincoln, eleven southern slave states eventually seceded from the Union to form the Confederate States of America. In April 1861 the Confederacy's firing on Fort Sumter started the Civil War.

Governor Alexander Ramsey was in Washington, D.C., when word reached the capital of Fort Sumter's surrender. The next day, April 14, Ramsey went to the War Department and offered to raise a Minnesota regiment of 1,000 for the Union. The following day President Lincoln called for 75,000 volunteers to be raised by the states to defeat the insurrection.[23] On April 29, with much enthusiasm, Minnesota organized the 1st Minnesota Infantry Regiment, which was then dispatched to Washington, D.C. Eventually Minnesota would send 15 percent of its population into the army during the war. As young men made up 25 percent of the state's population, this number was quite high.[24]

Naively, Lincoln believed that the rebellion could be put down by the small 15,000-man regular army supported by the newly raised 75,000 state volunteers, who enlisted for three months. The federal losses at Bull Run and Wilson's Creek soon dispelled that idea. On May 3, 1861, Lincoln issued a call to the states for an additional 300,000 men, this time to serve for three years. Under this new call, Minnesota pledged to contribute four additional infantry regiments and three companies of cavalry. Recruitment for the new regiments started that summer and continued through the winter. Much of the romance of warfare had dissipated by this time, and recruitment was slow. Yet C. C. Adams, a member of the 3rd Minnesota Regiment, later believed that it could have been worse: "If anyone had dreamed that in the course of a year our peaceful frontier would have been swept by Indian war, success in recruiting would have been much less than it was."[25]

Recruitment dragged to a point that the government issued bounties of money to men who would enlist. Minnesota was able to fulfill its quota of new regiments but soon faced another call for volunteers. The summer of 1862 brought new problems and

defeats for the Union. After a positive spring that saw Union
armies advance to the outskirts of Richmond, occupy much of
Tennessee, and move southward down the Mississippi River, the
summer proved a disaster. General George McClellan's Army of
the Potomac was defeated by Robert E. Lee in the Seven Days'
Battles and forced to retreat from Richmond, and Union attempts
to capture Vicksburg on the Mississippi River failed. These setbacks were followed by three Confederate offensives, into Mary-
land, Kentucky, and Missouri. In June and July 1862, fearing
that Great Britain and France might intervene in the war and
faced with mounting dissatisfaction with the overall war effort,
Lincoln issued a third call for men, this time for 600,000.[26]

There was still support for the war as shown by a popular re-
frain, "We are coming from the hillside, we are coming from the
plains; we are coming, father Abraham, 600,000 more."[27] For
Minnesota the call meant the raising of five new infantry regiments. Once more recruitment started off slowly, but many men
still did volunteer to fight even as casualties in the war mounted
at an alarming rate. The Civil War historians Earl Hess, Reid
Mitchell, and James McPherson have all written well-received
books on what motivated Union soldiers to enlist. The reasons
are numerous but also consistent: the need to save the Union and
to safeguard the republican form of government that the founding fathers had created, now in jeopardy from the conspiracy-
minded South that would destroy the Constitution. Often soldiers commented on their willingness to die "on the altar of
freedom," in order to protect the laws and rights that made all
American citizens equals. Also important was the need to prove
one's manhood. A true man stepped forward when called to fight
not only for his country but for home and loved ones. How he
carried out his duties, with self-discipline and in a civilized moral
fashion, rejecting such things as drunkenness and brawling, also
marked the individual as a man. Others fought to end slavery

and to continue to move the country in a progressive manner into the future.[28]

The findings of these historians are reflected in the personal accounts of the men joining the army in response to Lincoln's third call, men who would soon be serving on the Punitive Expeditions.

"In 1862 I thought myself quite a man, being then seventeen so made up my mind to be a soldier," wrote Charles Horton, whose family was from England and received lands in Minnesota following the Treaty of 1851, after joining Company D, 10th Minnesota Infantry. He added with some pride, "Three brothers out of four full blooded Englishmen enlisted to protect Old Glory or die in It's defense." At thirty, Pehr Carlson, 9th Minnesota Infantry, was much older than Horton yet echoed the younger man's willingness to defend his country: "The Union flag is my home and I am ready with my life to safeguard its freedom against its enemies." George Clapp, 7th Minnesota Infantry, agreed with Carlson, writing his wife that he was willing to die to "uphold the flag of my country." Clapp was thirty-nine when he enlisted, leaving his wife, Mariette, at home with their five children. "Before going into the service," wrote Clapp, "I counted the cost, and now feel compelled to go forward." James T. Ramer, 7th Minnesota Infantry, was raking grain with his brother when they heard of the call for five new regiments, writing, "I stepped off [the wagon], telling my brother Charles to take the rake, for I was going to enlist." Months after volunteering, Duren Kelley, 7th Minnesota Infantry, believed he had done the right thing. He wrote in a letter to his then girlfriend Emma Rounce that "I have never regretted the move for how could I stay out at home when all the boys were off for the wars." The following year he and Emma were married.[29]

Other men found comfort in their faith and drew upon it after enlisting. "I believe that leaving all the endearments of home and coming into the army in the midst of my present surrounding and circumstances," wrote Jacob Hamlin, 7th Minnesota Infantry, "has been the means of bringing me nearer to God. The ways of the Lord are mysterious and past finding out we do not always understand the designs of God's providence towards us and probably we never shall." In 1864 Hamlin was to die from wounds suffered at the battle of Nashville.[30]

Love of country and willingness to die for the flag were not reasons that made Christopher Byrne, an Irish immigrant, join the 10th Minnesota Infantry. He had heard the government was initiating a draft and, in a panic, volunteered to serve instead. "I am a soldier in the so-called Union Army, not from a conviction of fighting in a Just cause but the excitement of the time and the misrule of the administration has forced me," acknowledged a bitter Byrne. He went on to call the conflict an "unholy war." Thomas Hodgson, 8th Minnesota Infantry, also joined to avoid being drafted. His parents strongly opposed the war. They could "scarcely have been more opposed to it had they been life-long Quakers," remembered Hodgson.[31]

The desire to prove their manhood by joining the army and fighting for their country was complicated for those men who were married. Victorian-era mores dictated that a real man took care of his family. A husband's enlistment, lasting for years, did place hardships on those left behind at home. Captain John Jones, 3rd Minnesota Artillery, whose wife had difficulties with his leaving, wrote more than one letter trying to explain why he had to serve and encouraging her to focus on "the cause." Henry McConnell, 10th Minnesota Infantry, wanted his wife, Delia, to remember that she was "the dearest being on the Earth to me."[32]

Soldiers from Nebraska and Iowa who also served on the Punitive Expeditions shared the same views on enlisting and family as their Minnesota comrades. George Belden was a frontiersmen living in polygamy with several American Indian wives on the Northern Plains when word arrived of the war back East. "I can not describe how these tidings affected me," Belden recalled. "I could not sleep, and all night long walked up and down the camp." Soon after, he bid his wives good-bye and traveled to Omaha, where he enlisted in the 1st Nebraska Cavalry before later transferring to the 2nd Nebraska Cavalry.[33]

Siegmund Rothammer, 6th Iowa Cavalry, poured out his feelings to his wife, Rosanah: "Oh Love! My country is dear to me, and my love for it, and my family combined, caused me to make the sacrifice I did, conscientiously believing at the time, that it was my duty and that by so doing I could advance and better the conditions of those who were nearest to my heart. But how little did I think, what a great sacrifice I was making." He added, touchingly, "My only consolation on such moments is, to look on your likeness, and I am not ashamed to say, that many a tear has dropped on its glass, and many a kiss have moistened it."[34]

Unlike most other Union soldiers fighting in the war, men from Minnesota, Iowa, and Nebraska had another, more specific reason for joining the army: the Dakota War of 1862. Newcombe Kinney, 10th Minnesota, commented that most of the men in the regiment had some connection to the victims killed in the fighting: "Our regiment was made up mostly of farmers and of friends of the murdered whites." Amos Glanville, another soldier in the 10th Minnesota, decided "that my duty is to go where my country calls, and I will, God's grace assisting me, do all I can for this glorious cause." The 1st Minnesota Mounted Rangers was a cavalry unit specifically organized to serve in the war with the Sioux. One member of the regiment, Frank Griswold, wrote his parents why he had enlisted: "A horrible Indian raid upon our frontier has induced me to volunteer my services in a company of cavalry." Upon joining the 10th Minnesota because of the uprising, First Sergeant Thomas Jefferson Hunt sent his wife and three daughters back to Vermont to wait until his enlistment was over. His wife supported his enlistment, telling him to "go if you feel you ought, and God be with you." Although he did not join because of the Indian war, Charles Watson, 6th Minnesota Infantry, did not resent that it stopped him from fighting in the South, stating, "I have made up my mind long ago that I am willing to go any where that we are ordered."[35]

Watson was not the only Union soldier to discover he would not be engaging the Confederate enemy in combat but instead would face a much different foe. When the Civil War commenced, much of the regular army was stationed at numerous forts across the West. When these soldiers were recalled to serve in the East, replacements were needed for the regulars. Lincoln's administration decided that regiments of volunteers would be posted to the West, and by 1865 twenty thousand Union soldiers were stationed there. The volunteers, often from frontier states and territories, tended to hold a more pronounced racist attitude toward American Indians than had the regulars they replaced, so it was not surprising that, imbued with deep suspicion and loathing of Indians, they engaged in a series of wars with various tribes across the West. These wars were marred by atrocities and massacres, and deeply involved in several of these new conflicts were the Sioux.

In June 1861, companies from the newly raised 1st Minnesota Infantry were ordered to Forts Ridgely, Ripley, and Abercrombie as garrison troops to replace the departing regulars. They, in turn, were relieved by companies from the 2nd Minnesota Infantry later that year, and companies from the 3rd Minnesota Infantry and 4th Minnesota Infantry would then take their places. In April of 1862 Companies B and C, 5th Minnesota Infantry, were posted to oversee the reservations. Unlike other volunteers, the Minnesota soldiers treated the Sioux fairly and attempted to continue the regulars' policy of keeping the peace and enforcing the treaties.

Soon after their enlistments, three hundred soldiers from companies A, B, and C, 14th Iowa Infantry, led by Captain John Pattee, were ordered to the western outpost, Fort Randall in the

Dakota Territory. Here they replaced the regular army garrison for service back East. Sworn into the army in October 1861, Amos Cherry, 14th Iowa Infantry, soon was marching from Iowa City, Iowa, to the distant Fort Randall. At Clear Creek, Iowa, according to Cherry, women gave the soldiers a handmade flag while bands played, and a Miss Washburn called upon them "to prove true to this just cause and . . . that we as brave men of Iowa would maintain the honor of that beautiful emblem of our Countrys glory." This was followed by a feast thrown for them by the citizens of Grinnell, Iowa. The men were fed so royally that "our camp looked like one vast Bakery." They received a quite different reception at Bear Grove Station, Iowa. Here the war was not popular, and one woman declared that her son, serving with the 4th Iowa Infantry, "was a fool." Displeased, Cherry commented, "We found we was talking to a lot of sescisionists."[36]

Eventually, in December, the Iowans reached their destination. "Here we came . . . some wigwams and a few Indians. These were the first Indians we had seen. They were quite a curiosity to us all," wrote Cherry. Cherry was not impressed by the local Indian agent, who, he heard, "from all accounts is a rascall and cheets the Indians out of their just dues."[37] Cherry was concerned that the poor treatment of the Yanktons and Yanktonais could lead to an uprising against the Iowa garrison. He was mistaken, but a war with the Sioux did commence back in Minnesota, involving the Santees.

The coming of the Civil War only exacerbated the problems on the Dakota reservation. Faced with ever-increasing white settlement in the Minnesota River valley, the Dakotas confronted the clearly racist attitude exhibited by many of the emigrants. One individual wrote, "Minnesota was anti-slavery regarding the Negroes, but locally it was more anti-Indian." Yet the Santees were expected to assimilate into this hostile culture. Big Eagle, a leader of the Mdewakanton, argued, "if the Indians had tried to make the whites live like them, the whites would have resisted. . . .

The Indians wanted to live as they did before the Treaty of Traverse des Sioux—go where they pleased and when they pleased." Many older chiefs encouraged assimilation, while younger leaders advocated the traditional way of life. Their view was reinforced by contact with the still freely roaming Yanktonais. Assimilation was a threat to male honor and to the male role as hunter and warrior. Traditionalists formed soldier lodges to challenge the assimilationists, especially those Sioux converting to Christianity, promoting ritual and social customs.[38]

Always there was the problem of hunger. With so many people in the valley, hunting and trapping were becoming difficult, and it was no longer possible to feed the roughly six thousand Dakotas on the reservation. Indian traders continued to abuse the system, overcharging for their provisions and claiming much of the annuity monies. The brutal 1861–62 winter brought with it starvation. By summer 1862 the Santees were desperate for relief, and the annuity payment was late, not arriving until August. This desperation nearly caused an outbreak of violence at the Upper Sioux Agency when, in June, large numbers of Sissetons and Wahpetons gathered for the distribution of annuity provisions and money. "We went there because we wanted some food," Good Fifth Son remembered. "We . . . were in a starving condition."[39]

Indian Agent Thomas Galbraith, an incompetent political appointee, refused to release any of the food stored in the warehouses until the money arrived, while the Indian traders rejected all pleas to extend further credit to the hungry Sioux. Only the arrival of two companies of the 5th Minnesota Infantry and the quick thinking of Captain John Marsh saved the situation.

The reason the annuity was late had everything to do with the Civil War. The conditions in the treaty stated that the payment to the Santees must be made in gold, but the mounting costs of the war made gold difficult to obtain. Additional impacts of the conflict back East influenced the Dakotas' decision to go to war. The Sioux were not impressed with the volunteer soldiers who had replaced the regulars and had little respect for them. The fact that no military force, neither regulars nor volunteers, had been able to apprehend Inkpaduta, whose stature only increased as conditions worsened on the reservations, led many Santee warriors to question the fighting abilities of the army. Soon after, officers came to the reservation and recruited mixed-bloods for military service. This convinced many that the whites were running low on manpower and that few able-bodied men remained in Minnesota.[40]

Tensions were high when, on August 17, 1862, four young Santee men, out hunting, stole some eggs from a local farmer, then killed five settlers near Action, Minnesota. Fleeing back to the Lower Sioux villages, they told their elders what they had done. Believing all would be punished for this incident, a majority of the Mdewakantons and Wahpekutes decided upon a war with the whites. Less enthusiastic about fighting, far fewer Sissetons and Wahpetons, mainly younger men, joined in the conflict.

Although at first reluctant to become involved, the Mdewakanton chief Little Crow soon became the recognized leader of the rebellion. Born in 1820, Little Crow was forty-two, with six wives and twenty-two children, and had been chief for seventeen years at the start of the Dakota War of 1862. As a young man, he had led a questionable life of immoral behavior that included drinking and sexual promiscuity. At one point, upon becoming chief, two of his half brothers had tried to kill him. However, Little Crow matured as a leader of his people and was now well respected.[41]

On August 18 the war started with an attack on the Lower Sioux Agency. Thirty-one people, including Indian traders, agency employees, women, and children, died in the attack, with ten more persons taken prisoner. Survivors fled to the safety of Fort Ridgely. Captain Marsh, not understanding the severity of the situation, proceeded with most of the seventy-eight-man garrison toward the Lower Sioux Agency. Reaching the Minnesota

River, Marsh prepared to cross at the Redwood Ferry, only to be ambushed by the Dakotas. Marsh and twenty-three men died in the attack. The remainder of the soldiers made their way back to the fort as best they could.[42]

Left in command at Fort Ridgely was nineteen-year-old Lieutenant Thomas Gere. With only thirty men and the post filling up with panicked civilians, Gere sent a messenger racing for St. Paul with a report to Governor Ramsey. The Dakota War of 1862—a war that would leave hundreds of white settlers dead, divide the various bands and villages of the Dakotas, and lead to punitive expeditions—had commenced.

CHAPTER 2

The Dakota War of 1862

"LET IT BE A WAR OF EXTERMINATION"

Successful in its surprise attacks on the Lower Sioux Agency and against individual settlers, the Sioux offensive was blunted by two lost engagements. The first assault occurred at New Ulm, the nearest white settlement to the reservation. On August 19 the Dakotas moved against New Ulm. Soon fierce fighting broke out between the Sioux warriors and various quickly raised militia groups defending the town. Although almost the entire town was destroyed in the fighting, the defenders held and the Sioux withdrew in defeat. The next day, August 20, the Sioux tried to overwhelm the reinforced garrison at Fort Ridgely. Making good use of artillery, soldiers stopped the Dakotas from entering the post and drove the attackers off. The two losses were a serious check to the spreading of the war.

Meanwhile, having been informed of the uprising, Governor Ramsey was working to deal with the crisis. On August 21 he informed Secretary of War Edwin Stanton of the new war with a chilling telegram: "The Sioux Indians on our western border have risen, and are murdering men, women and children."[1] Still, even with this alert, the Lincoln administration initially did nothing about the uprising. The new crisis could not have come at a worse time for President Lincoln. After a spring that promised much for the Union, thanks to strong advancements down the Mississippi River and General George McClellan's approach to Richmond, the summer saw only setbacks. General Ulysses S. Grant failed in his first attempt to capture Vicksburg, and a Confederate army under General Braxton Bragg outmaneuvered Union general Don Carlos Buell and advanced deep into Kentucky, setting up a pro-Confederate state government and threatening northern states with invasion. Not only was McClellan defeated by Robert E. Lee outside of Richmond in the Seven Days' Battles, but in August Lee followed up his victory with a move northward, his intent to defeat a second Union army under General John Pope. Only Pope's Army of Virginia stood between Lee and Washington, D.C. The outcome of the current campaign was still in doubt when Ramsey's telegram reached the capital.[2]

The second step Ramsey took was to appoint the fifty-year-old Henry H. Sibley as a colonel of the volunteers, tasking him with preparing a force to rescue Fort Ridgely and the settlers caught up in the conflict. Sibley had first come to Minnesota in 1834 after earning a degree in law in Michigan, becoming a successful fur trader and politician. Although long-term political opponents, Ramsey and Sibley had over the years remained firm friends. Sibley was a mildly antislavery, Jeffersonian-style Democrat. He had been the first Minnesota territorial delegate to Congress before running for territorial governor against Ramsey in 1857. Sibley won the contest in a razor-close election, by a margin of 240 votes. In 1859, however, the new state of Minnesota went overwhelmingly for the new Republican Party. Ramsey was elected the first state governor, the legislature became controlled by the Republicans, and two Republican congressmen and one senator went to Washington.[3]

Sibley had declined to run for governor and remained non-committal as the sectional crisis deepened throughout the country. In the 1860 presidential election some Democrats, including Senator Henry Rice, an old trading partner of Sibley's and now a bitter enemy, supported a pro-southern approach while a majority of the party backed the nomination of Senator Stephen Douglas of Illinois. Although a state delegate to the Democratic conventions in Charleston and Baltimore, Sibley did not actively take a side but urged compromise to keep the party united. When war broke out the following year, Sibley, unlike many politicians, did not seek a military commission.[4] However, with an Indian war in his own state, he agreed to Ramsey's request to take command of the military offensive against the Sioux.

Five infantry regiments—the 6th, 7th, 8th, 9th, and 10th—were all recruiting in Minnesota when the uprising began, but only the 6th Minnesota Infantry, supported by some local militias and a few mounted troops, was well enough organized to serve against the Dakotas. In spring 1862, when first authorized to recruit, the 6th Minnesota Infantry had found few men ready to enlist. Not until later in the year, after the Union military setbacks and Lincoln's announcement of the Emancipation Proclamation, had recruits begun appearing. Enlistments were furthered spurred by news of the Dakota War. The men were recruited from various regions of the state and came from a wide variety of backgrounds and ethnicities. Company E was heavily German, and the men referred to themselves as Sigel's Guards, after a prominent German general in the Union Army. Twenty-four men in Company E had served in the military prior to their enlistments, and seventeen of these had been in European armies, including one man who had actually fought in the Battle of Waterloo.[5]

The 6th Minnesota Infantry was not the only regiment to see enlistments increase with the news of Sioux atrocities in the Minnesota River valley. Charles Horton, 10th Minnesota Infantry, acknowledged that "blood was in our eyes, we had been among the Indians all our lives and had no fear of them." Most whites placed blame for the war completely on the Dakotas. "A massacre . . . for extent of mortality and horrible details, was without a parallel in American history of the Sioux" was how Eugene Wilson saw the recent events, adding that the Sioux were "a fierce & warlike race." Wilson soon became a captain in the newly raised 1st Minnesota Mounted Rangers, organized to fight the Dakotas. Others were more pragmatic in their opinions of the causes for the conflict. Captain John Pattee of the 14th Iowa Infantry, serving in the Dakota Territory, saw things differently. The forty-two-year-old Canadian-born officer believed the citizens of Minnesota to be guilty: "It was conceded at last that the white people of Minnesota, but mostly the people near and connected with the agency, were responsible for this appalling calamity that chilled the blood of the white race of the United States."[6]

Although often criticized later for being too slow and cautious, Sibley gathered what forces were available and moved quickly into the valley, reaching Fort Ridgely on August 27. Five days prior to Sibley's arrival, the soldiers at the post had defeated a second attack, led by Little Crow. The Dakotas had suffered several setbacks but were still able to inflict punishment on their enemies. On September 2 a burial party, including Company A of the 6th Minnesota Infantry, was ambushed at Birch Coulee. After a desperate defense that lasted twenty-four hours, relief forces from Fort Ridgely arrived to rescue the defenders.

Sibley's forces continued to grow as companies of the various newly recruited regiments joined the campaign. As the soldiers entered the combat area, they encountered the destruction and death caused by the Santee war parties. Charles Johnson, 6th Minnesota Infantry, wrote of the regimental march into the valley: "Who shall describe the horrors and distresses witnessed in the march up the Minnesota [River]? The roads were literally lined with fugitive settlers, with their families, cattle and

household effects, terror-stricken and almost entirely unarmed."
Eighteen-year-old Charles Watson was also serving in the 6th
Minnesota Infantry. A devout Christian, Watson, usually an up-
beat man who took pride in being a good soldier, was depressed
by what he witnessed, writing, "I have seen a great many things
since I left home. I have seen some awful sights, men with their
heads cut off and their sculls all mashed to pieces."[7]

Corporal Duren Kelley, 7th Minnesota Infantry, missed his
fiancée, "my little darling" Emma, deeply, confessing, "What I
have to write is getting to be an old story for me to write and tell
you how much I love you . . . but I can't help it." Troubled by
what he had seen, he wrote to her, "I have beheld scenes of their
atrocities that would make the blood run cold. I have seen men—
soldiers—butchered by them—literally cut in pieces—their hearts
cut out and their bodies so mutilated that you would hardly mis-
trust they were once men." An enraged Kelley wanted to "kill
and spare not, obliterate the last traces of this detestable race";
twice he argued for the shooting of Dakota prisoners taken by
the army.[8]

"I went out in a northwesterly direction, 20 miles, I found
everything turned up side down, not a house escaped the ravages
of the miserable savages." Captain Leonard Aldrich informed his
brother that he had found bodies "mangled in every conceivable
way. Little children nailed up to doors of houses by their feet and
thus left to die with their heads hanging downward." Serving
with Aldrich in Company F, 8th Minnesota Infantry, George
Doud marched through the nearly destroyed New Ulm, noting,
"The town is now one complete reck." In his diary Doud related
more grim images, including "one girl about twelve years old was
found scalped and all of her garments was torn off from her. She
was fastened to the side of a house by driving nails through her
feet. her head was downward." He also remarked on women's
breasts cut off and pregnant women with unborn babies cut out
from the womb. William Paist, 8th Minnesota Infantry, wrote his

wife of a Mr. Eton, found later in the year. His head had been cut off and the flesh of his body eaten by animals. Paist recorded, "I remembered the sorrowful wife and 2 little children when they left here without hope of ever seeing their husband & father any more." Writing to his wife, Abby, George Adams, 6th Minnesota, related details of a patrol he had been on that discovered a woman and her child. They had been living in the woods for eight weeks: He reported, "She escaped from the Indians with two children and one of them died from starvation. . . . They were nothing but skeletons," having lived on leaves and a few raw potatoes. The woman had seen her husband killed and was still so terrified she couldn't sleep.[9]

As soldiers continued to skirmish with the Sioux and participate in burial details, the Lincoln Administration had come to view the war in a different light. There was a growing concern that Confederate agents were behind the uprising. Horace Greeley, the influential editor of the *New York Tribune,* believed so: "The Sioux have doubtless been stimulated . . . by white and red villains sent among them for this purpose by the Secessionists." Secretary of the Interior Caleb B. Smith agreed, informing Lincoln that after examining all the data he was "satisfied the chief cause is to be found in the insurrection of the Southern States." This caused Lincoln to claim Southern involvement in his State of the Union address to Congress in December.[10]

Lincoln was also under mounting political pressure to act on the crisis. Iowa's governor, Samuel Kirkwood, believed that the Yankton Sioux had risen to join the Santees and Iowa was now facing a terrible massacre. William Jayne, the governor of the Dakota Territory, agreed with Kirkwood, stating that the few thousand settlers of the territory were being challenged by fifty thousand Sioux. The war was devastating for the new territory, with over half of the settlers fleeing the area for safety; the only inhabited city to remain was Yankton, the capital of the territory. The *Mankato Semi-Weekly Record* reported that Sioux Falls had been abandoned by its citizens and later burned by the Sioux. From Minnesota, Ramsey continued his call for aid, sending a blunt telegram to Lincoln: "This is not our war . . . it is a national war."[11] Realizing the importance of the Midwest to the overall war effort against the Confederacy, supplying not only many men for the army but also vast amounts of foodstuffs, Lincoln finally took action.

On September 7, 1862, Secretary of War Edwin Stanton issued General Order no. 128 creating the military Department of the Northwest, consisting of the states of Minnesota, Iowa, and Wisconsin and the territories of Dakota and Nebraska, with departmental headquarters to be located in St. Paul. The head of the new department was Major General John Pope.[12] The opportunity to assign Pope to the department solved an embarrassing situation for Lincoln. Unhappy with the performance of General McClellan, Lincoln had hoped to replace him with Pope, a successful general who had shown leadership abilities in early campaigns in the western theater of the war. In summer 1862, Pope was ordered back East, where Lincoln gave him command of the newly organized Army of Virginia. When McClellan's Peninsular Campaign failed, Robert E. Lee and his Army of Northern Virginia were able to swing northward to challenge Pope. Here was Pope's chance to achieve greatness and replace McClellan. Although a talented officer, Pope was also outspoken, seemingly critical of the troops and officers he commanded in the Army of Virginia. He received little or no support from McClellan, who clearly realized what Lincoln was attempting.

What followed was the disastrous Battle of Second Bull Run. On August 29 and 30, Pope, outmaneuvered by Lee, suffered a crushing defeat that left Lincoln's plans in ruin. Pope, a loyal supporter of Lincoln and the war, was now a liability to the administration and the perfect choice for the Department of the Northwest, a department conveniently far removed from Washington. At least one soldier serving under Sibley approved of the appointment. Duren Kelley had never cared for Sibley, calling him a "cowardly old poltroon" for his cautious actions in the valley and noting, "We are apprised that General Pope is to take command of this division which news the men hail for joy as we don't like old Sibley at all."[13]

It was a difficult time for Pope. His humiliating loss at Second Bull Run was followed by the denigration of his quick removal to a remote area of the war. All of this occurred as Pope was suffering deep personal pain; just weeks before, his baby daughter had died. Pope's career had been badly damaged, his personal life was unsettled, and he understood that this new assignment marked his fall from grace. Yet it did not stop him from undertaking his current duties with energy and enthusiasm. On September 16, 1862, Pope formally took command of the department and immediately contacted General in Chief Henry Halleck. "You have no idea of the terrible destruction already done and of the panic everywhere," wrote Pope. "Unless very prompt steps are taken these states will be half depopulated before the winter begins." The frontier was alive with rumors of an expanded war. The local Ojibwas and Winnebagos were said to be preparing to attack, along with the Yankton Sioux. Pope requested that Halleck send four infantry regiments to Minnesota from Wisconsin and expressed his need for twenty-five hundred horses because of the great lack of cavalry.[14]

The following day, September 17, Pope wrote Sibley of his plans for a major offensive to be launched from Iowa into the Dakota Territory against the Yanktons and hostile Santees. Pope, excited by the rumors and the fears of the civilian population, believed the Yanktons to be hostile and part of the uprising. He wrote, "I think as we have men and means now we had best put a final stop to Indian troubles by exterminating or ruining all the Indians engaged in the late outbreak." Pope wanted the Sioux to be treated like "maniacs or wild beasts." Although so far in his campaign against the Dakotas Sibley had not shown such a desire for revenge, sensing the mood of his new commander, he responded in kind. They are "devils in human shape," he wrote Pope.[15] But the greater needs in other theaters of the Civil War soon ended Pope's plans.

To carry out the offensive, Pope wanted to use Iowa troops currently under the command of Brigadier General John M. Schofield, head of the Department of Missouri, who swiftly complained to Halleck, "I beg of you do not let him take them from me." On September 19 Halleck informed Pope that he was to cease his attempts to obtain Iowa troops meant for Missouri, adding, "It is not believed that you will require a very large infantry force against the Indians" and that Sioux numbers "cannot be very great." This rebuke was followed four days later by further rejection of Pope's intended offensive by both Halleck and Secretary of War Stanton. Stanton instructed Halleck to limit the amount of money Pope could spend and to refuse additional troops and equipment for his department. Halleck complied, informing Pope, "Your requisitions on the Quartermaster's Commissary and Ordnance Departments are beyond all expectations. . . . They cannot be filled without taking supplies from other troops now in the field." Stanton went even further, explaining that not only would no additional troops be sent to Pope, but Confederate general Braxton Bragg's invasion of Kentucky "requires that every man should be on the ground there who is not absolutely needed elsewhere" and ordered Pope to send all the men he could to Kentucky who were not "absolutely necessary."[16]

Halleck and Stanton had made it clear; regardless of Pope's attempts to make it so, the Northwest Department was not a priority of the war, especially with Lee's offensive in the East, Bragg's invasion of Kentucky in the West, including destructive raids by John Morgan and Nathan Bedford Forrest, and smaller Confederate forces threatening Missouri and western Tennessee. There would be no grand offensive against the Sioux in 1862.

Even if Pope's plans for an offensive had been approved, the attack on the supposedly hostile Yanktons would have proven erroneous. Neither the Yanktons nor the Yanktonais, outside of a few young men eager for war, became involved in the conflict. There were also deeply conflicting opinions among the Dakotas over the uprising. Heavily committed to the war were the Lower Sioux bands of the Mdewakantons and Wahpekutes, although not all agreed or supported the conflict. The Upper Sioux bands, the Sissetons and Wahpetons, were far less enthused. A number of influential leaders from both the Upper and Lower bands, including Wabasha, Wacouta, Traveling Hail, and Standing Buffalo, opposed the war or gave it mild support. Those Santees who were trying to assimilate or had converted to Christianity, such as John Other Day or Paul Mazakutemane, also spoke out against the war. Mazakutemane advocated that the fighting cease and all white prisoners held by the pro-war Dakota be released.[17]

Solomon Two Stars, a Wahpeton, years after the conflict testified that the majority of Sissetons and Wahpetons did not favor involvement in the war. In councils, Standing Buffalo, Scarlet Plume, and others made convincing arguments for not joining the Lower Bands against the whites. On August 28, 1862, following their victory at Birch Coulee, representatives from the Mdewakantons came to the Sissetons and Wahpetons, trying to persuade the Upper Bands to participate in the fighting. Iron Walker, Solomon Two Stars, Paul Mazakutemane, and Gabriel Renville, a mixed-blood, effectively countered every attempt to push the Upper Bands into a desperate situation. They blamed the Lower Bands for the war and for starting the conflict without discussions with the Upper Bands. Furious at this response, Lower Band warriors surrounded the camp of the Upper Sioux and threatened to kill any man who did not support the war. Prepared for such a move, the Upper Sioux men had armed themselves and stood ready to repel any attack. The Dakotas were standing on the brink of open civil war before the warriors from the Lower Bands backed down and left the area.[18]

For whites, the Dakota War of 1862 had come to be seen as including all the Santee bands, as well as the Yanktons and Yanktonais. It was seen as a unified war effort by the Sioux against the whites. Yet the exact opposite was true. Only a sizable minority of the Santees had come to the point of resistance against the hardships and oppressions of a reservation life that was hateful to them. The majority of Dakotas wanted no part of the conflict, and the Yankton and Yanktonais were only marginally involved in the fighting. So divided were the Dakotas over the uprising that after Birch Coulee, Sibley was able to recruit a body of Sioux scouts, including Gabriel Renville and John Other Day, to serve the army.[19] The war was tearing the Dakotas apart as a people, and the worst was yet to come.

On September 19, after a long period of preparation, Sibley's army left Fort Ridgely and continued its advance through the Minnesota River valley. Sibley now commanded a force of 1,600 men, consisting mainly of the 3rd, 6th, 7th, and 9th Minnesota Infantry Regiments. Wood Lake, the decisive battle of the war, was fought four days later. On September 23 Little Crow and some 740 warriors were waiting to ambush the advancing soldiers. Many of the men in the war party had been forced to join, and desertions were significant. By the morning of the battle Little Crow likely had only 300 men left. Big Eagle, a participant with the attackers, recalled, "We expected to throw the whole white force into confusion by the sudden and unexpected attack and defeat them before they could rally." The tactic might have been successful if not for a foray party from the 3rd Minnesota that moved ahead of the main column and unintentionally encountered the waiting Sioux. Heavily outnumbered, the Dakotas fought for two hours before being defeated and driven off. "I have had considerable fun today. Shooting the bloody aborigines," wrote Duran Kelley to his wife. "I tell you Emma, it does me good to see the Savage devils fall and to have the pleasure of participating."[20]

Sioux men fought on both sides of the battle, as those Santees who opposed the war fought with Sibley against their own people. "Our friendly Indians fought like tigers," noted Madison Bowler, 3rd Minnesota Infantry. "[John] Other Day got three scalps and three ponies. He shot his own nephew, and wouldn't scalp him." Bowler added that no mercy was shown to the wounded Sioux left behind; they were bayoneted by the vengeful soldiers. Little Crow was stunned by the loss: "I am ashamed to call myself a Dakota. . . . Our best warriors were whipped yesterday by the whites. Now we had better all run away and scatter out over the plains like buffalo and wolves."[21] With the defeat, the power of the pro-war faction lost control to those Dakotas desiring peace. In a little over one month Sibley, although criticized for his slow approach in pursuing the war, had apparently crushed the uprising.

Even prior to Birch Coulee, the peace faction among the Dakotas was trying to organize its resistance to the war. Those who did not favor hostilities with the whites formed a camp west of the Reverend Stephen Rigg's Hazelwood Mission buildings. Here a soldier lodge, an organization of experienced warriors whose task was to defend the village, was established to protect the supporters of peace. One of the early goals of the group was to obtain the release of the large number of white prisoners being held by the pro-war faction. At a meeting with the Mdewakantons, attended by a thousand people, representatives of the peace group argued for the prisoners' release, only to have their request denied.[22]

To encourage the peace faction, Sibley sent a letter to leaders of this group, assuring them that anyone who wanted to surrender would not be harmed. The fact was that harm seemed more imminent from the group's fellow Sioux. At one point three hundred mounted and armed warriors surrounded the peace camp, shouting war cries and demanding that the members of the village support the war. Soon after, under heavy pressure, the peace camp moved to a safer location. Its leaders then contacted Sibley about surrendering, wanting to know if he was sincere. In response, Sibley again stated that no harm would come to those who had not taken part in the fighting but insisted the white prisoners be returned. Following Birch Coulee, representatives of the peace faction again met with the pro-war leaders, near the village of Red Iron, a pro-peace Sisseton leader. Once more their desire for peace and the return of the captives was rejected.[23]

The loss at Wood Lake, however, finally moved the peace faction into a position of authority, and most of the prisoners were turned over to it. Red Iron's village was fortified, with the peace supporters digging rifle pits and setting up a camp guard to defend themselves and the white captives. When Little Crow came to his camp, Red Iron boldly threatened to fight him if he did not remove himself from the area. With his forces greatly diminished, Little Crow and some five hundred followers headed west. After his departure, messengers were sent to Sibley to report that the prisoners were safe and the Sioux wanted to surrender.[24]

On September 23, Sibley and his force entered the peace village, soon named Camp Release by the soldiers. With cries of joy and thanks to their rescuers, 269 white captives were freed. Paul Mazakutemane was present when the soldiers arrived and recounted, "And now General Sibley came with his army . . . when the white troops came near, I raised a white flag." Another supporter of the peace faction was Gabriel Renville. The mixed-blood Renville was thirty-eight, broad-shouldered, tall, and athletic. He had suffered during the war; he returned to his house to find it looted and everything he owned stolen. In late December, after writing "Having nothing to live on, and the outlook being very dreary," Renville went to Sibley to volunteer his services as a scout. He further suggested that Sibley hire other mixed-bloods and full-blooded Sioux to assist the soldiers. Initially Sibley had his doubts about hiring Sioux scouts and met with his officers to discuss the issue. He ultimately approved the recruitment of mixed-blood scouts, but when he confronted Renville over his recommendation of full-blood Sioux, Renville replied, "You told me to pick out reliable men. I have done so. There are full-blood Indians who are more steadfast and more to be depended upon than many of the mixed-bloods." Sibley agreed, and in February 1863 thirty-two men from among the peace faction members were organized as scouts, including Paul Mazakutemane.[25]

The day after his arrival at Camp Release, Sibley wrote a letter to several of the leaders of the village, including Mazakutemane and a man named Toopee. Calling them his friends who had nothing to do with the massacres of white settlers, Sibley assured them he had no intention of making war upon the innocent and asked them to "have a white flag displayed so that my men may not fire upon you." The same message was sent to those Dakotas who were hunting farther to the west and had mostly been absent during the fighting. Some 1,200 Dakotas, of whom 250 were men, were present in the camp. Others soon either surrendered or were captured and brought to the camp. Hoping to blend in, a number of Dakotas who had participated in the war had moved into the camp when Little Crow and the resisters had departed the area. When Sibley was apprised of this, he ordered measures be taken to apprehend the hostiles, causing some Sioux, both the guilty and the innocent, to flee the camp in fear of the coming punishment. Mazakutemane understood the fear: "Indeed we knew that the Americans were furious."[26]

Among those fleeing to the West was the family of Charles Eastman. Eastman, a full-blooded Dakota, was four years old at the time of the Dakota War and known by his Sioux name of Ohiyesa, meaning "the winner." Before leaving, "a yoke of oxen and a lumber-wagon were taken from some white farmer and brought home for our conveyance," Eastman remembered. To Eastman, the wagon was like a living animal, with wheels that squealed like a pig through lack of grease. Too young to understand what was happening around him, Eastman found the journey an adventure until an incident nearly killed him. While traveling in the wagon, older boys were enjoying themselves by jumping over the high sides of the moving wagon to the ground. Working up his courage, Eastman finally tried to jump from the wagon, only to first step on one of the wheels. The motion of the wheel made him fall beneath the wagon, avoiding being crushed only because a neighbor saw and rescued him. Upset and scared, Eastman blamed the whites for his misadventure and "rejoiced that we were moving away from the people who made the wagon that almost ended my life."[27]

Those Santees who had remained behind in Minnesota did encounter the wrath of the whites. "To-day we are having a court martial to try these friendly Indians many of whom have been foremost in the work of murder and theft, and will no doubt be either shot or hanged," wrote Madison Bowler to his wife, Elizabeth. Four hundred Dakota and mixed-blood men were put on trial by Sibley for possible atrocities committed during the uprising. Given the number of Sioux presently detained by the army, this included almost all the men, of whom 303 were found guilty of war crimes and sentenced to be hanged. Cool heads intervened on behalf of the many innocent Dakotas who had been condemned to die, and President Lincoln reduced the number to 38: even with this reduced number, several innocent men were executed. Those men pardoned by Lincoln were sentenced to one- to three-year prison terms at Davenport, Iowa.[28]

On December 26, 1862, the condemned men were hanged in the city of Mankato. Charles Watson, 6th Minnesota infantry, was present for the hangings and found them troubling. Showing no hatred toward the Sioux, Watson stated, "It was an awful sight to see thirty eight men just at the blow of an ax send them all to eternity." "A severe but deserved punishment" was how Jacob Hamlin, 7th Minnesota Infantry, found the sentence of hanging. Hamlin did feel some pity for the women and children of the men set to die: "There will be . . . squaws and children deprived of the means of living and left homeless upon these barren and almost boundless praires and unless the government pro-vided for them, they will certainly freeze and famish." Still, he could not help but feel they were responsible for their fate: "Little did they think when at the silent hour of midnight they crept stealthily from house to house murdering helpless women and children robbing and burning the houses . . . that they were bringing upon themselves such terrible punishment."[29]

The remainder of the Dakotas who had surrendered, some sixteen hundred people, were taken overland to Fort Snelling. Along the route furious white civilians attacked the defenseless Sioux, causing harm and injury while expressing their deep ha-tred. Although representing the peace faction, the Dakotas were treated as prisoners of war and kept under guard at Fort Snelling until their future could be determined.[30] Attention was now fo-cused on those Dakotas who were still at large and out on the prairies of the Dakota Territory.

There were an estimated six thousand Dakotas at the start of the war. Of these, two thousand were being detained at Fort Snelling, in prison at Davenport, or serving as scouts for the mili-tary. The other four thousand can be roughly divided into three groups. The largest, some twenty-eight hundred people, were mainly Sissetons and Wahpetons who, except for a number of young men, had taken no part in the uprising. A second faction of five hundred people was still following Little Crow, wanting to continue the conflict, and the remainder had fled from Camp Release fearing arrest. This last group, consisting of seven hun-dred Mdewakantons and Wahpekutes, was a mixture of resisters and peace supporters.[31] Given that in tribal societies one out of every four people is an adult male of fighting age, this would mean that up to a thousand warriors were unaccounted for by the military. Yet a majority of these men would either have been neutral or had favored peace during the conflict.

Little Crow, although decisively defeated at Wood Lake, still supported a continuation of the war. On September 23 Sibley sent Antoine Campbell to Little Crow, asking him to surrender. Campbell, a long-time friend to Little Crow, could not convince him to capitulate. "The long merchant Sibley would like to put the rope around my neck, but he won't get the chance," Little Crow responded with a laugh. Soon after, on September 26, Little Crow and a small force briefly attacked Fort Abercrombie. Little Crow now dreamed of creating a pan-Sioux alliance among the Lakotas, Yanktons, Yanktonais, and remaining Dakotas.[32] His efforts to recruit the neutral Sissetons and Wahpetons had already proven a failure. Even prior to Wood Lake, Little Crow had been unable to convince important leaders, including the Sisseton chief Standing Buffalo, to join the resisters.

When the war commenced, most of the Sissetons and Wahpetons were hunting buffalo in the Dakota Territory. Two popular locations for these hunts were in present-day southeastern North Dakota, around the Bear's Den region and along the lower Cheyenne River. One Sisseton group hunting along the Cheyenne River was from the village of Standing Buffalo. Standing Buffalo was thirty years old and had become chief four years earlier when his father stepped down as leader. A handsome man, Standing Buffalo was six feet tall with an athletic build. Practical and friendly as well, he was a good man and a successful leader. When two Wahpetons rode into his village and informed him of the outbreak of war, Standing Buffalo was shocked: "The news of all the wrongs that had been committed by my nation reached my ears and anguish took possession of my heart," and he wanted no part in the conflict. However, some of the younger men of the village thought differently and soon began to slip away, heading back to Minnesota to fight.[33]

Along with other chiefs, including Scarlet Plume and Waanaton, Standing Buffalo hoped to keep his people out of the war and stayed well away from the fighting. On September 15, near Montevideo, Minnesota, Scarlet Plume and Waanaton met with Little Crow in an attempt to obtain the release of the white prisoners. Four days later, Little Crow met again with the neutral chiefs, including Standing Buffalo, Scarlet Plume, and Waanaton, in an effort to convince them to join the war. One of the conference attendees, Little Paul, remembered that Waanaton spoke out against the war and wanted to send a letter to Sibley explaining their position. Another attendee, Light Face, heard Standing Buffalo state it was not right to fight the whites, saying, "I think it is not proper that we should be enemies of the whites, but I think we ought to write a letter to General Sibley." Little Crow argued his case but could not move the chiefs. "You have already made much trouble for my people," responded Standing Buffalo. "Go to Canada or where you please, but go away from me and off the lands of my people." Growing angry, he added, "You have brought me into great danger without my knowing of it before hand. By killing the whites it is just as if you have waited for me in ambush and shot me down."[34] Little Crow left in failure.

The same day as the conference, a letter dictated by Standing Buffalo was sent to Sibley. Standing Buffalo explained he had no part in the war and believed "the nation is about to sacrifice itself for the sake of a few foolish young men." He placed the blame for the uprising on the Lower Sioux bands and asked Sibley not to punish the Dakotas until Standing Buffalo could gather up his people and keep out of the way. To his dismay, this earnest effort to avoid trouble was quickly compromised when warriors from Standing Buffalo's village returned from the fighting, including the assault on Fort Abercrombie, with scalps and plunder and held a victory dance.[35] No chieftain was an absolute king; he managed his people through respect, persuasion, and good leadership. Young men wanted to be warriors, gaining fame and social advancement through war. Successful men of war were heroes. When elders or parents objected to participation in a war party, young men would still go, leaving at night to avoid any protests. A leader like Standing Buffalo could do only so much to restrain the normal desires of a warrior to gain honors and success in conflict. Yet how could Standing Buffalo now convince Sibley that his village was peaceful when members of the community he led had been involved in the conflict?

On October 3 Sibley replied positively to the letter sent by the chiefs. He wanted them to know that he knew the Sisseton leaders had not condoned the uprising and that they wanted to surrender to the army in order to show their innocence. Calling them friends, Sibley asked them not to come in at this time as "I have a great number of men who are very angry."[36] Instead, he wanted them to remain in their villages and he would come to them. Heeding Sibley was a decision the chieftains would come to regret. Sibley understood that the Sissetons and Wahpetons who wrote him wanted peace and had not participated in the war, yet this would not save them from a devastating military offensive in 1863.

Sibley's more tolerant approach to those Dakotas who were still free displeased Pope. Pope, under political pressure from Minnesota senator Henry Rice and eager to redeem himself after the Second Bull Run debacle, wanted a harsher approach. On September 28 he wrote Sibley that "it is my purpose utterly to exterminate the Sioux if I have the power to do so and even if it requires a campaign lasting the whole of next year." Pope further instructed Sibley that "no treaty must be made with the Sioux. . . . If they desire a council let them come in, but seize Little Crow and all others engaged in the late outrages." Tired of the criticism he was receiving and the stress of the military campaign,

Sibley was ready to step down and return to his civilian occupations. President Lincoln, however, had other plans, and on September 29, while Sibley was involved in the colloquy with Pope, he was promoted by Lincoln to the rank of brigadier general and given command of the new military district of Minnesota.[37]

Having been thus encouraged to remain in the military, Sibley did believe that the campaign season, if not the war itself, was nearing an end. Although Pope was still advocating further strikes against the resisters, on September 30 Sibley informed him that this simply was not possible. He had virtually no cavalry, was low on provisions and forage, and the grass was "so dry as to afford insufficient nourishment to the horses and cattle . . . ," concluding, "The campaign may be considered as closed for this autumn." Nor did Sibley see the remaining resisters as much of a threat. He reported to Pope that Little Crow and "a small band" of followers were moving toward Yankton on the James River while "the majority of his former adherents are slowly returning with their families to deliver themselves up to me." In early October, among those who capitulated were eighty-six lodges likely numbering some four to five hundred people. Sibley did note that two bands of Sissetons led by Sleepy Eye and White Lodge, linked to the massacre of settlers at Lake Shetek in 1862, were on either the Big Sioux or James Rivers but that the majority of the Sissetons "have been friendly throughout the outbreak and give strong assurances of amity" and that this "should insure them against injury by our troops."[38] Later actions proved Sibley wrong.

On October 7, Pope, in a report to Halleck based on Sibley's reports, explained the current situation in Minnesota by stating, "I think there will be no more Indian hostilities this season . . . ," but he still insisted that "a campaign should be made in the spring." Two days later Pope wrote Halleck that "the Sioux War may be considered at an end," indicating that he was pursuing the approval of a new campaign against the Sioux, not in order to win the war but to punish those he still held responsible for the conflict. Halleck was pleased by Pope's verdict on the uprising in Minnesota, since a possible Confederate invasion into Missouri was proving to be a concern. "How many regiments are ready for service in the Southwest?" queried Halleck. In answer, by the end of the year Pope had sent the 25th Wisconsin Infantry, 27th Iowa Infantry, and 3rd Minnesota Infantry southward, leaving only the mainly green 6th, 7th, 8th, 9th, and 10th Minnesota Infantry regiments and the 1st Minnesota Mounted Rangers scattered among various forts and outposts along the frontier region of Minnesota.[39]

Pope's announcement of the termination of the war did not find approval with the civilian population of the region. In response came calls for revenge upon, if not a deliberate genocide against, the Sioux. "It is not ended!" proclaimed the editor of the *St. Paul Press*. "What the people of Minnesota demand is not that the enemy shall retire . . . but that the war should now be offensive." The editorial concluded with "In God's name let the columns of vengeance move on!" The October 23 editorial in the *St. Paul Pioneer* agreed with the sentiments expressed by the *St. Paul Press*, adding that if Governor Ramsey allowed "a soldier of this state to be withdrawn until this matter is satisfactorily settled, the blood of his thousands [of] murdered constituents . . . cry out against him." Letters to the *St. Paul Daily Press* included one with the position that "we must do one of two things: either kill every Sioux Indian within our borders or drive the tribe out of the state." Another advocated, "Let it be a war of extermination."[40]

There was also political opposition to the ceasing of hostilities. Governor Ramsey wrote that "the Sioux Indians must be exterminated or driven forever beyond the borders of the state," insisting that "we whites are blameless . . . for the outrages of the Sioux." In the summer of 1863 Ramsey placed a bounty on male scalps by offering $25.00 per scalp but later raised it to $200.00. Dakota territorial governor William Jayne and other territorial officials, supported by reports from Indian traders, warned

Lincoln of a new organized spring offensive by the Sioux. The
Dakota territorial council and legislative assembly called on the
president for more military aid and approved of Pope's planned
1863 campaign.[41]

The desire for revenge and to continue the war against the
Sioux was apparent, but could an enemy be located? An Iowa
soldier stationed in the Dakota Territory wrote in a letter to the
Iowa City Republican that "the great tribes of the Sioux, Cuthands
and the Yankton are moving in concert," but no such alliance
actually existed. The Lakotas had not been involved in the war,
although two bands of the Lakotas, the Hunkpapas and the
Blackfeet, had heard of the conflict. Sitting Bull, a rising leader
among the Hunkpapas, was hunting buffalo at the mouth of the
Missouri River when the people of his village were met by Inkpaduta, the perpetrator of the Spirit Lake Massacre. Inkpaduta,
who had played only a minor role in the fighting back in Minnesota, informed Sitting Bull of the war and how the Santees had
been starved and mistreated by the whites. Encouraged by Inkpaduta to support his Dakota brethren, Sitting Bull declined,
wanting to be left alone to live the traditional ways of the
Lakotas.

Later, Little Crow may also have met with Hunkpapa and
Blackfeet leaders. He too wanted their aid to continue the war,
but the Lakotas wanted to know what would happen to the Santee prisoners held by the whites if they did join the uprising.
Little Crow told them not to worry; they would not be punished,
much as the Sioux were treated after Spirit Lake, because the
whites had a "soft heart" toward Indians. Again, no support was
forthcoming from the Lakotas. Although not concerned with
events occurring farther east in Minnesota, the Lakotas were
troubled by the rising number of white miners crossing over their
lands to reach the mining camps in the Rocky Mountains. In
1862 some five to six hundred miners came up the Missouri
River and crossed through Lakota territory, and in July of that

year, prior to the Dakota War, nine Hunkpapa chiefs met with the Indian agent Samuel Latte over the issue. Feather Tied To His Hair spoke for Hunkpapas when he told Latte that no more travel would be allowed and wanted the agent to "tell our Great Father what we say, and tell him the truth."[42]

Little Crow's attempts at a pan-Sioux alliance also failed with the Yanktons and Yanktonias. Following his disappointing meetings with the Sisseton and Wahpeton chiefs, Little Crow and his supporters, now down to three hundred people, had moved farther west to the Missouri River. In December 1862 he attempted to persuade the Yanktons and Yanktonais to enter the war, and while discussions were held for a month, once more Little Crow's efforts were met with rejection. The Yanktons in particular remained adamant in their determination to remain at peace with the whites, going so far as to send men to protect the white traders at Fort Pierre after Little Crow suggested the post be attacked. In the presence of their Indian agent, W. A. Burleigh, the Yanktons swore loyalty to the United States, pledging to "stand by it while they lived and die under its protection." Other Yanktons related news of certain Santees going to Canada to obtain arms and ammunition and being told by a white man there that soon the British would openly support the Sioux war against the Americans. Another Yankton chief, Strikes The Rees, journeyed to the camps of Sleepy Eye and White Lodge to negotiate a release of two white women and five children being held by them. The Yankton leader offered seven horses for the prisoners, but his ransom offer was met with contempt. In response, the Yanktons made it clear that the Santee resisters were on Yankton land and would be attacked if they did not hand over the captives. The prisoners were given to Strikes The Rees.[43]

Nor were the Yanktonais persuaded to enter the conflict, although some young men did participate in the fighting, so with the Lakotas, Yanktons, and Yanktonais not open to embracing the struggle, only the Dakotas remained as a possible opponent

to the army if the war were to continue. Here too there was little
support for hostilities. Forced onto the plains in the fall, the
woodland Sioux suffered great hardships. The buffalo had left
the region, and with the coming of winter food and shelter proved
difficult to obtain. Many people died from hunger and the bitter
cold weather. The suffering was great that winter, with horses dying and the people surviving mainly on fish. Those who survived
camped together, resisters and peace faction, in the Devil's Lake
region of the Dakota Territory, close to the Canadian border.
Some six hundred lodges spent the winter there, including the
village of Standing Buffalo, who, fearing the whites would come
to see him as a supporter of further warfare, remained nervous
dwelling so close to the resisters. In early November, sick of the
terrible conditions, the first Sioux crossed the border into Canada. Over the next year, Dakota bands totaling a thousand
people made their way across the border. They pleaded with
British officials for sanctuary based on their support for Great
Britain during the War of 1812, promises made to them by King
George III to protect their culture and freedom, and the fact
that part of their traditional homeland was now part of Canada.
British representatives allowed the Sioux to stay, calling them
"alien Indians."[44]

As a military opponent, the Dakotas were a shattered people.
With 2,000 tribal members under arrest or detained by the
whites, another 374 Santees (men plus their families) employed
as scouts for the army, and roughly 1,000 Sioux seeking asylum
in Canada, only some 2,500 Dakotas remained at large on the
plains. Of these, 300 were resisters, following Little Crow, along
with at least three small resister villages under Sleepy Eye, White
Lodge, and Inkpaduta. A large majority of the Sioux were those
who had remained neutral or supported peace during the war.
There were likely only 100 to 200 men still willing to continue
the struggle. A force of this size would be able to mount small
raids upon the settlers in Minnesota and along the borders of

Iowa and the Dakota Territory, but not enough to seriously challenge the armed might of the United States. Pope may have
wanted a campaign and Minnesotans may have feared renewed
violence, but the Santees were simply too devastated to put up
much resistance.

Still, factors did exist that would motivate a punitive expedition against the Dakotas, a campaign that stressed the need for
revenge or punishment for those who had started the bloodshed.
This campaign would come in 1863 and inflict new destruction
not only on the handful of resisters but also on those who favored
peace and who had had no part in the war. The called-for "Columns of Vengeance" would march.

CHAPTER 3

Preparing for the
First Expeditions

"TO CRUSH THE SIOUX LILLIPUT
UNDER THE PONDEROUS
HEEL OF STRATEGY"

The desire to take revenge was a strong motivator for the 1863 campaign against the Sioux, as was Pope's personal plan to promote the significance of his Department of the Northwest. But the foremost argument for a punitive expedition to advance onto the plains of the Dakota Territory was the firmly held belief that the Sioux had not been defeated and were, in fact, preparing a massive new offensive against the white settlers.

Rumors abounded over what Little Crow was preparing for the spring. Pope was convinced that the Santee leader had formed a large army consisting of Santees and Yanktonais, with the Lakotas, who were being armed by British traders out of Canada, soon to follow. It was believed by the Americans that these forces were gathering around Devil's Lake, known as Minnewakan to the Dakotas, and that the way to stop the upcoming invasion was an expedition to smash the new Sioux alliance before a second uprising took place. The editor of the *St. Paul Pioneer and Democrat Weekly* criticized the army for not attacking Devil's Lake—where, he maintained, five thousand hostile Sioux were dwelling—during the winter. The surveyor general of the Dakota Territory, G. D. Hill, wrote to the commissioner general, J. M. Edmund, that the Santee Sioux were still causing problems in the territory and "recently shot two men within four miles of my office, the effect of all this is to create a general panic." In the spring, minor raids into Minnesota only intensified arguments for an expedition.[1]

Although it was accurate that many Dakotas wintered at Devil's Lake, few of those encamped there favored further hostilities with the United States. Red Eagle, a Sisseton at Devil's Lake, knew that no alliance for a new war existed, stating, "They were friendly to the whites." In March 1863 Standing Buffalo, also camping at the lake, wrote another letter to Sibley reaffirming the innocence of his people and his willingness to bring his village in to surrender at Fort Abercrombie if Sibley would guarantee the lives of his followers. Even as the editor of the *St. Paul Pioneer and Democrat Weekly* proclaimed a force of five thousand hostile Sioux, he admitted that "A large portion of the Indians are anxious for peace but are fearful if they give themselves up they will be killed." Trying to surrender was dangerous. While on patrol, fifty Sioux scouts under Renville discovered fifteen lodges of Santees returning from Canada who wanted to give up. Recognizing two men who had committed atrocities during the uprising, a scout named Star shot one of them, a grandson of Inkpaduta, while he sat on the ground. The other man tried to run for safety but was also killed.[2]

The feared alliance of the Yanktonais and Lakotas with the Santees was a myth—Little Crow had tried but had been rebuffed for his efforts—and the Indian agent Henry Reed reported on the lack of warlike behavior by the other Sioux bands: "There are again many friendly Indians of the Sioux who are looking to you to be sustained in their friendly relations."[3]

In early February Little Crow was encamped at Devil's Lake with only one hundred men. Undaunted by the rebuff to his latest recruiting efforts, he soon left, this time to try and create an alliance with the Mandans and Arikaras, traditional enemies of the Sioux. His delegation was fired upon when they approached the two tribes. Failing with the Mandans and Arikaras, Little Crow then pursued an alliance with another long-time foe of his people, the Ojibwas in northern Minnesota. Near Pembina, Little Crow met with representatives of the Ojibwas, only to encounter further rejection.[4] One must give Little Crow credit for his convictions; he had attempted alliances with the Lakotas, Yanktons, Yanktonais, Mandans, Arikaras, and Ojibwas, and he tried to persuade the peace faction of the Dakotas to join with the resisters. In every case he was met with refusals to join a new campaign against the whites. Outside of his immediate followers, only a handful of Santees were still willing to resist, and many of these, like Inkpaduta, were willing simply because they could not surrender to the whites without being severely punished.

In April Little Crow journeyed to Canada. At Fort Garry he met with representatives of the British government to ask them for weapons and ammunition or possible refuge. Governor Alexander Dallas made the position of the British clear: there would be no support given to the resisters, and Little Crow must leave and not return to Canada. Secretary of State William Seward had already written the British foreign minister over the issue of British military support of the Sioux and had received his assurances that no such aid would be forthcoming.[5] Once more, Little Crow's diplomatic overtures had failed.

With the coming of spring, many of the Santees left in order to begin hunting buffalo. This included Standing Buffalo with six hundred lodges, who moved to the Bald Hills on the Cheyenne River. By May Little Crow had returned to Devil's Lake and was still advocating war. At this point the rest of the Santees gathered around the lake were wary of the Mdewakanton leader and clearly desired peace. Little Crow was becoming a pariah among his people.[6]

The coming spring was not kind to the peace faction of the Dakotas held in a concentration camp in Minnesota. In December 1862 Minnesota senator Morton Wilkinson had introduced two bills in the United States Senate for the removal of the Sioux and Winnebagos from Minnesota. Under these bills, the tribes would forfeit all lands held by them in Minnesota and be moved to a new reservation in the West. In February and March 1863 the bills passed Congress and were signed into law by President Lincoln. For the 2,000 Sioux detained at Mankato and Fort Snelling, the winter had proven costly, with 143 people dying; now they were faced with the loss of their homes and the annuity money they needed to survive. By May the Dakotas were preparing for the move to their new reservation at Crow Creek, located eighty miles above Fort Randall in the Dakota Territory.[7]

The Santees were a defeated and shattered people, yet Pope was still convinced they posed a threat. He wrote, "There is no sort of use to make a treaty of peace with them; such treaties amount to nothing as they are only kept by Indians as long as they find it convenient." A military campaign against them, argued Pope, "will give the government the opportunity to make a final and favorable disposition of a large number of troublesome Indians, so as to secure perfect quiet in the future." In February Pope had made his plans known to Sibley: "As you know it has always been my purpose to make a vigorous campaign against the Indians as soon as possible in the spring."[8]

Initially, Pope's plan called for three columns advancing against the Sioux. Two would come from the east—the first under Sibley based at Fort Ridgely, and the second from Iowa moving by way of the Big Sioux River. The final column, based at Fort Randall, would campaign along the Missouri River. Also, a small force would remain in Minnesota to shadow the Ojibwas around Red Lake.[9] This plan would change over the coming months and meet with opposition from various groups, but the fact that a punitive operation versus the Santees would happen was never in doubt,

once more bringing Sioux men, women, and children into conflict with the volunteer soldiers from Minnesota, Iowa, and Nebraska sent against them.

Several Minnesota regiments had already seen some combat
in the Dakota War, but the 6th, 7th, 9th, and 10th Infantry Regiments who served on the upcoming expedition had been raised
to fight against the South. However, other units were organized
to serve in the West, especially after the uprising began. On September 9, 1862, the 6th Iowa Cavalry was brought into being
under a special order from the War Department. The regiment
was to protect the northern frontier of Iowa during the Dakota
War. Enlistments for the new unit proved slow, occurring between January and March 1863. Most of the soldiers came from
the northern counties of Iowa and tended to be older than men
who had joined earlier Iowa regiments, and many were married
with children.[10]

The 7th Iowa Cavalry was also formed to serve on the western
frontier, around the same time as the 6th Iowa Cavalry. Commanded by Colonel Samuel Summers, the 7th Iowa started to
gather men in the summer of 1863. Again, with slow enlistments,
not until July did the regiment number eight companies. To fill
out the ranks, Companies A, B, and C of the 41st Iowa Infantry,
already stationed at Fort Randall in the Dakota Territory, were
transferred to the unit. The men of these companies had joined
in 1861 and came with nearly two years' experience on the frontier. Also transferred to the new regiment was a veteran company
of cavalry from Sioux City, Iowa. Formed in 1861, the company
had spent the next year and a half patrolling the borders of Iowa.
At the time of the uprising, the Sioux City company was the only
active military unit serving along the Iowa border with Minnesota. Armed with Gallager carbines, Colt .44 pistols, and dra-
goon sabers, the 7th Iowa Cavalry was assigned to the Military
District of Nebraska, scattered across Nebraska, Kansas, and
Colorado.[11]

One of the problems encountered by Sibley during his Minnesota River valley campaign had been the lack of cavalry. If the army were to pursue the Sioux onto the prairies of the Dakota Territory, this issue had to be addressed, and so in the fall of 1862 the 1st Regiment of Mounted Rangers was raised. Many of these enlisted men had lost loved ones in the uprising and were veterans of the fighting in the valley.[12]

The Civil War and the Dakota War of 1862 not only affected the United States and Sioux at a national level but forever changed the lives of those individuals who became embroiled in the conflicts. These wars affected individuals, families, and communities, and as far as the wars' disruptions to the normal flow of life, experiences of the white soldiers and Indians were quite similar.

Upon enlisting, soldiers broke the direct connection they had with family and community, yet fighting for one's country also implied defense of family and community. Most men joined companies made up of soldiers from their hometown or county, and the resulting sense of community played a key role in keeping men in the army and their morale high. How one performed as a soldier in battle and as a person off the battlefield soon became known back home. Approval of friends and family was important to soldiers.[13] For them, the most direct contact with the community they had left behind came through letters—of which, the soldiers believed, there were never enough.

When Sergeant George Clapp joined the 7th Minnesota Infantry, he left behind his wife, Mariette, and their four children, Maria, Harrie, Belle, and Isadore. At age thirty-nine, Clapp was older than most men who enlisted. "I did expect to get a letter from you before this but have been disappointed everyday as the mail arrives for the company for a long time I have received only one letter from you since my arrival here," a dejected Clapp wrote Mariette. Sergeant George Adams, 6th Minnesota Infantry, had been married to his wife, Abby, for ten years before enlisting. Missing Abby and his four-year-old son, Frank, George instructed his wife, "You must write often and good long letters." In October 1864 Adams died from typhoid fever while serving in the South. Corporal Henry Synder served in the same company as George Adams. "We have had three mails since we have bin here But tharr has not Bin any for me," a mournful Synder wrote his wife, Maria. Synder was greatly concerned over the health of his two children, Charles and Rachel, who both had been ill. "I have felt very anxious to here from them But I have maid up my mind thet they are Better or else I should have heard Before this time." Philip Osborn also longed to hear from his family, writing home, "I have bin to the post office and no letter yet I wish I cold git a letter from home it seems so long sence I hav heard from home." He then added what was foremost on his mind, "Oh how I wod like to see my wife and children."[14]

As would be expected, married soldiers were the most devoted to those families back home. Letters kept them in touch with that other life, the nonmilitary life, they had left behind. Much of the correspondence between husbands and wives was tender and showed a close, loving relationship. Henry McConnell, 10th Minnesota Infantry, called his wife, Delia, "the dearest being on Earth to me." Upon receiving a picture of his wife, Abby, George Adams wrote her that "it made my heart feel glad, it was the thing that I wanted, it pleased me the most of anything you could have sent." He further noted that the photo was of "the very girl I used to court. . . . I could almost see you. I imagined just the way you look when you set by the table." Henry Hagadorn, 7th Minnesota Infantry, wrote in his diary how he "received a letter from my wife this evening in which I was very glad to hear that they were all well which is of much comfort to me at this time in these lonely hours which I pass alone in my tent."[15]

Soldiers drew strength from news that all remain well for their families at home. When Hagadorn received word that his wife and children were in good health, he found it "the most pleasant news that I could hear and it gives me great courage to endure the soldiers life in great patience and look forward with great pleasure for the happy day, that day when peace shall again bless this once peaceful and happy land." Many soldiers were concerned for the financial well-being of their families. "I giv Samuel my nots and 6 dollars in money to give to you and I will tell you what I want you to do[.] git James Greer to tend my bisness," instructed Philip Osborn to his wife. Osborn acknowledged his "pore hand" in writing, but knowing his wife could not read, told her "you will have to git someone to read for you."[16]

When John Leo, 10th Minnesota Infantry, failed to hear from his wife, Annie, he became convinced that he had said or done something to upset her in his last letter. Her lack of correspondence after that caused him to write her, "I concluded that I must have said something wrong in it and wish you to answer this and let me know if it is so, and also what it was as if I am guilty it is through Ignorance and am not to be blamed." For Thomas Cheetham, 8th Minnesota Infantry, concerns over his wife, Mary's, health were more serious. Cheetham was from Great Britain and had married Mary in 1855. In the seven years of their marriage they had three children, Caroline, Emily, and Charles. Thomas was devoted to his family: "I am a poor homeless fellow my Dear wife, I wish you was where I could see and talk to you but we must do the best we can for the present and pray for a better time to come." That better time was not to be. Mary was unwell, and although it was not realized at the time, suffered from tuberculosis. She died on July 22, 1863, while Cheetham was on the 1863 expedition against the Sioux.[17]

Soldiers also wrote to their children. The letters were filled with love, concern for physical and mental well-being, and advice. What the content of this correspondence also shows was a departure from the more stern, disciplined, and controlling parental approach of the eighteenth and early nineteenth century to a more modern view of an affectionate and child-centered family.[18]

To his son, Wesley, Philip Osborn wrote, "You must be a good boy and not cry and I will send you a present. You and William must cut wood fead the sheep and pigs and calvs and I will send you something nice." George Clapp wondered "if Bell, Harrie and Maria will forget their father at night when Mother puts them to bed and in the morning when they arise I shall think of them often and not only them, but you all while on the march, in the camp on guard duty during long and tiresome hours of the night while you quietly asleep and perhaps dreaming that you see me or of bright visions of happy days to come." Writing directly to his daughter Isadore, Clapp was glad she was reciting Bible verses in church and called upon her to come to Christ: "Will you not now embrace the savior of sinners heed his pardoning voice whispering that your sins are all forgiven." William Paist, 8th Minnesota Infantry, missed his son so much that "if I had you here I would almost eat you up. Save me all the kisses. You can write me a little letter Ma will hold your hand but you must tell her what to say." Paist concluded by adding, "I have kissed your picture everyday." Thomas Cheetham also yearned to see his son Charles: "Tell my son father wants a kiss and wants him to come and see him. . . . I want to see you all so bad it makes my heart beat." He ended the letter as he often did, hoping Mary felt better. "May God restore you to health is my prayer from your loved husband."[19]

Bonds to their communities at home and concern over loved ones influenced the spiritual lives of many soldiers. Soldiers pondered their relationship with God, as well as the religious lives of their families, and often worried whether being in the army would affect their moral beliefs or if their families would come to feel that their morals had declined since leaving home. Corporal Duren Kelley, 7th Minnesota Infantry, was engaged at the time of his enlistment in August 1862. He missed his soon-to-be-wife, Emma, writing her, "I would give one months wages to see you tonight and have one sweet kiss." Kelley became deeply troubled when he learned that Emma was reading novels and not regularly attending church. "You say you don't go to meeting every Sunday. You know that won't answer. And about those novels what shall I say," chastised Kelley. "See here Emma," he urged, "you must go to the meeting regularly. You know for I am not there to take care of you and I am afraid that you would get to reading novels and that would not look good on Sunday." Emma responded by asking him to read the Bible once a week and kidded him about his morals now that he was in the army. Kelley felt her request to read the Bible a "very reasonable request." Then he added, "Now I wish to exact one promise from you, that you read a chapter of the Bible as often as you read a novel."[20]

John Smith, 10th Minnesota Infantry, a faithful Christian, did "firmly believe and trust that God shall overrule the present rebellion so that Truth, Right and Liberty shall triumph." Yet he was amazed at the wide disparity of morals shown by the soldiers he served with: "What a curious anolomy [anomaly] is soldiering. Some spend their time in card playing, others round saloons loitering. Others smoking and chewing tobacco. Others in cursing and swearing and using obscene language. Others drinking and carousing. Some growling and dissatisfied with every thing that turns up. While others in talking politics and all manner of talk. Others are still and meditative. While others endeavor to live in conformity with Truth and Justice and act with good will unto their fellow men."[21]

Even among the religious, disputes could arise. When a Mr. Cox, a closed communion Baptist minister, attempted to become the regimental chaplain for the 7th Minnesota Infantry, Jacob Hamlin objected. "I consider a minister of that order unfit to preach to any but his church," wrote an irate Hamlin. "If a soldier was dying desiring to have the sacrament administered to him he would not do it, neither would he baptize one except by immersion."[22]

The importance of family, marriage relationships, and children to soldiers serving in the army would have been wholeheartedly accepted by the Sioux they were to face on the upcoming expedition. Kinship was an essential part of the Dakotas' social fabric. It was through kinship that the Sioux learned about social harmony. The author and scholar Ella Deloria, a Dakota, explained: "By kinship all Dakota people were held together in a great relationship that was theoretically all-inclusive and co-extensive with the Dakota Domain. Inside of Dakota society, no one was alone; one was always related to someone else. Through kinship one had a mother and father with your father's brothers and male cousins serving as your secondary fathers. Your mother's sisters and female cousins became your secondary mothers. Upon marriage, your spouse's relatives became your relatives."[23]

Loyalty was always first to one's family. Families were very close, with strong bonds between brothers and sisters. If parents should die, grandparents or older brothers or sisters would assume the raising of the younger children. Children were never left as orphans or alone. With so many kinship ties, children were automatically cared for and loved. With such intimate kinship ties a major disaster, such as an attack on the village that left significant numbers of people dead, had a major social impact.[24]

Marriage was a primary form of kinship. The Sioux had three classes—upper, middle, and lower—based on birth, accomplishments, and economic wealth, and rarely did anyone marry outside of their class. Susan Bordeaux Bettleyoun, a Lakota, added another factor to whom one married through which the bravest men obtained the prettiest women. She further noted that "women were the property of the parents and male children of the family, they had to be obedient and go wherever they were sold or given." But women could have a say in who they married, although the family would make the final decision. Oscar One Bull, also a Lakota, described getting married as "when the man was ready to marry a woman he selected one and if she satisfied him, he married her. He merely brought her to his tepee where she lived with him: that was the marriage. There was no marriage ceremony." Upon becoming married, Sioux men, for the most part, were devoted husbands and fathers. The Reverend Samuel Pond, a missionary to the Santee Sioux, noted, "We could not expect lovers among them to be very demonstrative, but evidently many husbands and wives were very much attached to each other."[25]

The Sioux loved children; a couple that proved to be barren were believed to have committed some offense. Relationships between parents and children were filled with tenderness, respect, and love. Children were cherished and rarely punished, and never spanked or struck physically. Children grew up in a close-knit extended family of parents, grandparents, sisters, brothers, cousins, and secondary mothers and fathers. A very close bond existed between fathers and sons. Luther Standing Bear, a Lakota, recalled that his father "played often with me. It was a pastime with him to lie on the ground on his back and with his legs crossed to toss me up and down on one foot." While playing this game of horse, Standing Bear's father would sing warrior songs to his son.[26]

By the spring of 1863 Pope's plans for the upcoming expeditions against the Sioux were being finalized. It would be a two-pronged offensive. The first prong, under the command of Sibley, was to consist of two thousand infantry and eight hundred cavalry with artillery support. Sibley was to advance to Devil's Lake, still seen as the center of resistance, and defeat the Santee resisters he found there. Devil's Lake was roughly six hundred miles from Fort Ridgely, the base for Sibley's column. The second prong, based at Sioux City and to consist of two thousand cavalry and three hundred infantry plus artillery, was to move up the Missouri, then rendezvous with Sibley after "showing the flag" to intimidate the Lakotas, Yanktons, and Yanktonais.[27]

The first serious issue to arise was who would command the second prong of the offensive. In late 1862 Brigadier General

John Cook was assigned command of the newly created 1st Military District, Department of the Northwest. The headquarters for the new district was Sioux City. Cook was ordered by Pope to begin preparation, including making contacts for supplies and hiring steamboats, for the upcoming punitive expedition.

At some point Pope found Cook to be incompetent and unable to meet the requirements for a field command. Pope wanted to replace Cook with a personal friend and former staff officer, Brigadier General C. W. Roberts. His request was approved by the commander of the army, Henry Halleck, but he was overruled by Secretary of War Edwin Stanton. Stanton believed Roberts too inexperienced for the command, his only qualification being that he was Pope's friend. Stanton wanted a different officer for the position, Brigadier General Alfred Sully. Sully was an experienced Indian fighter who had served over twenty years on the frontier; he had seen action in the Seminole War, Rogue River War, and First Sioux War, and against the Cheyennes. Currently Sully was in command of the 2nd Division, 3rd Corps, of the Army of the Potomac, mostly recently seeing combat during the Battle of Second Bull Run. The forty-two-year-old career officer was ordered to Sioux City to take command of the second column of the expedition.[28]

Instead of appreciating the aid of a veteran officer like Sully, Pope resented Sully's being assigned to his department. He declared Sully to be too old, too ill, and too drunk to be given a field command. Pope still wanted Roberts and worked actively to have Sully removed. In May Pope wrote Halleck that Sully had arrived at Sioux City but stated that his health was not strong enough for an active campaign. Pope suggested two officers who could replace Sully, including Roberts. Halleck moved quickly to blunt Pope's negative attacks, replying, "Sully is the man for that place." Conceding the argument, Pope responded to Halleck, "As you desire I have sent Sully" and added he would "do the best I can with the means at my command."[29]

Pope was also irritated with Sibley, the other column commander. Sibley had concerns with the operation. First he requested that contraband slaves from St. Louis be attached to his column to be used as teamsters for his supply wagons. Pope granted this request, sending 260 men along with their families to Sibley. Sibley also wanted more troops, but this request was strongly rejected by Pope, who insisted that the five and a half regiments already serving under Sibley were more than enough to defeat the Sioux. Pope informed Sibley that the column of 2,000 men was half the size of the entire old regular army prior to the Civil War, and that given the manpower needs of the Union after the Battle of Murfreesboro and with the upcoming campaign against Vicksburg, no more troops were available.[30]

Sibley also lacked support for the offensive operations put forth by Pope. Sibley was concerned that too many men were being taken away from the Minnesota frontier, leaving the area defenseless. Clearly unhappy with Sibley, Pope responded that six and half regiments would be left to protect the frontier and added, "I shall not refer your letter to Washington, where I am sure it will occasion as much surprise as it did me."[31]

Sibley was not the only voice questioning Pope's expeditions. There was both public and political opposition to the campaign. That the 2nd Nebraska Cavalry was to serve on the expedition was not popular with the governor of Nebraska, who believed the regiment necessary for local defense. Halleck informed Pope that "he twice begged to have the order countermanded, which I refused." Complaints also arose from the Dakota Territory. Agent Henry Reed wanted troops to be stationed at Fort Pierre and Fort Benton: "We have from Fort Randall to Fort Benton a distance of some eighteen hundred miles . . . not a single military post not a civil office of any kind." Secretary of the Interior J. P. Usher also wanted troops for the Dakota Territory, making the request to Stanton. The secretary of war replied, "A regiment of cavalry was ordered to Sioux City . . . will be part of the expedition." However, Stanton stated it was up to the commander of the department to determine how best to use the regiment. The commissary general, J. M. Edmunds, spoke out against the expedition, insisting it would "only afford protection of a temporary character and in the immediate vicinity of the force for the time being." Newton Edmunds, the new governor of the Dakota Territory, also opposed the expeditions, calling them expensive, useless, cumbersome, and slow. He advocated that a line of military posts be created across the southeastern region of the territory to ensure the peace. Such a series of forts would also mean a steady source of money and military contracts for the citizens of the territory.[32]

A more direct political attack came from the United States Senators from Minnesota, Henry Rice and Morton Wilkinson. Rice, a member of the Committee on Military Affairs, had opposed the appointment of Sibley, claiming there were already too many generals in the army, but the truth was that Rice, Sibley's former business partner but now bitter enemy, did not want his rival promoted. His efforts had failed when on September 29, 1862, Sibley had been promoted to brigadier general and given command of the new military district of Minnesota. Undeterred, Rice had then focused his attentions on having Pope removed as commander of the Department of the Northwest. A Democrat, Rice realized his chances of reelection were slim, and he had hoped that if he could oust Pope, he might be made the new department commander. Pope, who soon became aware of the political maneuvering, had called upon General Halleck for assistance, referring to Rice as "a reckless and ruined speculator and Indian trader." Halleck had promised Pope his full support, and once more Rice's plans were blocked.[33]

Rice may have failed in his earlier attempts to discredit Sibley and have Pope replaced as commander of the Department of the Northwest, but the expeditions gave him more ammunition to fire at his opponents. Rice and Wilkinson went to see Halleck, complaining that the expeditions would leave Minnesota defenseless. They wanted Sibley's column to be reduced to a third of its current size, with majority of the troops to remain in Minnesota. Although the senators were men of considerable political influence, Halleck supported Pope and refused to cut the size of the column. Undaunted, Rice and Wilkinson then proceeded to meet with Secretary of War Stanton. They asked that an independent cavalry battalion be authorized for service along the Minnesota frontier. Edwin A. C. Hatch, a friend of Rice's, was to be given command. Stanton agreed to the battalion, which started recruiting in July 1863, to the great annoyance of Pope and Sibley. Pope quickly blocked the attempt to make Hatch's battalion an independent unit, placing the new cavalry battalion under his command.[34]

Pope's plans were met with further complaints from Minnesota citizens. The editor of the *St. Paul Press* scoffed at the need for such a large offensive operation, calling Sibley's expedition an attempt "to crush the Sioux Lilliput under the ponderous heel of strategy." The *St. Cloud Democrat* voiced its lack of enthusiasm for the operation because it would draw needed troops away from the border: "The withdrawal of the cavalry from this garrison [Sauk Center] is looked upon with considerable alarm."[35] At stake were the very lucrative military contracts to feed and supply all the various forts and outposts created to protect the border. If Pope's expeditions proved successful, many of these posts would be closed, the troops sent elsewhere, and the contracts disappear. For many in Minnesota, it was more profitable for the army to remain on the defense, providing a steady income for the local economy.

The awarding of contracts by the War Department could involve large amounts of money. Fort Ridgely, just one outpost, had numerous contracts with local businessmen and farmers. Just two contracts, one for thirty-five thousand bushels of oats at $1.11 per bushel and another for fifteen thousand bushels of corn at

$1.17 a bushel, cost the government $61,350. The economies of local communities close to Fort Ridgely prospered. Jacob Nix, a butcher from New Ulm, received the beef contract at 5.2 cents per pound of beef delivered, Thomas Welch, a banker from Henderson, provided firewood at $3.75 a cord, and partners Henry Behake and Theodore Crone of New Ulm sold fifteen hundred bushels of oats to the fort at 37 3/8 cents per bushel.[36]

Needless to say, such profits only increased the demand for even more troops to be stationed in the state. An exasperated Pope believed that the settlers in Minnesota would not be happy until a regiment, or at least a company, was stationed "in the front door of every settler's house in the country." Pope argued that a successful offensive campaign would end the Indian war and allow for the transfer of troops to the more vital theaters of war in the South. But bowing to the "carping and finding fault" people of Minnesota, Pope did agree to leave soldiers behind so that the "timid, spiritless population of foreigners along the frontier will not abandon their villages and farms." Even with this compromise, Pope discovered his plans were still opposed: "There came up a terrible outcry from the whole people west of the Mississippi, through the newspapers, that they were being abandoned." Bluntly, Pope stated that there were people in Minnesota who absolutely refused to allow any troops to leave the state.[37]

Pope's 1863 punitive expeditions were not some isolated events that occurred in the West as the Civil War raged back East. During the Civil War, a number of wars and expeditions were carried out against various American Indian tribes. Pressures over increased white settlement, the demand for tribes to give up lands and move to reservations, and the Civil War were some of the factors in a heightened level of warfare in the early 1860s. The volunteer units stationed in the West, replacing the regular soldiers who had served there prior to the Civil War, often sought conflict with Indians. Coming from western states and territories, the volunteer soldiers took a more hard-line approach to

relationships with nearby tribes. Certain officers came to repre-
sent this more racist view of Indians. In summer 1862 Brigadier
General James H. Carleton began his campaign against the Mes-
calero Apaches with these instructions to his command: "There
is to be no council held with the Indians, nor any talks. The men
are to be slain whenever and wherever they can be found."[38]
After defeating the Apaches, the following year, 1863, Carleton
was successful in forcing the Navahos onto a reservation. Brigadier General Patrick Edward Connor led volunteer troops against
the Shoshonis, Bannacks, Utes, and Sioux in various campaigns
during the same time period, and in 1864 came the infamous
Sand Creek Massacre, perpetrated by Colorado soldiers under
the command of Colonel John Chivington. This event led to a war
with the Sioux, Cheyennes, and Arapahos that swept across the
Northern Plains, leaving hundreds dead.

Further, as Pope organized his expeditions, 1863 proved a key
year in the Civil War. In May, in the eastern theater, the Union
Army of the Potomac lost the Battle of Chancellorsville, allowing
Lee's Army of Northern Virginia to invade the North. The cli-
mactic battle of the invasion came in July, at Gettysburg. Also in
May, in the western theater, General Grant placed the city of
Vicksburg under siege. At stake was the control of the Mississippi
River, and Vicksburg fell to Union forces in July. In the fall, Union
and Confederate armies engaged at the Battle of Chickamauga.

For the men preparing to serve on the punitive expeditions,
thoughts of the Sioux, the coming campaign, and the events occurring back East were often on their minds. Many of the soldiers had enlisted to fight against the Confederacy but were now
being called upon to fight a totally different opponent. For others,
this was a chance to avenge the terrible assault unleashed against
unsuspecting settlers.

In war it is not uncommon for soldiers to demonize their enemy. Early in the conflict, Union soldiers often wrote highly negative things about the Confederate soldiers they faced in battle.

Southerners were portrayed as traitors, cowards, and savages who needed to be punished for attempting to break the Union. One captain serving in the 91st New York Infantry believed that "a rebel against the best government the world ever saw is worthy only of one of two things to wit a bullet or a halter." However, as the war went on, Union soldiers' views changed, with many coming to see Confederate soldiers as honorable and courageous.[39]

In the same vein, those Union troops readying to march against the Sioux often used racist and demeaning terms about them. The most common expressions were references to American Indians as "savages," "bloodthirsty savages," or, as Henry Hagadorn, 7th Minnesota Infantry, wrote, "our savage enemy." Other terms included "Mr. Lo" and "Mr. Red." After serving against Southern soldiers and American Indians, A. P. Connolly made this comparison: "In the South we fought foeman worthy of our steel, soldiers who were manly enough to acknowledge defeat, and magnanimous enough to respect the defeat of their opponents. Not so the Redskins. Their tactics were of the skulking kind; their object scalps, and not glory. They never acknowledged defeat, had no respect for a fallen foe, and gratified their natural propensity for blood."[40] Never would the soldiers fighting the Sioux change their opinions of their foe. The Sioux remained savages and inferiors who were bloodthirsty.

The desire for revenge, or actual extermination of the Santees, motivated many soldiers. With great relish Eli Pickett, 10th Minnesota Infantry, looked forward to the "retribution which awaits the . . . accursed Indians." In a letter to his wife, Philena, Pickett stated, "I know that my hatred for the Indian is great . . . so great I believe I could murder the most helpless of their women and children without a feeling of remorse." Pickett also believed the expeditions could benefit his state: "This Indian war will not only rid Minnesota of the Indians, but will bring millions and millions of dollars to our state." Knowing he could soon die in combat, Pickett concluded by adding that he "has given all for his countries good" and even offers his life "upon the alter of liberty." In strong agreement with Pickett's views was A. P. Connolly, who thought the upcoming campaign was being fought "for the final extinction of the Indians." And Duren Kelley wrote to Emma: "This is going to be a tremendous expedition. If it don't do execution somebody will be to blame . . . the Indians had better say their prayers for they are surely going to be snuffed out."[41] Not mentioned was the fact that most of the Santees the soldiers would face were from the peace faction and had not participated in the war. Dangerously, all the Sioux were starting to be found guilty of being hostile simply because they were Sioux.

Other soldiers were not that belligerent toward the Dakotas: they were just bored with serving at the small posts along the frontier and wanted some excitement. Duren Kelley felt that "it is pretty certain that I shall go with the expedition which will suit me better than laying around this dull town [Winnebago City, Minnesota]." Eager for action, William Paist had a great desire to "try my pluck on either an Ingen or a rebel and I don't care which."[42]

Henry McConnell was not sure of the destination of the expedition: "Rumor says that we are to go somewhere but where it is not known. Some say across the plains." Wherever it was bound McConnell did not mind, as he was bored and "would much prefer a change and more active service, the danger I consider no greater than remaining here." Yet in writing to his wife, Delia, McConnell did express one reservation about leaving: "I should prefer going, but if we remain I can have the satisfaction of hearing from you often and perhaps of seeing you occasionally." Upon learning that his regiment, the 10th Minnesota Infantry, would be participating on the expedition, McConnell was disappointed with the news—"My heart filled with sadness thinking how soon I must leave here and all prospects of seeing my loved ones again for months and months"—but was thankful that the regiment was not heading south that year as men were being "slaughtered by thousands."[43]

G. Merrill Dwelle, Jones Artillery Battery, had seen action in the east as a sharpshooter. Wounded at the Battle of Antietam, Dwelle had been mustered out and then commissioned as a second lieutenant in the artillery. To Dwelle, the whole expedition was a waste of money and "a grand humbug." Other men were more pragmatic in their response to the expedition. "I have made up my mind along ago that I am willing to go any where that we are ordered," acknowledged Charles Watson, 6th Minnesota Infantry.[44]

Although most were willing or desired to serve on the coming expedition against the Sioux, many soldiers still believed the conflict with the Confederacy was a priority. As Duren Kelley wrote to Emma, "I should pray that our regt. Might be sent South. I have confidence in the men that I don't believe they would ever flinch place them where they would, only give us a chance at Old Jeff's rag-muffins and we should be heard from." Sergeant George Clapp was more concerned with Northern Democratic support for the Southern cause. He denounced them as the "miserable so called Democratic Party," whom he accused of being "in league with our enemies of country. They have been sought by all the means in their power to destroy our government preferring that of Jeff Davis whose cornerstone is slavery. Unconditional loyalty to the government is all the soldiers in the army will endure." Still, in spring 1863 Clapp was positive on the outcome of the war: "It is my opinion the war with the Southern Rebels is fast being brought to a close. All the news we have had for the last ten days seems to indicate a speedy termination." John Smith was also waiting for the end of the conflict: "I hope and pray that this unnatural war may soon end and that truth and righteousness may triumph." Yet he did wonder how this would be achieved when "so much sin and selfishness are rampant among our soldiers and officers."[45]

Throughout April and May the various units that were to participate in the campaign began the march to Camp Pope, the rendezvous point for the expedition, located near Fort Ridgely. "We received our orders on Sunday to start today for Fort Pope or Redwood," wrote Corporal Thomas Montgomery to his parents. "A great many of the wives and friends of the soldiers were up yesterday to see us and some still remain." The march through the Minnesota Valley impressed Henry Hagadorn. In August 1862 Hagadorn had moved to Minnesota from New York and had immediately thereafter enlisted. He found the area he traveled through a "beautiful rolling pararie [sic] with meadow and water in abundance and the soil excellent." The valley was also the center of the previous year's fighting and slaughter, and the signs of the conflict were still apparent. As Thomas Montgomery noted, "The devastation occasioned by the Indians last August becomes visible dozens of houses burned to the ground and the bones and carcases of animals lying strewed around."[46]

Eli Pickett reflected on the scenes of carnage—"It seems their inate savage desire for blood had been so long pent up that when it once got loose no earthly consideration could prevail to stay the hand of savage [unclear]"—and viewed the fighting as a "great carnival of blood." Members of the 8th Minnesota Infantry went to a St. Peter hospital to see victims of the uprising. Thomas Hodgson called it a "ghastly sight" and said the "tales of woe and horror that these poor victims could tell would fire one's blood against the redskins." While on a patrol near Camp Pope, Corporal Henry Synder, 6th Minnesota Infantry, discovered eight bodies: "Nothing left of them but their bones which were very much scattered." John Leo was with the 10th Minnesota during its march to Camp Pope. The evidence of Dakota raids was everywhere, "the distruction of their hands was visible in the shape of dead horses and cattle and the graves of two white men." When passing through the Lower Sioux Agency, Leo noted the presence of Sioux burial scaffolds containing four or five bodies. He wrote, "It was some

satisfaction to find that some of them went to the spirit land or
some other land before they were sent for."[47]

The destruction found in the valley moved nineteen-year-old
John Nelson, 6th Minnesota Infantry, to poetry. In his poem entitled "Minnie-ha-ha!," Nelson wrote:

> Minniehaha laughing water
> Cease thy laughing now for aye
> Savage hands are red with slaughter
> Of the innocent today
>
> Have they killed my Hans and Otto
> Did they find them in the corn
> Go tell that savage monster
> Not to kill my youngest born[48]

That spring, stories of raids and minor skirmishes convinced the
soldiers that the frontier was still vulnerable. On April 24 a Santee raiding party consisting of some fifty to one hundred warriors attacked the small community of South Bend in Watonwan
County, Minnesota. The garrison, twenty-one men of the 7th
Minnesota Infantry, fought off the surprise attack. They sustained a loss of one soldier killed and two others wounded, along
with the deaths of a small boy and two women. Soon after, another attack, likely by the same war party, occurred on the unfin-
ished stockade at nearby Madelia, Minnesota. A detachment of
twenty-five men of the 7th Minnesota Infantry gathered up
local civilians and rushed them to the stockade, where they
defeated the Sioux assault. Further raids continued throughout
the summer.[49]

There is little doubt that the images of the destruction in the
valley, coupled with new raids, led soldiers to believe that those
Santees still free in the West were hostile and threatened the
frontier communities of white settlers, increasing their desire for

revenge. Meanwhile, those Dakotas who had surrendered or never participated in the war were beginning to be removed from Minnesota, banished to the new reservation of Crow Creek 150 miles up the Missouri River from Fort Randall.

On May 4 and 5, as Lee was once again defeating the Army of the Potomac, at the Battle of Chancellorsville, 1,318 Sioux, mainly women and children, were herded onto two steamboats, *Davenport* and *Northerner*, and departed Fort Snelling. Aboard ship, the discouraged Dakotas did not know where they were destined. The journey was not well handled, having been compared by later writers to the Middle Passage for African slaves, but on June 3 the Dakotas arrived at their new reservation. With the government supplying flour and meat, they started to plant potatoes, corn, and other vegetables in the hard, difficult soil. In July their efforts to feed themselves were dealt a devastating blow by a severe drought. The corn died, and the other crops produced little food as the grass burned and dust blew through the area. There was game in the region, but few had anything with which to hunt. Slowly, the Dakotas started to starve, but they would not suffer alone. In June 2,000 Winnebagos, completely innocent of any role in the uprising, were also removed from Minnesota and sent to Crow Creek.[50]

Also in May, Pope had tried to expand the theater of operations with an invasion of Canada. Pope was concerned that the Sioux were crossing the border and would avoid the punishment he so desired to inflict upon them. An earlier request by Pope to enter Canada had been firmly denied by Halleck, who spoke for the president, fearing a possible war with the British. On May 19 Sibley wrote Pope of reports that Little Crow was moving into Canada, adding that if he was not allowed to follow, "the main objective of the expedition may be frustrated." Once more Pope asked permission from Halleck for the right to invade Canada, informing the commanding general that the Hudson Bay Company, the powerful fur trading business located in Canada, had no issue with such a military action on the part of the United States. Halleck replied that government officials were speaking to representatives of the British government over the issue. Until then, "care must be taken that our troops do not cross the frontier in the eagerness of pursuit." As Little Crow did not remain in Canada and the British government never approved an American military intrusion into Canada, the issue became moot.[51]

Pope was focused on events dealing with his department, but soldiers in the 6th and 7th Minnesota Infantry found news of the war back East far more compelling. On May 9 word arrived of a Union victory at the Battle of Fredericksburg. In his diary, Henry Hagadorn stated that while on dress parade the men learned of "the news of our great victory at Fredericksburg and the 6th and 7th regiments gave cheer after cheer for the brave soldiers and their glorious cause." As cannons were fired three times to mark the occasion, many men rejoiced at the news, assuming that the war would soon be over and they could return home.[52]

The next day word arrived that cut short the soldiers' jubilation. "We recd news this PM that instead of victory we have been defeated at Fredericksburgh which was recd with great sadness," wrote Hagadorn. The following day at dress parade the real story of the loss at Fredericksburg was related to the men. "How changed were the feelings from that of 48 hours previous," noted Hagadorn. The regiments "marched to their quarters in perfect silence with anguish in their hearts." Hagadorn concluded his May 11 entry with the pained "alas: alas: my country where is thy boasted liberty," as he wondered if the defeat came from the incompetence of General Ambrose Burnside, commander of the Army of the Potomac, and, if so, why the government did not know of this.[53]

Ever optimistic, within days Hagadorn accepted a new rumor, about the fall of Richmond. A captain from the 6th Minnesota Infantry had a copy of the *St. Paul Press* that reported the capture of the rebel capital: "The air resounded with shouts of joy from the hearts of more than 1,000 soldiers and the 12lbs cannon burst forth it fire and smoke which reverberated from hill to hill . . . not of deadly strife in battle but in joy for the great Union victory." Once more men dreamed that the war would soon cease: "They now look for a speedy closing of this great rebellion," remarked Hagadorn.[54] Shortly thereafter, the good news was again proved false.

Having twice been disappointed, Hagadorn was more cautious when at the end of the month, four cavalrymen rode into camp with reports of the fall of Vicksburg on the Mississippi River. He simply noted the rumor in his diary without commentary. This was not the case with George Clapp, who eagerly wrote his wife that "good news reaches us . . . of victories in various parts of the South. Vicksburg is reported captured by our forces under Gen Grant . . . soon we shall hear of the downfall of Richmond and Charleston. Heaven will bring order out of confusion."[55] Although Grant had placed Vicksburg under siege, the city did not fall until July 4.

With such hope for the end of the war, the realization that the reports had all proven to be erroneous led soldiers to once again pine for their families and home. Ill in bed, Hagadorn took time to write, "I received a letter from my wife this evening in which I was glad to hear that they are all well which is of much comfort to me at this time in these lonely hours which I pass alone in my tent with no one to comfort me in my sickness. . . . Oh home sweet home how I long for home." Upon learning that his wife's illness was getting worse, Thomas Cheetham urged her to "tend to your medicine. . . . You must take the best of care of yourself and may God help you." Realizing that his wife might be dying, Cheetham added that if God saw fit to call her home she should "above all things be prepared."[56]

By early June most of the troops going on the expedition had arrived at Camp Pope, located some twenty-two miles above Fort Ridgeley. Charles Watson, 6th Minnesota Infantry, found it a pleasant spot: "This is a beautiful place it lies in the valley of the Minnesota [River] on the second rise of ground the camp is laid out nice and there is quite a number of buildings such as hospital, store house, guard house, headquarters and a place to keep ammunition stores." Nearby Fort Ridgely became a massive supply depot for the column. Enough supplies for twenty-five hundred men, including fifty thousand rounds of ammunition and forage for a thousand horses, were gathered there. The now abandoned Lower Sioux Agency was stripped of all available lumber, blacksmith equipment, and carpentry tools.[57]

A. P. Connolly estimated that 3,052 infantry, 800 cavalry, and 146 artillerymen were assembled at Camp Pope. Writing shortly before the expedition left, Amos Glanville, 10th Minnesota Infantry, described the column as consisting of "three regiments of infantry and regiment wagons; one regiment of cavalry and wagons; battery and wagons; two hundred and twenty-five quartermaster and commissary wagons, containing ninety days of rations for the expedition, or as some estimate, three hundred thousand rations for man and beast . . . ammunition train and three or four hundred beef cattle. The whole, when underway, stretches out several miles."[58]

Among those who prepared for the expedition were four hundred teamsters hired to drive the more than three hundred wagons accompanying the column. Of these drivers, three hundred were African Americans from the South. In a letter to his parents, Thomas Montgomery referred to them as "a heavy squad of niggers for teamsters," while Duren Kelley wrote, "There will be about three hundred niggers along, enough to stock a plantation." The African Americans were not the only members of the expedition to experience the racist attitudes of the white soldiers. The Sioux scouts brought their families with them into camp. Jon Leo found the Santee women to be wanting in comparison to white women: "All the females we can have the pleasure of seeing now is the very amiable handsome looking but sooty squaws when we look at them and think of those we once had the privilege at least to looking at, we turn away in disgust."[59]

Individually, the soldiers also got ready to depart for the West. Each soldier was responsible for a wide assortment of equipment and rations. Glanville noted what was included: "a haversack stuffed with 'hardtack' and pork; a canteen filled with water; a knap sack stretched to its utmost capacity with clothing; an overcoat on top; a Springfield [rifle] and bayonet; and a supply of ammunition accouterments. The whole combination, in its completeness, including a spare cone and conepick, tarpaulin, makes one feel more like a pack mule than a soldier." Part of the food rations were desiccated vegetables for use in soups. The vegetables were not highly thought of by the troops. Captain Theodore Carter, 7th Minnesota Infantry, sarcastically called them "desecrated vegetables" and described them as "various vegetables cooked and mixed together, dried and pressed together into a sheet iron can from 1 to 2 feet square."[60]

One purpose for the vegetables was to help combat illness while serving in the field. The health of soldiers was a serious problem in the Civil War, causing far greater casualties than actual combat. "Our company is getting very small," Charles Watson wrote his father. "There will be thirty men less this year than there was last." Another way for soldiers to improve their health was to cut their hair short to prevent lice. "I tell you it is a fine thing for there is no chance for the lice and another thing it requires no combing," a contented Duren Kelley informed Emma.[61]

On June 6 Sibley arrived at Camp Pope, and four days later he took formal command of the expedition. Sergeant James Ramer, 7th Minnesota Infantry, recalled that "Gen Sibley arrived at 5 o'clock the cannon was fired and the whole camp was called out to salute him." Impressed by Sibley, Connolly believed he had "gained the confidence and universal respect and love of the soldiers."[62]

Sibley's promising assumption of command was soon marred by personal tragedy. On June 13 the general received word that his seven-year-old daughter, Mary, who had been ill for weeks, had died. She had been his favorite child, and he referred to her as "my dear lamblike little Mamie." A father in mourning, Sibley stated, "How dear to us this gentle child was." Mary was the third, but unfortunately not the last, child of Sibley and his wife, Sarah, to die.[63]

Sibley was not alone with his thoughts of home and the approach of a campaign with an unforeseeable future. Many men contemplated the coming expedition and the families they were leaving behind. Henry Synder took time to pen one last letter to his wife, Marie, before leaving: "Keep in good heart and do the best thee can. For I do not think it will Be a very long time Before I will be back with thee and the children then we will see some good times yet in this world of trouble and care." Synder asked Marie to give his love to their children and to "save a large portion for thy self fore thee is one that I owe the most of my love to." Ever concerned about how his own wife Marie was handling their being apart, Captain John Jones, Light Artillery Battery, encouraged her to "bear up and meet your trials cheerfully, you must not despair, you have our children to care for and watch over. Let that be some comfort to you. . . . We must submit and sacrifice so that we may hereafter live in peace."[64]

Other soldiers were concerned over how they would perform in the campaign. In a letter to his mother, Thomas Montgomery acknowledged there would be "many hardships greater than we can now image but we hope to have Courage to overcome all cheerfully, and be able to come back safe in the fall." Charles Watson's thoughts turned to death: "May my life be spared through this campaign if not may I so live so as to meet you all in that upper and better world." Duren Kelley desired to "bag an Indian this summer," yet was pleased to learn that his wife, Emma, was trying to get him discharged from the army. If that happened,

Kelley "would come home willingly." Also ready to leave the army was Henry McConnell. To his wife, Delia, McConnell confessed, "I should be the happiest man on earth if I thought I could come home for certain next fall. . . . I pray and hope that I can. I am getting more tired of the service everyday and so is everybody else that I see."[65]

On June 15 Enoch Eastman, a teamster on the expedition, wrote a brief entry for that day: "Orders received today for expedition to start tomorrow morn at 4 o'clock. . . . Orders that any sutler found selling intoxicating drink to soldiers or officers shall be court-martialed and dismissed from service."[66] Sibley's expedition marched out of Camp Pope the next day. Pope's long-anticipated campaign to wreak havoc on the Dakotas had commenced.

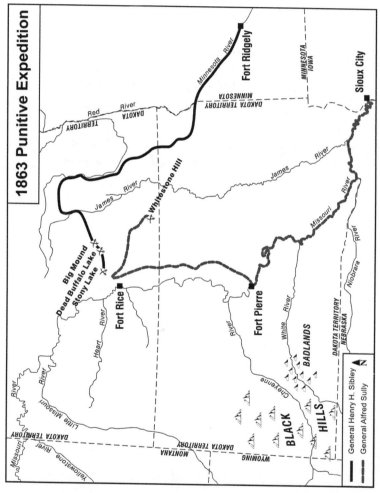

1863 Punitive Expedition

Fort Ridgely
Minnesota River
Red River
DAKOTA TERRITORY
DAKOTA TERRITORY
MINNESOTA
MINNESOTA
IOWA
Sioux City
James River
Whitestone Hill
James River
Missouri River
Big Mound
Dead Buffalo Lake
Stony Lake
Fort Rice
Heart River
Fort Pierre
White River
BADLANDS
DAKOTA TERRITORY
NEBRASKA
Niobrara River
Cheyenne River
BLACK HILLS
WYOMING
MONTANA
DAKOTA TERRITORY
Little Missouri River
Missouri River
Yellowstone River

N

General Henry H. Sibley
General Alfred Sully

Copyright © 2013, University of Oklahoma Press.

CHAPTER 4

Sibley's Expedition Departs

"ONE DAY WAS MUCH LIKE ANOTHER"

On June 16, 1863, before dawn, the roughly two thousand men of Sibley's column left Camp Pope. "Great noise and confusion at 3 O'clock" was how teamster Enoch Eastman remembered the morning. The column extended some distance: the wagon train alone was five miles long, with the last units not leaving Camp Pope until noon. The scouts led the way, followed by pioneers, a detachment of cavalry, the artillery, wagon train, and infantry, with more cavalry bringing up the rear. Cavalry also protected the flanks. The standard daily march for the expedition was one hour of marching, followed by a ten-minute break, starting at four A.M. and continuing until five or six P.M. Each man carried equipment weighing some forty pounds.[1]

Few of the men could have known that the chief opponent of the expedition would be not the Sioux but rather Mother Nature. The coming weeks saw brutally hot temperatures and a long, sustained drought that dried up the lakes and rivers, making fresh water difficult to obtain. The first day provided a foretaste of what the soldiers could expect, with the temperature reaching

100 degrees. "We suffered from the heat, the dust and the weight of our knapsacks, gun and equipments, from the first day," A. P. Connolly reflected. After the campaign, in his memoirs Connolly was more descriptive: "It was a season of drouth such as was never before known in the West. The prairies were literally parched up with the heat, the grass was burned up, and the sloughs and little streams were dry. The fierce prairie winds were like the hot Siroccos of the desert, and great clouds of dust, raised by the immense column, could be seen for miles and were viewed with wonder."[2]

After a march of six to eight miles, the column stopped for the day at what was named Camp Crooks, a beautiful location close to the Minnesota River. Not until noon did the march resume on June 17, but the column made better time, covering twelve miles and camping at the site of the Battle of Wood Lake. Wood Lake was a symbolic victory for the troops. "Where gallant Colonel Marshall of the Seventh [Minnesota Infantry] had made the biggest charge ever made in an Indian battle," Captain Christian Exel, 6th Minnesota Infantry, wrote with pride. "This action had decided the fate of the Indians under Little Crow and had brought a start to our commanding general." Enoch Eastman echoed that belief, stating Wood Lake had "resulted in the discomfiture of the Indian and the final delivery up of white prisoners."[3]

The current camp, named Miller, was near the abandoned Yellow Medicine, or Upper Sioux, Agency; Enoch Eastman described it as "a heap of ruins. A great number of scythes, pieces of iron and what fire could not consume lying about in every direction." Some soldiers decided to take small measure of revenge upon the Santees. "The boys burned some deserted Indian houses," noted Ransom Walters, 7th Minnesota Infantry.[4] It was likely that the homes belonged to those who had not supported the war and were innocent of any actions occurring during the fighting.

On the third day of the march the column crossed the Yellow River, reaching Hazelwood Creek five miles above the agency.

Amos Glanville, tired of the heat, was concerned over the lack of rain: "There hasn't been any rain since we left. . . . The prairie is rent with large cracks. But, so far, we have managed to get water by hard scratching i.e. digging. Every night a detail is made to dig after water." This changed on June 20. Having reached Camp Release, the soldiers awoke at four A.M. to a change of weather. "Drizzling rain and so cold that I suffered with two coats on . . . a most disagreeable day," grumbled one soldier. With a sharp wind blowing, the men, shivering in their overcoats, pushed forward eighteen miles that day. Although miserable in the weather, Captain John Jones could still write that evening to his wife with optimism that "I think when the Indians see . . . the number of our men, they will think that all the warriors of the United States are after them."[5]

On June 21, a Sunday, the column rested for the day after four days of marching. Kelley explained to his wife, "As it is Sunday we are laying over. A very good arrangement as it affords an opportunity to read our bibles and meditate on the errors of our ways." That day also brought the first rumors about the Sioux. "Rumors say that Standing Buffalo and Sweet Corn are at Stone Lake with a band of warriors waiting to give themselves up . . . but I have some doubts about this being true," Henry McConnell told Delia in a letter. Duren Kelley felt the same way about Standing Buffalo and Sweet Corn's desire to surrender: "Now this may be so but I don't believe it."[6] A large portion of the Dakotas living on the plains were from the peace faction of the Santees; Standing Buffalo was a key leader of those who had not participated in the war and was recognized as such by Sibley. Yet soldiers doubted that any Sioux could be trusted, and Pope had demanded a harsh campaign of punishment against them. Future events would be determined by how Sibley decided to view the Santees he would soon confront.

For Thomas Cheetham, having a day of rest or whether Standing Buffalo could be trusted was not foremost on his mind. He had just received word from his wife, Mary, of what he most feared—she was dying. Mary wanted to know what should be done with their three children—Emily, Charles, and the youngest, Caroline. A heartbroken Thomas replied, "You have asked me some <u>very hard questions</u> for <u>me</u> to <u>answer</u> as <u>you</u> said. You spoke of giving the children away. If you think it best to let Mrs Wheaton have one of them, do so, as it is a good steady place. If she will let you, had better let her have Caroline as she needs a steady place and steady hand to take care of her. Almost anyone can get along with Emily and I will see that Emily and Charles have good care." Cheetham added he would pay for room and board and send money for clothes. Longing to be with his wife, Thomas wrote tenderly, "Dear Mary keep up your courage and may God prolong your days that we may meet again on earth. If not, my prayer is that we may all meet again in heaven to part no more forever."[7] Thomas and Mary did not see each other again; Mary died one month later. Nor did Thomas reclaim his children. Following the war, he left them with their foster parents and remarried.

By June 22 the hot weather had returned, and the soldiers were finding it difficult to obtain wood and water. Encamping at the end of "a very severe march" that had left "all much exhausted," Arthur Daniels, 6th Minnesota Infantry, found to his displeasure "very filthy and green" water that he declared "the worst water we had ever seen." Daniels survived the expedition but died of disease in a Memphis hospital one year later at age twenty-one. Sibley had ordered no stopping for water during the march, even though the army passed through a river. A defiant Henry Hagadorn stated, "The boys declare that they will get water at every opportunity here after let come what will." There was also no wood for fires in the camp except for two or three old barrels. A glum Hagadorn wrote, "We now began to see what hardships we have to endure before we get to Devil's Lake and back to civilization."[8]

The heat and lack of good drinking water continued. The twenty-third of June proved a brutal day. "Today, in terrible heat, we march fifteen miles through a deserted and grassless sandy prairie whose gloom and monotony was only ameliorated by a few prairie fires," observed an exhausted Captain Exel. Daniels found the "weather hot, grass dry . . . water . . . only in sloughs, and then offensive and impure." A more vivid description was presented by Oscar Wall, 1st Mounted Minnesota Rangers: "had nothing but prairie slew water to drink and it was so filthy that I had to strain it between my teeth and spit the young frogs out or swallow them as I chose."[9]

The difficult conditions of drought, heat, and lack of water hampered the expedition for the rest of the campaign. In five weeks Sibley's column was able to march only two hundred miles. The weather was so dry that hardtack boxes broke apart and had to be repackaged and reloaded. Many of the men had brought along pet dogs that now either died of thirst or had to be mercifully shot. Combined with the above problems were swarms of grasshoppers that devoured what grass there was, leaving little for the horses and mules to eat. So severe were the issues of heat, lack of water, and grasshoppers that the column was almost forced to retreat.[10]

Thankfully, June 24 proved to be a better day. The army crossed the Yellow Earth River, "a pretty little stream" with good water, according to Exel. Reaching the Big Stone River, the expedition was now in the Dakota Territory. Along the river, men took time out to fish, as "our mouths were getting quite sore from eating much hard tack," explained Amos Glanville.[11]

The next two days the column marched over a "dead prairie" situated between Big Stone Lake and Lake Traverse. The men were able to catch five thousand fish while camped by Swan Lake, but they also discovered the bodies of other whites killed by Sioux raiding parties the previous year. "Found the remains of four white persons which was killed last fall," noted Sergeant

James Ramer, 8th Minnesota, in his diary. Enoch Eastman related a further discovery of two more bodies at the burned-out
Myrick Trading Post. "General Sibley with a carriage, attendants
and twenty horsemen went out near evening and the remains
were decently interred." Soon after, soldiers located an Indian
grave where "some inquisitive unthinking men dug it open and
exposed the corpse in the air," wrote a disapproving Eastman.[12]

Lewis Paxton was not concerned with fishing or discovery of
bodies. Paxton had only resided in Minnesota for four months
before enlisting in the 8th Minnesota Infantry. A meticulous man,
Paxton spent his free time keeping strict accounts of how much
money he spent and how much money he was owed. His entry for
June 25 read, "Major Smith came and paid me $26. I paid
Thompson $25. I still owe him $15. Two companies paid off."[13]

Sibley halted the army, worn down by the heat and lack of
water, for a three-day rest near the Lake Traverse area, a region
that John Pettibone, 6th Minnesota Infantry, believed to be "the
most romantic place I ever saw." Pettibone was to die of illness at
Helena, Arkansas, in August 1864, serving against the Confederacy. On June 27 the men relaxed, washing their clothes and
bathing. There were still problems with the water supply. "The
worst thing I have to contend with is the water. We have to drink
slough water principally and frequently have to wade into water
above our knees to procure it and then strain it through our hand-
kerchiefs, or chew it, one of the two," a sarcastic Kelley wrote
Emma. For the first time the soldiers tasted buffalo meat. While
on patrol, members of the 1st Minnesota Mounted Rangers shot
some buffaloes and brought the meat back to camp. Amos Glanville found the meat "rather tough," but John Jones wrote Marie
that it was "very sweet and tender too." Thomas Jefferson Hunt
echoed Jones's opinion, declaring "it was the sweetest meat I ever
tasted," while Eastman thought "it is sweet and much more tender
than this grass fed beef though somewhat coarser."[14]

As June 28 was a Sunday, church services were held by Chaplain Light, 7th Minnesota Infantry, and Chaplain Lathrop, 10th Minnesota Infantry. Sibley had proclaimed that every Sunday would be a day of rest during the campaign, confident that "we shall march farther, week after week, by resting on God's day, than we should by marching through the seven. . . . If God be not with us, we shall fail of accomplishing the desired objects, and one way to secure the presence and assistance of God is to remember the Sabbath day to keep it holy." The service conducted by Light moved Jacob Hamlin: "We are all seated on the ground in a semi-circle around the preacher, some holding their knees in their hands, others reclining upon their elbows but not withstanding this we have a excellent meeting and the gospel seems to sound sweeter to us soldiers here in the wilderness than ever before."[15]

Meanwhile, other men from the 7th Minnesota Infantry discovered another pastime. Along some nearby bluffs, they encountered a Sioux burial ground. They proceeded to tear the graves up, scattering the bodies over the ground. While traveling to Camp Pope, G. Merrill Dwelle had seen similar destruction of Sioux graves. "One thing I was sad to see," he wrote his sister Carrie, "was wherever there was a grave of an Indian the body was dug up and allowed to rot above the ground. With all the boasting of our civilization are we not almost as barbarous as they?" Angered by these acts, Sibley ordered punishment for anyone found disturbing the burial sites. Eastman found Sibley's position to be "a sensible order." Another man from the 7th found time to wander away from camp and become lost. James Ramer noted in his diary that "this morning a man from Co K strayed a little to far from camp and has not returned. He is supposed to be lost." Sibley ordered a mounted detail to search for the missing soldier, whom they located the next day ten miles from camp, where "he had layed down to die."[16]

While the men rested in camp, rumors started that two Dakota villages, likely those of Standing Buffalo and Sweet Corn, were in the Dakota Ridges—a series of bluffs located fifteen miles to the west. Excitement ran through the camp, and Sibley sent two companies of cavalry to investigate. However, Kelley remained doubtful: "I place no confidence at all in the Indian scouts and very little in Gen Sibley." The cavalry returned the next day after finding no evidence of the villages. Discouraged, soldiers wondered if it even mattered, believing that the drought would make the column turn back anyway.[17]

Sibley had no intention of retreating. On June 29 he ordered Lieutenant Colonel John Averill with three infantry and three cavalry companies to escort a train back to Fort Abercrombie. The next day, after paying the men, the advance continued. A twenty-mile march brought them to Camp Bradley, where once again Arthur Daniels encountered "very filthy water."[18]

Now more than 130 miles to the west of Camp Pope, any excitement the soldiers felt at the start of the expedition had waned. Captain Ole Paulson, 9th Minnesota Infantry, summed up the feelings of many: "One day was much like another. We saw nothing but sky overhead and the prairie underfoot; the sun burned mercilessly." Men suffered from mirages. Theodore Carter recalled, "We could see far ahead of us a beautiful lake with timber all around it . . . men would start calling water, water as the column suffered from lack of water." Yet the lake proved an illusion. A depressed Exel described the region as being "characterized by many small, clear lakes with sandy shores. Without these lakes this vicinity would be a desert where neither human being nor animals could live, with the exception of grasshoppers which populate the prairie by the millions and make life fearfully unpleasant for us." Exhausted from the day's march, Daniels was briefer, writing, "We are very fatigued."[19]

On July 1 a new problem emerged in the form of a prairie fire. "The flames spread, becoming one vast sheet, sweeping over the prairies," wrote A. P. Connolly. "A very roaring cataract of fire, the billows of which reached to the clouds." The horses and mules reacted to the flames with fear, nearly leading to a stampede. Soldiers started a counterfire that saved the column.[20]

The next few days were among the worst encountered on the expedition. Reaching the appropriately named Skunk Lake, soldiers immediately noticed a terrible smell, a smell so bad that, as Exel insisted, "It is hard to believe that there could be a place with a worse smell." However, the lake was full of fish, and officers and men made rafts and went fishing. The water itself was barely drinkable, being "warm and green." The first soldiers who arrived in camp dug a well for fresh water, and then sold it to the later troops as they arrived for ten cents for a canteen and fifty cents for a gallon. Combined with the bad water was the plague of grasshoppers. Exel commented that they "increased terrifyingly in numbers as well as in size and are destroying every vestige of green which has survived the drouth."[21]

The third of July dawned with rising temperatures. Exel wrote, "Today the heat was fearful . . . many soldiers fell half dead by the wayside; others had to sit down in order to rest; again others had such strong nose bleeding that they could no longer march, but had to sit or lie down. . . . Many a poor devil, tired and sick, had to drag himself over the prairie." Ambulances were sent to carry the fallen but "were soon filled to overflowing." Eastman declared it "the worst day we have had since we started. The air so close you could hardly breathe, and many fell down with the heat, as soon as they got into camp." "The earth like an oven, the air like the blast of a furnace" was how Lieutenant Colonel William Marshall, commander of the 7th Minnesota Infantry, remembered the day.[22]

After a march of twenty miles in the heat with no water, the soldiers made camp near a lake containing foul water. "It was a greenish-yellowish muddy mixture of such terrible taste that even in our dried-out, thirsty state we could not drink it," wrote a frustrated Exel. Desperate, men started to dig wells in the hope of finding better water. Soldiers from the 7th Minnesota Infantry found water after digging some fifteen to twenty feet down. A guard was placed on the well to ensure the water would be distributed equally. Although Sibley had ordered no alcohol be brought on the expedition, certain officers, lacking water, drank champagne instead.[23]

On the Fourth of July, bracing themselves for another difficult day, the soldiers had barely starting marching when it started to rain. "It made us feel like new-born children," Exel rejoiced. After advancing ten miles, Sibley called a halt for the day along the Cheyenne River. Exel wrote, "It flows through a deep valley that cut through the midst of the prairie and is lined by trees and populated by fish." Wells were dug that produced good water and the column was to remain by the river for a week.[24]

The short march gave the men a chance to celebrate the holiday. As Eastman recorded it, "Thirty-nine guns were fired by the battery in honor of the states and territories." Thirty-five men from the 6th Minnesota picked up their commander, Colonel William Crooks, and carried him around the camp as a brass band played. Crooks was popular with his men because "he thinks a great deal of his boys and they of him," Charles Watson told his father. Soldiers bought oysters, sardines, and peaches from the sutler, making a great feast.[25]

For some officers, the celebration started to get out of hand. "Gambling and drinking everywhere. Major drunk . . ." was how Lewis Paxton saw things. Theodore Carter also remarked on the number of high-ranking officers who became intoxicated. Soldiers were quick to criticize officers who they felt were incompetent, cowards, or drunks. Carter was still hard on higher-ranked officers, especially those from West Point. They were, Carter argued, "with few exceptions . . . hard drinkers and in two cases at least, drunkenness caused the loss of lives of soldiers and property of the government." In order to be a successful general,

Carter further maintained, you needed a vivid imagination, an ability to make the most of every occasion, and the disposition to claim everything in sight as being your work.[26]

Carter may have been critical of certain officers, but Corporal Thomas Montgomery was earnestly trying to become one. Montgomery was a member of Carter's company in the 7th Minnesota Infantry. A Lieutenant Cutter, an unpopular company officer, had resigned his commission, leaving a lieutenancy position open. Nine men, including Montgomery and Carter, vied to fill the vacancy. In a letter to his parents, Montgomery went into great detail about the lieutenant's examination for the position. It consisted of questions dealing with the "school of soldier and company," duties of line officers, the evolution of a company, skirmish drill, army regulations, and writing and spelling. It was so difficult that two men dropped out before even taking the examination. Montgomery scored the highest, and reported that "this announcement was received by the boys with 3 hearty cheers and congratulations." His promotion was short lived, as on July 10 Lieutenant Cutter returned to the company after his resignation was denied. The other two company officers were not pleased with Cutter's return, as they did not "like him at all," wrote a disappointed Montgomery. Later in the war, Montgomery, like other ambitious enlisted men, transferred to a colored regiment in order to become an officer.[27]

In the midst of celebrating the Fourth, certain soldiers took time for some solemn reflection. Thoughts turned to the war back East and experiences on the expedition. "The great and glorious day has dawned," wrote Exel. "But the heavens are not clear; they are gloomy and clouded like the political horizon of our glorious union which is so close to destruction. Does nature want to present us with a mirror of what is happening in the United States? Does nature want to tell us that our country is in danger and its sons are more desperately needed in Pennsylvania than on the deserted praires of the dakotahs? May our comrades there be victorious!" Yet a mournful Exel commented that the column kept marching "in a western direction, deeper into the wilderness, without hope of ever seeing a redskin. How will the whole thing end?" Henry Hagadorn was more positive about his experiences in the West: "I sit on the bluff ½ mi from camp and look on the scene before me my mind wanders, back to the East and my Native State but of all the beauties there I have seen none that will compare with this spot so wild and uninhabited and so far from civilization."[28]

Unknown to the soldiers was the death of the chief leader of the resisters. Little Crow, having failed everywhere to create a new alliance for continuing the war and with his request for assistance from the British government in Canada denied, could do little else than gather a few followers for a raid into Minnesota. By now there was a bounty of five hundred dollars on Little Crow's head, placed by the War Department upon the request of General Sully. On July 3, near Hutchinson, Minnesota, Little Crow was killed by farmers while he and his son, Wowinapa, were picking wild berries. The sixteen-year-old Wowinapa escaped and started a long, desperate journey to return to his people far to the west.[29]

On July 5 excitement raced through the camp with the report that the Sioux were nearby. "The Indians have made a junction and are at Devil's Lake in force, and intend coming out to meet us, on the prairie, five days march this side, and fight a great battle," wrote an eager Eastman. Sibley accepted the hostile intentions of the Dakotas, ordering the men to dig entrenchments. A cautious man, Sibley took this precaution throughout the campaign, to the disgust of Alfred Hill, 6th Minnesota. The men were often tired and hated doing the task, as many felt it unnecessary. Especially, Hill grumbled, for an enemy they "neither respected or feared."[30]

Although it is understandable that the soldiers desired combat, especially since they wanted a measure of revenge on the

Santees, it is unclear why Sibley felt so threatened. Sibley was very aware that the majority of the Dakotas the column was approaching were from the peace faction. He had been in correspondence with Standing Buffalo and other Santee leaders on several occasions, instructing the Sioux chiefs to remain where they were until he could come for them in the West. As a long-time Indian trader, he was knowledgeable about the Santees, their numbers and leaders, and had even fathered a mixed-blood daughter. Knowing that many of the leaders had not participated in the war, Sibley was not motivated by revenge on this campaign. Still, he was preparing for trouble and soon engaged the Dakotas in combat.

This willingness to see the situation as dangerous likely came from Sibley's understanding of Pope's desires for the campaign. Pope had been quite direct in what he wanted the expeditions to accomplish. These were to be punitive expeditions, to punish and destroy the Santees still at large. Pope needed military action to justify the importance of the department he commanded. Where the majority of the Santees looked for peace and an end to hostilities, the army was intent on war.

Following the celebrations on the Fourth, the expedition remained for six days in what was called Camp Hayes, awaiting the arrival of a supply train from Fort Abercrombie. On July 9 the supply wagons arrived and the column prepared to advance once again. The heat and the plague of grasshoppers made many doubt they would ever reach Devil's Lake. Writing to his wife, Mariette, George Clapp told her, "It is the belief of many wise men in the command that we can never reach our point of destination on account of food for the animals." However, Clapp supposed "our General knows how to manage his business and I don't borrow trouble." The drought had also led to the death of 120 cattle, making feeding the men more difficult.[31]

Clapp was not the only soldier who found matters depressing and needed to voice his concerns. "I fear it will not be to accomplish much," Thomas Montgomery opined in a letter to his parents. "For there is one opinion prevalent that we will not see any hostile Indians this summer; but it may be a mistaken one. Some think we may meet the Indians in force within a few days march but I rather think we will not." Captain John Jones was more hopeful they would find the Sioux "in two or three days. . . . I hope so, and that God in his mercy . . . will ever be on our side and give us the victory." Jones was still worried over how his wife, Marie, was handling his absence. He wrote that he knew she missed him but urged her to draw strength from the knowledge that he fought for "the cause." Sibley was also dealing with issues of a personal nature. He had received word that his son Frank was now ill. Having just lost one child, Sibley was thrown into depression worrying over his son. Unable to sleep well, he suffered from nightmares.[32]

The supply train also brought news of Lee's invasion of Pennsylvania. There was great concern over the outcome of Lee's Confederate offensive into the North. "But unfortunately the decisive battle in Pennsylvania had not yet been fought, and the speculations about the situation which we discovered in the paper were not very encouraging," noted Exel. In his diary Sibley wrote, "I feel much depressed to-day . . . by the gloomy news of the advance of the rebels." Thomas Morton, 7th Minnesota Infantry, included the news from the East in his rant against the army in general. Upset over the "red tape" of the military, Morton complained about the poor food, that "the hardtack is spoiling" and the pork had gone bad. If this was how the government ran the war, Morton raged in a letter, they should just grant the Confederacy its independence and be done with the war.[33]

On July 11 the advance continued, with the days that followed passing much like the earlier days. The heat caused the marches to end early in the day, the men entrenched each camp, and the lack of good water persisted. Every night the soldiers dug wells, up to sixty at a time, to try and find better water than that available from nearby lakes. The bad water led to increased illness among the soldiers. Glanville noticed that "the teeth of a great many became loose and other symptoms similar to mercurial salivation, rendered a large number unfit for duty."[34]

After a month of arduous marching, Sibley finally received definite word from some Red River hunters on the location of the Dakotas. On July 17 three mixed-blood Chippewa men rode into camp. They informed Sibley that the Sioux were no longer at Devil's Lake but retreating toward the Missouri River. The villages of Standing Buffalo, Red Plume, and Sweet Corn, numbering six hundred lodges, were west of the James River and moving westward. The next day Sibley advanced to a more defensible position named Camp Atchison, located fifty miles southeast of Devil's Lake.[35]

Sibley prepared to split his command, leaving behind at Camp Atchison those men too ill or unfit to continue the advance, along with supplies and a guard. One of those to be left behind was Henry McConnell. McConnell had gone for a bath in the river and encountered poison ivy. "My legs very badly, my right leg commenced breaking out and inflaming from my foot clear up to my knee and many places perfectly raw," a pained McConnell told his wife, Delia. As guards, Sibley chose Companies C and G, 6th Minnesota Infantry; Companies C and I, 7th Minnesota Infantry; Company D, 10th Minnesota Infantry; and some cavalry and a battery of light artillery. Heavy earthworks were thrown up to enclose the area sheltering the 600 sick soldiers and guards as well as 150 wagons and supplies being left behind. The sod walls were four feet high and encompassed a two-acre area. Twenty-five days of rations were loaded into wagons, one wagon per company, for the 1,500 infantry, 500 cavalry, and 100 artillerymen preparing to continue the advance.[36]

As Sibley organized his slimmed-down expedition, the men were shocked by a murder. Among the men serving as soldiers on the expedition were several full-blood Santees and mixed-bloods. A. P. Connolly had three Santees in his company of the 6th

Minnesota Infantry. One, Joe Alord, was said "to have a grudge against his people. He said they had always treated him badly, and he wanted to fight them. The second Sioux, named Miller, embraced assimilation and was a devout Christian, and the third Connolly referred to as "Walker."[37] There had been no trouble between the white soldiers and their Santee and mixed-blood comrades.

On July 18 a shot rang through the camp. A Lieutenant Fields, Company G in the 1st Minnesota Mounted Rangers, had shot a mixed-blood private serving in Company L of the same regiment. It was unclear what caused the assault, but the soldiers placed the blame on the lieutenant, now under arrest. Thomas Montgomery wrote his brothers that the attack was "apparently unprovoked" and that he "saw the poor fellow shortly after he was shot through the body." Oscar Wall wrote in his diary that "the Lt. will be tried tonight or to morrow if he gets his just dues he will soon depart this life." Another unnamed soldier agreed with Wall: "The Lieutenant is under arrest and if he gets his due he will be shot." However, at the trial Fields claimed that the mixed-blood soldier had drawn his saber and was waving it around at him before the lieutenant shot him in self-defense. Fields was acquitted.[38]

While soldiers in the 1st Minnesota Mounted Rangers mourned the loss of a comrade, Sibley suffered with the death of another child. He received word that Frank had died from his illness, and he continued to have nightmares for the rest of the campaign. William Paist also received a letter from home, from his daughter Lilly. In an effort to coax her father to return, Lilly told him that if he did not come home soon, his wife would marry someone else. Paist was touched by his daughter's transparent attempts, but it did remind him of how badly he missed his four children. "I look at their pictures everyday, oh I want them to be good children and mind their Ma and teachers and when Pa comes home they will get some nice presents," Paist wrote his wife, Henrietta.[39]

Further news dealing with the war back East reached the expedition while still at Camp Atchison. Word arrived of the Battle of Gettysburg and the capture of Vicksburg. "Our papers confirmed the news from the war," wrote Paist, "but oh at what a cost. Yet it will not do to stop now it must be gone through until effectually and peace fully restored or millions of unborn husbands brothers and sons will yet bite the dust in future wars that will spring up out of our unsettled nigger difficulties." Paist asked Henrietta if she thought the war was nearly over, adding, "I am heartily tired of it. I want to be with you so bad." Hagadorn called it "glorious news." Charles Watson, however, was concerned over the losses suffered by the 1st Minnesota Infantry at Gettysburg: "They say that the first regt is nearly all killed or wounded that is bad news."[40]

Rested and ready, the reduced column pulled out of camp on July 20, but the army had not proceeded far when it encountered a large number of mixed-blood Chippewa hunters led by a Catholic priest, Father Andre. The one hundred hunters, along with several hundred women and children, were hunting buffalo, and "they made a really fine appearance, riding like Arabs of the desert," noted William Marshall. More important to Sibley, the hunters had seen the Santees. They confirmed the earlier report Sibley had received, that the Dakotas were heading for the Missouri River. Long-time enemies of the Santees, the mixed-blood Chippewas further claimed that the "Sioux intend to fight," George Clapp wrote his daughter Isadore.[41] Even though they were currently moving away from the army and Sibley knew that the leaders were peaceful, this news only increased the desire for battle among the soldiers who had journeyed so far to the West looking for revenge. Sibley encouraged this feeling by giving a speech to the men, urging his troops to "give them such a dressing as they would not soon forget." The men cheered their commander.[42]

Father Andre had reported that some fifteen to twenty lodges of Santees still remained at Devil's Lake. To confirm this, Sibley

ordered two companies of the 7th Minnesota and one cavalry
company to scout the Devil's Lake area. The patrol returned on
July 22, having discovered no village, but they did capture the
half-dead, emaciated son of Little Crow, still trying to return to
his people. "The scouts found him in the weeds with out any
thing to load his gun with he had shot a wolf with the last charge
he had," remembered Thomas Morton. For the first time, from
Wowinape, Sibley learned that Little Crow was dead and not with
the Dakotas whom the expedition would soon encounter. Charles
Watson was pleased with the news of Little Crow's demise and
hoped that "if we are prospered we will doe something with the
rest of them in a day or two."[43]

By July 22 the column had crossed the James River, currently
dry because of the drought. The men passed over without getting wet and advanced forty-eight miles. That same day, a cold
and windy day good for marching, the soldiers met with six more
mixed-bloods. The hunters claimed the Sioux were only one day
away, with a village consisting of eleven hundred lodges and five
thousand warriors. A terrible exaggeration, but Hagadorn found
the rumor troubling: "if this should prove true I fear that they
will be too much for our boys." Montgomery too voiced concerns
over upcoming events, writing his parents that "I shall endeavor
by God's help to live in accordance, while I do live, and if called
to give up my life as a sacrifice for my country trust it will be all
well with me."[44] Two days later the army found the Santees.

CHAPTER 5

The Battles of Big Mound, Dead Buffalo Lake, and Stony Lake

"WE MUST FIGHT FOR OUR CHILDREN"

Bloketu is the Dakota word for summer. "When the new-born birds try to fly, summer is here. . . . The buffalo calves, the ones born in the spring, turned dark" was how Oscar One Bull, a Lakota, remembered the season.[1] For the Lakotas, Yanktons, and Yanktonais, May was the traditional month to break winter camp and start following the buffalo. When food supplies were low, hunting became a priority. Wintering at Devil's Lake had been difficult for the Dakotas, and the need for food was great. Standing Buffalo and the various other Sisseton and Wahpeton chieftains who favored peace banded together to pursue a buffalo hunt. As they traveled, remaining to the east of the Missouri River, they received word that Inkpaduta's smaller, resister village was encamped near Long Lake, while several villages of Lakotas had crossed the Missouri River and were also hunting buffalo.[2]

By midsummer, on July 23, the Dakotas were at Big Mound. The previous day, Inkpaduta with six to ten lodges had met up with this larger group and now resided near the Sisseton and

Wahpeton camps. Joining with Inkpaduta were two other small resister camps, those of White Lodge and Lean Bear. The three villages totaled around fifty lodges, perhaps two to three hundred people, all located to the west of Big Mound. Three to four miles south of Big Mound was a group of Mdewakantons numbering one hundred lodges, roughly four to five hundred people. Finally, the Sisseton and Wahpeton village, consisting of three hundred lodges of nearly fifteen hundred people, lay southwest of Big Mound and four miles from Inkpaduta's village.

Of these groups, the leaders Inkpaduta, White Lodge, and Lean Bear—firm in their resistance and already considered outlaws by the military—realized that surrender was not an option for them. The Mdewakantons to the south consisted mainly of those who had participated in the uprising; however, the group did contain a number of people who had not favored the war, and many, weary of living in the west, far from their kin, desired to surrender. The majority of the Sissetons and Wahpetons had not been involved in the earlier fighting, but there was concern among them about those young men who had gone against the advice of their elders and participated in the conflict.[3]

Iron Hoop, Daniel Paul, and Good Singer, all Sissetons or Wahpetons, later insisted that the three groups camped around Big Mound were not together but hunting separately. They did not mix and were not even friendly to one another. According to these men, it made the Sisseton and Wahpeton leaders nervous and unhappy that there were resisters dwelling so close to them. Most of the Santees camped around Big Mound were only trying to survive and wanted to surrender; Standing Buffalo and Sweet Corn, along with other leaders, were waiting for Sibley to arrive in order to do just that. Only a small group still favored resistance and continuation of the conflict.[4]

For the Santees, July 24 started out like any other day. The men prepared to go hunting. Iron Hoop recalled, "Early in the morning, it was reported that there was buffalo east of us, and we got together and started in that direction to hunt buffalo." Daniel Paul was among the men heading eastward. He wrote, "There was in sight quite a dust rising; out of sight, but they could see the dust of somebody moving, and it was supposed that they were buffalo." It was not long before the hunters realized they were mistaken. "One man on horseback went quite aways ahead and got up top of a hill and immediately turned around and come back towards where we were, and said that all the Americans in the land were close," remembered Iron Hoop.[5]

After the discovery of the army so near, the reactions of the Santees prove interesting. First, the women did not start taking down the lodges. If an attack was expected or feared, the immediate expected response would have been for the Santees to pull down the lodges and get the women, children, and elders out of harm's way. Further, the men did not start to prepare for war. For the Sioux, warfare involved the painting on of symbolic colors and wearing of feathers and objects such as bear claws. Rituals were performed to prepare medicines that would protect or heal the warriors while in battle.[6] Although the Santees had time to prepare for battle, they did not; this meant the warriors were not expecting to fight. Instead, for most present, here was the opportunity they had been waiting for—a chance to surrender and end the tension with which they had been living for months.

For several days, scouts brought word to Sibley of Sioux sightings, sending throughout the column a wave of excitement that a village might be close. Still, many soldiers wondered if they would ever make contact and believed the expedition was becoming a waste of time. "Our wild goose chase is a standing joke," grumbled Amos Glanville, and on July 24 Arthur Daniels wrote, "Truly, we know not what a day may bring forth." At one P.M. that day, this view abruptly changed. Sibley was in front of the column with his staff checking out possible campsites when scouts raced in announcing contact with the Sioux. The soldiers immediately anticipated combat, while Sibley ordered ten men from each

company to start digging entrenchments as well as wells; the
wagon train was corralled near a small salty lake. Sometime between two and three P.M. three Santee men appeared on the surrounding hills and were soon joined by others.[7]

The first to make contact with the Santees were the Sioux
scouts serving with Sibley's column. Little Paul rode right up to
the Santees and starting shaking hands. Gabriel Renville, who
had been vocal in his opposition to the war, was more cautious:
"Some of them wanted to shoot me, but through the bravery of
O-win-e-ku who was a relative of mine and took my part, I finally
met and shook hands with them." Although contact was peaceful,
one mixed-blood scout, Antoine Campbell, told a different story
to Sibley. Campbell reported that the Santees were acting hostile
and that the general "had to look out, them Indians say they are
going to fight, and they are going to." Campbell further stated
that through a relative he had been passed a message from Scarlet Plume, a leader of the antiwar group, that the Sioux intended
to trick Sibley and murder him.[8]

Even so, Sibley sent word that he wanted to meet with Standing Buffalo and other leaders and that he had no intention of
making war upon them, only those who had participated in the
uprising. At first excited, the soldiers began to relax, breaking
ranks to pitch tents and dig for water. James Hart, 10th Minnesota, did not think the Santees were looking for a fight but,
rather, that "they were out on a buffalo hunt." In his diary James
Ramer noted, "The Indians seemed to be friendly & said they
did not want to fight but surrender." The fact that Sibley did not
immediately strike the village annoyed a number of the men. A
frustrated Ole Paulson complained, "There stood the soldiers
armed to the teeth, burning with the desire to have permission
to fire on the blood thirsty savages. But we had to wait patiently
until the word of command was given." Thomas Morton disagreed
with Sibley's approach, maintaining that the general should have

"demanded their surrender and if they refused pitched in and cleaned them out." Critical of Sibley, Oscar Wall claimed, "Old Sibley is not worth a nish to fight. If they had have let Colonel McPhail have his own way the reds would have been cleaned out." Thomas Jefferson Hunt did not understand why Sibley would not attack, as the Sioux "were brave against the feeble and defenseless and gloried in torturing a captive" but would not stand against a real military force.[9]

As both sides waited for the chiefs to arrive for a conference, a number of Santees came down to the army camp. Their interaction with the army began smoothly. The soldiers even gave out crackers to some of the young Santee men. For Daniel Paul it was a time for a reunion with his father, who was serving as a scout for the army, and when he went to the camp to see him, his father took him to meet Sibley, with whom Paul shook hands.[10] Soon various tribal leaders were approaching the army lines. Suddenly, only three hundred yards way, their hopes of a peaceful surrender were broken asunder with a senseless murder.

Doctor Josiah S. Weiser, regimental surgeon for the 1st Minnesota Mounted Rangers, was from Shakopee, Minnesota, and had lived among the Dakotas, learning their language and serving as their doctor. Believing he saw men that he knew, Weiser and his African American orderly rode out of camp to a nearby hill, where scouts were meeting with some young warriors. One of the Santee men was Handsome Boy, the brother of Standing Buffalo, who was having a conversation with Alexis LaFromoise, a mixed-blood scout. Weiser arrived and began to shake hands with the men he recognized. Although several of these warriors had painted their faces for war, everything appeared calm until a member of Inkpaduta's band, often referred to as Tall Crown, pulled a gun and shot Weiser in the back, perhaps mistaking the doctor for Sibley. The scouts quickly fired, wounding one man. The warriors returned fire and hit a scout, Salon Stevens, in the hip. Soon after, the scouts drove the young men away. Behind them, Weiser's assistant raced back to the camp, screaming, "They've killed the doctor!"[11]

There was no conspiracy to murder Dr. Weiser. Everything up to that point had been peaceful and incident free. The news of the killing sent the soldiers into a rage. A. P. Connolly called it "treachery, pure and simple." Charles Watson was pleased that peace efforts had failed: "The ball was noe open. And pitchin was the game." Always a pragmatist, Theodore Carter commented that he felt that Weiser had been killed by some young warriors operating on their own. He did not believe that the majority of the Sioux wanted to fight but that it was more probable "that all that they tried to do was to keep our forces in check while they got their families away."[12]

The killing of one man did not automatically mean that peace was unattainable. Sibley could have seen the incident for what it was, the foolish actions of some young men. However, having listened to Campbell's reports and under pressure by Pope to pursue a more aggressive approach, Sibley ordered his army to prepare for combat: the Battle of Big Mound had commenced.

The first casualties for the Santees were the chiefs and elders who had ridden out to meet with Sibley. Caught in the open, they were shot down by the scouts as they turned to flee. Witnessing what happened, Iron Hoop related, "A few old men that had gone to the front, expecting to have a talk, were caught by the soldiers and killed." Standing Buffalo was not among them; he had not yet left camp when the fighting starting. Stranded in the soldier's camp was Daniel Paul, still visiting with his father. He stated, "Immediately a cannon was fired toward the south where there were a great many Indians on the top of a hill, and they all dropped down behind the hill." Frantic that his son might be murdered by the soldiers, Paul's father rushed him to Sibley and requested Daniel be enlisted as a scout. Paul remained safe for the remainder of the battle.[13]

When the fighting started, the 6th Minnesota Infantry were on the left flank of the line next to the lake. The 10th Minnesota Infantry were next in line but had been charged with protecting the camp. On the right flank was the 7th Minnesota Infantry, along with the 1st Minnesota Mounted Rangers. Sibley ordered Colonel Samuel McPhail, commander of the Mounted Rangers, to retrieve Weiser's body. Advancing toward the hill, the cavalry discovered the ground to be so rough that Companies A, D, and E dismounted, sending their horses back to camp while Companies B and F stayed mounted. Major George Bradley, 7th Minnesota Infantry, was ordered to support the dismounted cavalry with Companies B and H of his regiment. Aiding the attack was an artillery piece sent up to the top of a small hill protected by 10th Minnesota's Company B.[14]

Big Mound was one and a half miles away, with a series of hills, broken terrain, and a ravine running directly east of the camp lying before the soldiers. The Sioux were trying to hold a defensive line along the ravine. The artillery opened fire on this position with spherical-case shot as the dismounted cavalry and infantry pressed forward. Watching with the 10th Minnesota infantry, Glanville remarked that he saw "some splendid artillery practice." Falling back from the ravine, the Sioux rallied on a hill to the east. Ole Paulson describe the scene: "The great sugar-top swarmed with Indians: The artillery fired a few shells in their midst and cleared the hill." The cavalry then charged and captured the position.[15]

With the attack processing nicely on the right, Lieutenant Colonel William Marshall, commander of the 7th Minnesota Infantry, requested that five more of his companies be brought forward in support. Companies A, E, F, G, and K came forward at the double quick, racing up one peak as they deployed into a skirmish line to the left of the dismounted cavalry. Both the infantry and cavalry started a steady advance, flanking the Sioux as they pushed toward the summit range to the right of Big

Mound. George Clapp wrote his wife that he was proud of how the 7th Minnesota Infantry performed in the engagement: "Not a man flinched at all or showed any sign of cowardice." Describing one tough area, an "extended rocky eminence" held by the Sioux, Thomas Montgomery recalled that the men were "cheered on by our gallant colonel," with Marshall yelling, "Up and on the devils. Give them Hell boys." To a man, Montgomery's company rushed forward. "The balls whistled past up close and fast."[16]

Much of the firing was long range; the Sioux were badly outnumbered and lacked the firepower the soldiers possessed. Armed with bows, shotguns, and even old flintlock muskets, the Dakotas could not close with the advancing soldiers, especially when they were supported by artillery. Newcombe Kinney, 10th Minnesota Infantry, recalled that "their old flintlock guns . . . would not carry the distance, . . . although some would bravely ride close." Iron Hoop agreed that the Santees could not compete in an up-close battle with the soldiers and that "the Indians started to run away" or retreat from the onset of the engagement. Sibley further acknowledged this fact in his report on Big Mound, writing that the Sioux were constantly driven back "until, feeling their utter inability to contend longer with our soldiers in the open field, they joined their brethren in one common flight."[17]

Because of their ability to advance steadily against the Santees, soldiers who fought at Big Mound often dismissed the combat efforts of the Sioux. However, adapting to the realities of the battle, including the superior arms of the soldiers, the Dakotas were actually quite successful in their tactics. A Sioux warrior would fight for personal glory and honor, for horses or revenge on an enemy. But one of the primary duties of a warrior was the protection of those people, including his family, who could not defend themselves. A warrior was to be brave; Standing Bear, a Lakota, remembered his father telling him, "Son, I never want to see you live to be an old man. Die young on the battlefield." Now, with the soldiers threatening the capture of the villages and harming the young and elderly, the warriors, although they preferred fighting from an ambush, chose to block the army for as long as possible to allow the women time to take down the lodges, gather up their possessions, and flee from the danger. What soldiers saw as a constant retreat was, in truth, a skilled delaying action by experienced warriors.[18]

The warriors made sure that the soldier's attention was upon them and not on the defenseless in the villages. The warriors gathered behind the hills, using them as cover, keeping up a level of fire that slowed down the advancing soldiers. When the army gained one hill, the warriors retreated to another hill, starting the process of retreat and fight all over again. In his diary Charles Bornarth, 7th Minnesota Infantry, described the Sioux tactic: "Then with a tremendous yell they would discharge their pieces making the dust fly by the sinking of their balls losing distance in front of us," then, with another yell, the warriors would fall back to the next hill. Montgomery also mentioned the actions of the Sioux: "The Indians in numbers on the hills in our front dancing and waving their blankets before us in sign of defiance." Two leaders in particular, Standing Buffalo and Inkpaduta, proved skillful in their defensive actions during the fighting.[19]

Another delaying tactic occurred when the Dakotas put pressure on the army's left flank, threatening the soldier's camp and supplies. In response, Colonel William Crooks ordered Companies E, I, and K of his 6th Minnesota Infantry regiment and Company A of the 9th Minnesota Infantry to advance as skirmishers to drive off the attackers. Supporting the counterattack was Lieutenant Whipple's battery of artillery commanded by a Lieutenant Whipple. Never making contact, the soldiers drove the Sioux back over two miles. Still, as a jubilant Arthur Daniels believed, "Our men are chasing and chastising the savages severely."[20]

Meanwhile, Marshall and the 7th Minnesota Infantry had also advanced two miles. Finally reaching the last row of hills, Marshall could see the villages fleeing across the prairie one and a half miles away. The terrain made a mounted charge on the villages inviting, so, riding to McPhail, Marshall encouraged the commander of the 1st Minnesota Mounted Rangers to initiate such an attack. McPhail initially hesitated, causing some men in the 7th Minnesota Infantry to see his lack of aggressiveness as cowardice. "So much for the cowardice of one miserable coward. Let his name go down to posterity associated with cowards," a furious Clapp wrote his wife. If McPhail had acted, Clapp continued, "a hundred or two of the red murderers of men, women and children on our frontier could have been slaughtered." Montgomery concurred with Clapp, stating McPhail had "let's them slip off."[21]

McPhail did order the cavalry to advance. As it did, lightning from the darkened skies overlooking the battle struck John Murphy of the 1st Minnesota Mounted Rangers, killing him immediately. "A thunderstorm arose just as a cavalry charge was beginning. . . . It burst in all its fury, as they neared the Indians. One flash of lightening seemed to envelop an entire company," noted Glanville. With their villages and loved ones in danger, the Sioux put up their strongest opposition of the day. Periodically the warriors would charge the soldiers before making a rapid retreat. Five times McPhail led a charge to break through the Sioux defenders, one of which was met by an extremely brave man. Wrapped in an American flag, a warrior stood his ground and fired through the uniforms of two soldiers who were approaching him. Private Archy McNee returned fire, only to miss. Unable to reload his musket, the warrior used it as a club, nearly unhorsing Private Andrias Carlson before being hit numerous times by pistol fire and then sabered to the ground to his death. During the various charges, one man, Gustaf Stark, was killed and another, Andrew Moore, seriously wounded.[22]

McPhail continued to push forward nearly fifteen miles, reaching the area of Dead Buffalo Lake. Here, late in the day, the

Sioux put up their final defense in the rushes and wild rice that surrounded the lake. After a fifteen- to twenty-minute skirmish, the Santees broke off the engagement, and with that the battle ended. The villages and most of their possessions and food were, for now, secure, and the people living in them had survived; the tactics of the warriors had saved them.

Behind them the men of the Mounted Rangers proceeded to scalp the dead Santees left on the field. "Many of the cavalry, who were from the communities where they committed the depredations and where they and their friends had lost loved ones, now showed no mercy and scalped Indians marked the way the cavalry had gone," Newcombe Kinney explained. The cavalrymen took at least thirty-one scalps, and Charles Watson claimed that the men of the 6th Minnesota "have 40 of their topknots in our possession," something Sibley found distasteful. "I am ashamed to say that all were scalped. Shame upon such brutality! God's image should not be thus mutilated or disfigured," he wrote in his diary. Sibley ordered the practice of taking scalps to cease. However, the scouts continued to bring in scalps from their patrols to prove to the soldiers that they were fighting against their people. McPhail condoned these actions, explaining to Sibley that that was the only way to know if what the scouts were saying was true. Sibley then rescinded his earlier order on scalping, allowing the Sioux to be treated like wild animals to be hunted and skinned.[23]

Having advanced anywhere from ten to eighteen miles, by the evening of the battle the army was badly spread out, and attempts to reassemble were plagued by miscommunication. During the later stages of the engagement, Sibley had ordered most of the 6th Minnesota Infantry and five companies of the 10th Minnesota Infantry to participate in the pursuit of the retiring Santees. Realizing that after an eighteen-mile march to Big Mound, and with the coming of night, the infantry would not be able to close with the well-mounted Sioux, Sibley then ordered the 10th Minnesota, now five miles from the camp, to return; he also instructed the 6th Minnesota Infantry, who had advanced nearly ten miles, to bivouac in the field. The 10th Minnesota proceeded back to the camp, not arriving until ten that night; Company B became lost and did not arrive until the next morning. Exhausted, having had neither food nor water for most of the day and night, the soldiers collapsed to the ground, with Glanville observing, "Had nothing to eat since the morning of the 24th." Initially, the 6th Minnesota Infantry did stop their pursuit and were preparing to camp on the prairie when confusion with the orders led officers to instruct the men to march back to the main camp. Marching all night, they reached camp as reveille was being sounded. Some did not make it back at all, overwhelmed by fatigue and sleeping where they fell. Thomas Jefferson Hunt was left behind during the march. He reported, "I fell over a stone and made no effort to rise. No comrade was to be seen or heard, nor was I certain I was going in the right direction; and properly concluding that I should lie there until daylight I went to sleep."[24]

Conditions were even worse for the men of the 7th Minnesota Infantry and the cavalry. Having continued the advance far to the west, Marshall did not order his men to make camp on the prairie until nine P.M. His command was badly disorganized, as John Danielson of the 7th Minnesota Infantry stated: "Our forces were in fact scattered in small squads and without command. Many not knowing where the next move was to be." Having found buffalo robes left behind by the Sioux, the men wrapped themselves up and started to sleep on the ground. When McPhail rode into the improvised camp, he immediately urged a return to the main camp over ten miles away. Reluctantly, the men were woken, brought to their feet, and directed to return to the encampment. The lack of water was keenly felt; only a brackish slough was encountered. Clapp found the water "in a miserable slough near the Indian camp." He filled his canteen, took one drink, and then gave the rest away to other suffering men, as he "could not bear their cries for water and keep any in my canteen." Ambulances with water were dispatched to the men in the field, but they had only proceeded a short distance from the camp when, spooked by the sounds of the night, they took flight, retiring back to the camp. Not until the next morning did the men reach the camp, with Carter observing that they "came straggling back, tired, hungry and thirsty."[25]

Sibley's failure to keep control over the pursuit of the Santees had caused the troops to march some forty miles, along with fighting a battle, during the course of one day. So exhausted was his command that the day following the battle was mainly one of rest and reorganization; the column advanced five miles to a better campsite and buried their dead there. Casualties among the soldiers were low; four men had been wounded and three men—Dr. Weiser, John Murphy, and Gustaf Stark—killed. Later, Andrew Moore also died from his wounds.

Two men, George A. Brackett, the beef contractor for the expedition, and Lieutenant Ambrose Freeman, of the 1st Minnesota Mounted Rangers, had been away from camp hunting antelope when the fighting commenced around Big Mound. Unaware of the combat, the men continued their hunt, lazily enjoying the day while shooting at the fast-moving antelope. Stopping to water their horses by a small lake, they were joined by three Dakota scouts from the expedition, led by Chaska. Chaska, thirty-two years old and an affirmed believer in assimilation, lived in a white-style house, wore white civilian clothes, had both his children educated in school and had opposed the uprising. During the war, he saved a number of whites from death or captivity. Wearing a straw hat, Chaska rode up to the hunters, curious to know why they were so far from camp, and shortly thereafter a war party of Sioux appeared three miles away. First assuming the new arrivals were a cavalry patrol, the group soon realized their mistake when the warriors attacked. Freeman was struck by an arrow and fell, mortally wounded. Another warrior fired at Brackett and missed, while Chaska returned fire, wounding Brackett's assailant. Mounting their horses, the scouts and Brackett made a run for it and were chased for four miles until they were surrounded near a small marsh. Bravely, Chaska yelled for Brackett to dismount and hide in the marsh while he and the other scouts tried to lure away the Sioux war party. Brackett crawled into the high grass as Chaska and the scouts led the Sioux from the marsh.[26]

Owing his life to Chaska, Brackett wandered across the plains for the next seven days, living on frogs and what water he could find before reaching Camp Atchison. Back in Sibley's camp it was believed that Brackett had died. A rumor emerged that instead of protecting Brackett, Chaska, had, in fact, killed him and Freeman, then placed the blame on a roaming Sioux war party. Quietly, certain soldiers decided that Chaska would have to be punished for his actions.[27]

Estimates on the losses suffered by the Santees, and how many warriors were engaged, varied. James Ramer believed twenty Sioux had been killed. Sibley reported forty-two causalities among his opponents. Standing Buffalo later claimed thirteen had died, and Little Six placed the number at twenty-six, with most being "old men and women who could not get away." Daniel Paul maintained that only five Sioux had been killed: "I saw them all. The fifth was a very old woman, and the others were old men." Sibley also reported that he had fought a Sioux force of some one thousand to fifteen hundred men. Given the size of the village, this was a vast exaggeration. Carter placed the number at five hundred, a more likely figure, then added sarcastically that he was not surprised that the number was enlarged, as it had been his experience that when officers made their battle reports "the enemy nearly always exceeds the attacking force in numbers, and always fights desperately."[28]

For many of the soldiers, Big Mound was their first time in combat. In researching the experiences of soldiers fighting in the Civil War, the historians Earl Hess and James McPherson found that after having been in a battle, few men wanted to endure another. Henry Cross, a soldier from Massachusetts, wrote home that "a battle is a horrid thing. You can have no conception of its horrors." After his first fight, an Indiana soldier acknowledged, "Got to see the Elephant at last and to tell you the honest truth I don't care about seeing him very often any more." Combat in the East consisted of large armies fighting over great sections of land with an amazing amount of smoke, noise, and confusion, often unable to even see the enemy. This was not the case in the West, where much smaller forces faced foes that often did not want to engage in close combat and fought in wide open spaces. In the East, regimental losses could range as high as 50 percent after a major engagement, not including the numerous men who died from disease. Far fewer losses, from either combat or illness, occurred in the West.[29]

At Big Mound soldiers did not hesitate to engage the enemy. "They were not afraid to face the music, Minnesota may well be proud of her Regiments if they all fight as well as these have done," John Jones informed his wife, Marie. However, George Clapp wanted Mariette to know that "when the balls of the enemy flew past our heads the thickest I though of my wife and five children and asked God to spare my life for their sake." Yet he still felt "impelled to obey by such an inspiration as I never experienced before. Life was dear to me as ever but duty uppermost in mind."[30]

On July 26 Sibley continued his pursuit of the Sioux. The warriors had been able to protect their people and, briefly, their villages and their material contents, but as these items slowed the retreat, they were abandoned along the way. Sibley's men encountered a wealth of food, buffalo hides, lodges, and other objects as

they advanced. "There were quantities of jerked buffalo pemmi-
can, robes, furs ect. [*sic*]," remarked Glanville. A. P. Connolly
noted, "The praires as far as the eye could penetrate on either
side presented this condition of abandonment by the Indians of
their property and winter's supply of food." All such goods, along
with the lodges, were burned by the soldiers.[31]

Also discovered were the dead bodies of those killed in the
fighting and several elderly women and small babies left behind
during the retreat of the Santees. The women and children were
treated fairly by the soldiers. Connolly was moved to compassion
by the things he witnessed, and by something he found: "In the
sand on the bank of the lake, I found a tiny pappose moccasin,
and could see the imprint and count each separate toe of the little foot in the sand, as it probably was dragged along by the anxious mother, who was too heavily laden to carry her little baby. I
thought—poor, helpless child, not in the least responsible for its
unhappy condition." Connolly went on to observe that blame for
all the suffering could be placed solely upon the Santees for starting the war.[32]

Connolly and other men may have had pity on the young and
elderly, but no soldier commented on the fact that the majority of
the Santees whose villages they had destroyed and who were now
economically devastated by the battle, left with no food or shelter
for the winter, had had little or nothing to do with the uprising.
To the men on the expedition, all the Sioux they encountered
were guilty of crimes against the civilians of Minnesota and
needed to be punished. "Poor Indians! They had to pay for the
outrages which they had committed," wrote Ole Paulson.[33]

Although Connolly believed Big Mound was a decisive victory,
Sibley came under harsh criticism from many of the soldiers, who
felt he had failed to inflict enough revenge on the Sioux. Paulson
thought Sibley had been deceived by the "crafty Redskins" who
lied about their intentions to surrender, only to buy time to escape.
"Sibaly completely out generald . . . ," complained John Pettibone,

6th Minnesota Infantry. "We whaled them out as clean as we could with the leaders we had." Oscar Wall firmly believed that "the Reds would have been cleaned out . . . so bad that they would never draw a gun to their faces against the white man again" if McPhail had been allowed to command.[34]

As the army regrouped in preparation for continuing its pursuit of the Santees, the Dakota leaders met to look for a way out of the dangerous situation in which they found themselves. Stopping at Dead Buffalo Lake the night of the battle, the chiefs gathered to determine a course of action. Surrender was impossible with the solders hot for vengeance. Inkpaduta's bravery during the fighting was recognized, but many were angry with him, believing it was his followers who had brought this disaster upon them. Already the villages were in a state of mourning over the dead. Women were weeping and wailing, cutting their hair off to their necks and slashing their legs to draw blood. The men painted their faces black and cut ornaments and fringe off their clothing. If a father had lost a child, he cut himself in sorrow. Those in mourning put on rags, refused to wash, and started to fast. Normally possessions, including lodges, would be given away, but after the loss of the lodges and their material goods, there was little for them to part with. Unlike the Lakotas, the Santees buried their dead, but even here there was little time for a formal funeral.[35]

The next morning, wanting no more trouble, Standing Buffalo and the Northern Sissetons, along with many of the Wahpetons, broke from the main group and fled toward Canada. "We, the Sissetons hid and got away from there—went off in another direction," said Little Fish. Iron Hoop later testified that the pro-peace Santees went with Standing Buffalo while Inkpaduta and the other resisters, along with the Mdewakanton, continued heading towards the Missouri River to the west, although other non-resisters were likely part of that group. The family of the writer of Mdewakanton and Wahpeton descent, Charles Eastman, was pro-peace and still with those Santees fleeing toward the Missouri River. Eastman related the hardships of the Sioux trying to escape the pursuing army: "In our flight we little folks were strapped in the saddles or held in front of an older person, and in the long night marches to get away from the soldiers, we suffered from loss of sleep and insufficient food. Our meals were eaten hastily, and sometimes in the saddle. Water was not always to be found." As they retreated they encountered the Lakotas, still buffalo hunting. Meanwhile, Standing Buffalo and his people fled across the border to Manitoba.[36]

At five A.M. on July 26, the soldiers were once more on the march. It was a cold day, and the soldiers put on their overcoats and wrapped blankets around themselves. Sioux scouts were sighted, and Companies A and B of the 6th Minnesota Infantry were sent ahead as skirmishers. Sibley ordered no weapons to be fired that day unless the Sioux attacked, but when a deer bounded out from the nearby bluffs, the hungry men, longing for fresh meat, could not resist shooting the animal. Hearing the firing, Sibley believed an assault was underway, and for a time the column was thrown into confusion. By noon the army had covered fifteen miles and reached Dead Buffalo Lake. Along the way the scouts, moving in front of the column, had found an old man hiding under a blanket and an elderly woman. "She was nearly scared to death when we found her, poor old thing," wrote Edwin Patch. James Ramer discovered "a number of bodies that had died from wounds received on Friday" indicating such a flight by the Sioux that it had been impossible to care for their seriously wounded, who were left behind upon death.[37]

The plans to camp at Dead Buffalo Lake were soon interrupted. "All of a sudden the Indians hove in sight. Their numbers were formidable and, being mounted on swift fresh ponies, they circled around us with impunity, filling our ears with their, anything but pleasant, music," wrote an amazed Glanville. Connolly was also surprised that "the savages came swooping down on us, and it seemed as though they sprang up out of the earth, so numerous were they." More troubled by the attack was Thomas Jefferson Hunt, who claimed, "We were suddenly met by the whole Sioux nation, naked and mounted."[38]

The remaining Santees had been reinforced by their Lakota brethren. The Lakotas were from the Hunkpapa and Blackfeet bands. There were likely a variety of reasons why the Lakotas joined the fight: kinship ties, the threat to their own nearby villages, the frustrations still felt over the First Sioux War loss and the desire for honor and glory for the younger warriors. Black Moon was one of their chiefs, and likely present was another upcoming Hunkpapa leader, Sitting Bull. As at Big Mound, the Sioux were not attempting to defeat the army but delay them. Their main attack was aimed at the mule and cattle herds, to limit the mobility of the soldiers and reduce their food source.

To block the assault, Sibley ordered John Jones's artillery section to a high hill six hundred yards in front of the camp, along with two companies of the 6th Minnesota Infantry, commanded by William Crooks. Jones raced his battery to the hill and commenced firing a half a dozen rounds at the attackers. One Sioux, an elderly man present at the attack, remembered the artillery: "There was a heap of indians made a break for Sibley's wagon train . . . Sibley shooting guns that would make a noise going through the air, then all load up again & shoot second time, kill heap more indians that time." The artillery fire halted the attack and forced the Sioux to retreat, which Arthur Daniels referred to as "another beautiful skedaddle." The rest of the 6th Minnesota Infantry was brought up for support and proceeded to drive the Sioux back a mile and half from the camp. Daniels commented that the "Indians were immediately in our front, on ponies, riding backward and forward and evidently trying to feel us a little or draw us on" and called these attempts a "farce."[39]

The first attempted attack stopped, the Sioux now moved to the left flank, to make another run at the mules and cattle.

Marshall was surprised by the attack. He wrote, "Suddenly as the spring of concealed tigers fifty to a hundred mounted Indians dashed in upon the camp from the North. Many of the teams were out on that side getting hay and it seemed almost inevitable that they would be gobbled up." Companies A and L of the 1st Minnesota Mounted Rangers counterattacked, with Captain Eugene Ware of that regiment recalling that "it was a smoky day, and the horses of whites and Indians stirred up the dust, and the contestants mingled with each other, it was often difficult to distinguish friend from foe." The soldiers were impressed by the attack; Connolly thought that "there were those among them who knew something of the tactics of war." It was likely Chief Gray Eagle who led the assault. "He was finely painted, and his head profusely decorated with feathers," according to one soldier. Clapp respectfully called Gray Eagle "a bold, reckless chief" who, along with his followers, "dashed right into our camp mounted on their fleetest ponies." Gray Eagle was killed in the attack. John Platt of the 1st Minnesota Mounted Rangers also died when he confronted a dismounted wounded warrior. When Platt's pistol misfired, the warrior quickly shot him. Platt, mortally wounded, died two days later. Scout Joe Campbell saw this exchange and fired, mortally wounding the warrior in turn. As the man died, angry army scouts scalped him. After a fifteen-minute melee, the attackers were driven back.[40]

Long-range firing continued until three P.M., when the Sioux retired. The Battle of Dead Buffalo Lake had lasted three hours. Alfred Hill, 6th Minnesota Infantry, proudly proclaimed that the Sioux had been "repulsed in fine style." Connolly described it as a decisive engagement, and Arthur Daniels noted that the Sioux who attacked them seemed different from those at Big Mound. Theodore Carter characteristically downplayed the fight, referring to it as "the celebrated Battle of Dead Buffalo Lake" and believing far fewer Indians participated than were commonly stated; "I know, for I watched them thru my field glass." Sibley reported that nine Sioux had been killed, but John Pettibone wrote that the soldiers recovered only five bodies from the field. The army had one man killed and several wounded.[41]

Once again, the Sioux had been successful in delaying the army's pursuit. The battle, along with a serious lack of water, had worn out the horses, and the army was unable to pursue their attackers until the next day. It was a long, fatiguing march of twenty miles to the next campsite, called Camp Ambler, at Stony Lake. Horses and mules began to give out and died during the advance. Along the route of the march the soldiers followed a trail of discarded materials from the Sioux as they moved rapidly toward the Missouri River. Both sides were suffering from the drought, heat, and conflict.[42]

On July 28 Oscar Wall took time to jot down a quick entry in his diary: "Start out this morning in pursuit of our blood thirsty enemys." The morning opened with fog. The wagon train, not in its usual four-wagon-wide, close-in column, was spread out in a single wagon column, with the 7th Minnesota Infantry protecting the left flank. The 10th Minnesota Infantry served as the vanguard, and the 6th Minnesota Infantry and 1st Minnesota Mounted Rangers were on the right flank. Out ahead rode the scouts. At four-thirty A.M. the head of the column was one and a half miles away, with part of the wagon train still in the camp preparing to leave. Daniels acknowledged, "We were taken by surprise this morning as we were leisurely coming out of camp."[43]

The Battle of Stony Lake opened with the scouts racing back to the main body shouting, "They are coming! They are coming!" The announcement was met with cheers from the soldiers. "We had gained the first ridge, west of camp, when we heard the unmistakable sound of rapidly advancing Indians," wrote Glanville. Soon a single Sioux warrior appeared on a hill waving a blanket; this was followed by a mounted charge of several hundred Sioux. Sibley called the attack "one of the most magnificent sights" he had witnessed. Newcombe Kinney was equally

impressed: "Every Indian was at his best in point of paint, feathers and trappings. They were a wonderful sight—terrifying and
fascinating at the same time. They too were fighting for their
families, as well as their own lives." Unsettled by the assault, Clapp
wrote Mariette that "for a moment I thought we should meet with
considerable damage and loss of life." Paulson admitted that the
men under his command "became terror-stricken" by the charge
but recovered quickly when he ordered them to fire. "Then they
awakened as though from a trance and their vollies echoed in the
hills." "We gave them our usual compliments byway of a little
cold lead," agreed Clapp.[44]

The artillery was rushed to the front and soon opened fire on
the incoming Sioux. The artillery "poured a rapid and destructive fire from as many different points," Sibley later reported. The
rounds had a telling effect, and the attackers "scattered as if they
thought every hair in their heads was a snare drum and they
were all playing Yankee Doodle," recalled Wall. With the aid of
the cannons, the assault was "in a short time repulsed," noted
James Cornell, 6th Minnesota Infantry.[45]

The repulse discouraged the Sioux. They had believed that
they would surprise the soldiers in their camp, only to find them
already awake and prepared. "We are too late; they are ready for
us," one man called out. This time the delaying attack had not
worked. Still, shouts of encouragement were heard by the soldiers. Warriors calling, "We must fight for our children," and
"Remember our children and families, we must not let them get
them," only reinforced the importance of the stalling attack to
protect the warriors' loved ones, giving them more time to move
away from the approaching army. Other Sioux were indignant
over the soldiers' failure to fight with individual honor. Where
was the glory or desire for personal honor when one used artillery and long-range rifles to keep the warriors at bay? One chief
motioned by waving a blanket to stop shooting. He then yelled to

the soldiers, "Put up your shooting wagons [artillery] and long knives [sabers] and we will fight you like men."[46]

The Sioux spread out along the width of the column, some five to six miles, hoping to find an opening that would allow them to attack the wagons. "Signal men could be seen waving signal flags on certain parts of the field which was always followed by a rush of Indians to that quarter," one report noted. Colonel James Baker, 10th Minnesota Infantry, wrote, "They were well mounted, and moved about with the utmost rapidity and with their characteristic hideous yells." At one point the cavalry charged the right flank of the Sioux line, forcing them to retire, but mainly the fighting was long range, doing little damage.[47]

Realizing that the goal of the Sioux was to delay the expedition, Sibley ordered an advance through the attackers. Sibley created a square, with cavalry out front and infantry to the flanks and rear, to protect the wagons, livestock, and artillery in the center. Connolly found it "a beautiful sight to see the regularity with which the column moved" and proclaimed the Sioux "did not impede out progress in the least." With "yells of disappointment and rage," the Sioux fired a few final shots and departed, reported Sibley.[48]

This time the delaying tactic had failed. The army kept pushing on, undeterred by the brief fight at Stony Lake. In his comments on the battle, Sibley gave in to bountiful exaggeration. He called the skirmish "the greatest conflict between our troops and the Indians," estimating that his command faced between 2,200 and 2,500 warriors that included Little Crow's followers and the Yanktonais, whom Sibley called "the most powerful single band of the Dakotas." Unable to stop himself, he concluded that "no such concentration of force has so far as my information extends, ever been made by the savages of the American Continent." The more pragmatic Carter more accurately reviewed the last engagement. He believed only 100 to 150 Sioux attacked, with the

main purpose, as with Dead Buffalo Lake, being to fight a holding action. Reflecting on the three fights with the Sioux, Carter
concluded that "I believe that most of the Indians at Big Mound
and at this camp, were peaceable, but the comparatively few hostiles brought on the trouble, as the Action murders brought on
the Outbreak." The engagement at Stony Lake lasted somewhere
between forty-five minutes and two hours. Sioux losses were either three or eleven killed. One soldier recorded the taking of
eight scalps from the Sioux dead.[49]

Later in the day the soldiers captured a young Yanktonai man.
Having come to observe the battle, he had fallen asleep under a
buffalo robe. A scout riding by saw the robe and bent down to
pick it up. The man leaped up and started to run "swiftly, in a
zig-zag manner," wrote Connolly. "Some thirty shots were fired,
all hitting the robe, but still he kept on with the same zig-zag motion, so that it was impossible to hit him." Finally, Connolly stated,
"He now stopped, dropped the robe, and threw up both hands,
in token of surrender." The soldiers were impressed by his bravery, and the Yanktonai man was taken to Sibley. The man told
Sibley that he and his father, a chief, had come to see the fighting
but had taken no part in the engagement. Sibley was much taken
with the twenty-year-old man, soon releasing him with a letter to
his father, praising him for remaining out of the conflict. Sadly,
days later, as the lad approached some miners waving the letter, a
nearby group of Lakotas prepared to ambush the whites; the
miners shot and killed the Yanktonai youth and were then themselves murdered by the Lakotas. "This was another sad chapter
of this unholy war," a solemn Connolly wrote.[50]

That evening, the army encamped on Apple Creek, not far
from the Missouri River. All around them were signs of the desperate flight of the Sioux. "Near our camp in a ravine, a large
amount of jerked buffalo meat, buffalo skins and other Indian
property, were found and burned. The fleeing families have suffered a great deal from the hardships of their hasty march, as we

can see from the number of graves of children we find on the march," wrote Carter.[51] The expedition had not been stopped at Stony Lake, and now the Sioux were forced to make an immediate crossing of the Missouri in order to outrun their attackers. Supplies, food, lodges, and wagons had to be abandoned in their hurry to cross.

Charles Eastman's family left behind the lumber wagon that he had come to despise after his nearly fatal accident. Now his family prepared to move across the Missouri River. Eastman remembered that "the Washechu [white men] were coming in great numbers with their big guns, and while most of our men were fighting them to gain time, the women and the old men made and equipped the temporary boats, braced with ribs of willow." The crossing was not easy: "Some of these [boats] were towed in the water and some by ponies. It was not an easy matter to keep them right side up, with their helpless freight of little children and such goods as we possessed." Frank Jetty, a mixed-blood, had fled from the army with his mother and sister. During the night of July 28, his family crossed the river. "They started to improvise boats with small trees on which they tied buffalo hides. All during the night the Indian swimmers guided these boats across the river with ropes held in their teeth. Thus, all who could not swim and the women, children and belongings were carried across," wrote Jetty.[52]

Some of the Sioux were still fighting. Sitting Bull was out leading a raid against the approaching army. In June Sitting Bull had been hunting near Apple Creek when he encountered a patrol from Sibley's army. Attacked, Sitting Bull and his people fought back. "I did not want to fight the Whites, but I did not want them in our Buffalo land . . . ," stated the rising Lakota leader. Now, as the army closed on the Missouri River, Sitting Bull's war party struck at a military supply train toward the rear of the column. The Sioux could not close because of the rapid fire of the longer-ranged weapons of the soldiers guarding the train. "The soldiers had many guns and fired rapidly, bullets were flying all around us," noted Sitting Bull. Unable to do much damage to the train, capturing only one mule, Sitting Bull did count coup on a mule skinner.[53]

On July 29, at two A.M., reveille was sounded in the army camp, "a sound we have almost learned to hate," grumbled Arthur Daniels. At daybreak the column marched for the Missouri, reaching the river at eight A.M. They arrived to see the last of the Sioux crossing the river. "They were riding ponies, some ponies carrying a squaw and three or four papooses. They plunged into the water and swam across," reported John Smith, 10th Minnesota Infantry. Left behind was a large quantity of wagons and buggies. Soldiers counted 175 such vehicles, along with an amazing find of a new, bright red J. I. Case threshing machine separator pulled by oxen that made more than one man wonder about its appearance.[54]

As the army approached the timbers that grew along the river, Companies A, B, F, and G, 6th Minnesota Infantry, were sent forward as skirmishers. Spread out along a half-mile front, with men spaced five paces apart and supported by two artillery pieces, the skirmishers advanced. Daniels wrote that it was a severe way to march, "for it is necessary to keep the line as nearly straight as possible, and a little sway in the center, throwing either flank forward a little, causes the other flank to march in quick or double-quick time, to gain the alignment." At eleven A.M., after marching two miles through the timber, the 6th Minnesota Infantry reached the river. The Sioux had crossed, and Daniels believed that "both seemed to realize the farce was finished—they evidently enjoying the thought with gladness, and we with great bitterness." Edward Patch also expressed disappointment: "We are all disheartened that the Indians outwitted us though we drove them from Minnesota and through the Dakota Territory." The Sioux had escaped, but not without losses. Soldiers found the bodies of a number of women and children who had drowned during the river crossing. Newcombe Kinney wrote, "We drove the Indians across the Missouri and the women and children were drowned, many of them."[55]

Having marched many miles, the men "suffered from thirst," recalled Carter. Now, reaching the Missouri River, the first thought on the minds of the soldiers was water. "After having for weeks drank the brackish water of the prairie lakes, we drank this sweet though turbid stream," a grateful Connolly wrote. As they drank, the men came under fire from warriors shooting from the west bank. The soldiers returned fire, keeping "up a brisk firing," stated Duren Kelley, until artillery fire forced the Sioux back from the river. Soon after this brief skirmish, exhausted from the days of marching and combat, soldiers dropped to the ground and quickly fell asleep. So fatigued were the men that "when they would fire off a cannon we did not hear it," wrote Charles Watson.[56]

By evening, concern had arisen over the whereabouts of two men, Lieutenant Frederick Beaver and Private Nicholas Miller. Beaver, an English gentleman, had come to America to hunt buffalo and had joined the army with the coming of the Dakota War. He was serving on Sibley's staff and had carried orders to Colonel Crooks before trying to return to Sibley's headquarters at night. Miller was a member of the 6th Minnesota Infantry and had likely become lost. Rockets were fired that night to aid the lost men in finding their way back to camp. The gesture was futile, as the next day the bodies of the two men were found. Beaver had taken a wrong trail and been ambushed. He had fought back, emptying all three of his revolvers before being killed by three arrows and a bullet. James Ramer noted that "the Lieut was tomahawked & his having hairy whiskers they skinned his chin . . ." Half a mile away, the lost Miller also died in an attack. Several soldiers noted that Beaver was a Mason, so he was accorded a Masonic burial.[57]

In his report of the campaign, Sibley was very pleased with what the expedition had accomplished, calling the results "highly satisfactory." During the Minnesota Valley campaign, Sibley had shown understanding of the divisions inside the Santees and had reached out to the peace faction when establishing Camp Release. He had also corresponded with the Sissetons and Wahpetons who had remained neutral during the conflict. Now, perhaps trying to impress the more vengeful Pope, Sibley was merciless in his evaluation of the Sioux he had opposed on the expedition. Sibley wrote that the taking of "vast quantities of subsistence, clothing, and means of transportation" would leave "many, perhaps most of them, to perish miserably in their utter destitution during the coming fall and winter." Sibley voiced his disappointment that he could not wipe out all the Mdewakantons and Wahpetons, but took solace in knowing that "the bodies of many of the most guilty have been left unburied on the prairies, to be devoured by wolves and foxes." Preparing to end the campaign, Sibley issued General Order 51 to the troops, which built on his earlier report. "You have routed the miscreants who murdered our people last year . . . and driven them in confusion and dismay across the Missouri River," Sibley proclaimed, but acknowledged that "it would be a gratification if these remorseless savages could have been pursued and utterly extirpated, for their crimes and barbarities merited such a full measure of punishment."[58] Left unreported were the numbers of women and children killed, that the Lakotas had not committed any "crimes and barbarities," and the fact that Standing Buffalo and most of the other Dakota chiefs had been prepared to surrender before the fighting even began.

On August 1, after camping near the Missouri River for two days, the expedition headed for home with the band playing "The Girl I Left Behind Me." The men appreciated the announcement of the return march. "Joy prevails in camp this morning homeward bound is the cry in all quarters the boys all rejoice think that we may again be permitted to place our feet on the soil of civilization again," wrote a pleased Oscar Wall. There were only fifteen days worth of food left; the men, horses and mules were worn down, and little more could be accomplished. However, Arthur Daniels did not look forward to returning over the drought-ridden plains: "It is almost enough to make one sick to think of going again over the dreary waste," he admitted. "All, I think, are sick of Indians, and Indian war." Daniels disagreed with Sibley over the success of the campaign and was still bitter toward the Sioux, "who is as treacherous and cowardly as he is wild, and only brave, when . . . he can steal upon his victim with serpent-like stealth, and glory over him thus fiendishly slain." Daniels was not the only one to still desire further revenge. Some soldiers left behind beans laced with strychnine for the Sioux to discover.[59]

The column had barely left the camp when Sioux warriors started reoccupying the abandoned area. The 6th Minnesota Infantry was serving as the rear guard and did an about-face to counter the threat. After a few volleys the Sioux fell back. It was the start of a long, difficult day, hot with thick air from the smoke of a prairie fire. Assuming that water would be available on the march, the soldiers quickly emptied their canteens. With mirages of lakes appearing in front of the column, men began to cry, "Water, water!" wrote Connolly, but "We march and thirst again, and the beautiful lake seems just as far away." Not until later in the day, after marching eighteen miles, did the expedition reach Apple Creek. "The famishing men make a run for it, and do not stop until they are in waist deep, and then they drink their fill and replenish their canteens," concluded Connolly.[60]

The first day of the return march was one of great physical difficulty, but the following day, August 2, was one of cruel injustice. That evening Edwin Patch noted in his diary, "Tonight one of our Indian scouts died suddenly—sick only an hour." The dead scout was Chaska, who had died of poisoning. Although Brackett was at Camp Atchison, safely recovering from his week-long ordeal, no one serving with the main column was aware of his survival, and rumors still existed that Chaska, the man responsible for saving Brackett's life, had secretly murdered him. Wanting revenge, a member of the 6th Minnesota Infantry obtained poison from a hospital clerk and administered it to Chaska. Within a short while, Chaska died. On August 3 he was buried, to the sorrow of Patch: "This morning we buried the remains of poor Chaska in his lonely grave. We feel his loss as he was one of our best scouts." Days later, when the column reached Camp Atchison, a very alive Brackett greeted them, praising Chaska for his survival. A solemn Carter reflected, "Chaska was exonerated, but just the suspicion of treachery had cost him his life." Connolly also felt the loss, saying of Chaska: "He was faithful among the faithless."[61] Chaska had embraced assimilation, protected white settlers and Bracket, and had served alongside the whites against his own people. Yet, in the end, his being Sioux led the men he had befriended to murder him.

CHAPTER 6

Sully's 1863 Expedition

"YOUR MOVEMENTS HAVE GREATLY
DISAPPOINTED ME"

Sibley claimed his expedition had been a great success, inflicting severe punishment on those Santees who had participated in the Dakota War. However, one key element in the
operation had been absent—Brigadier General Alfred Sully's column. Sully's expedition was to have been the anvil to Sibley's
hammer. Pope had intended Sibley to strike against the Sioux at
Devil's Lake and then drive them westward into the waiting arms
of Sully's force. Sully's column consisted solely of cavalry, in order
to give it the mobility to be in place for the decisive defeat that
would annihilate the perpetrators of the uprising. Yet Sibley fought
a solo campaign, reaching the Missouri River with no blocking
force in place. Sibley had fought three engagements with the
Sioux, always with the question, Where is Sully?

As with Sibley's expedition, the second prong of the operation
assembled over the spring of 1863, but in Sioux City, Iowa. Initially, Brigadier General John Cook, a volunteer officer from Illinois, had been given the task of organizing the expedition.
Cook started the preparations and met with leaders of the

Yankton Sioux in an effort to keep them at peace. Found wanting as a top leader of the expedition, Cook was replaced by Sully, over the strong objections of Pope.

The 6th Iowa Cavalry, eight companies of the 2nd Nebraska Cavalry, Company I of the 7th Iowa Cavalry, and an artillery battery were to compose the strike force under Sully, along with three companies of the 45th Wisconsin Infantry, who were to both build and garrison a fort at a site chosen by Sully. The 6th Iowa Cavalry had been organized in the winter of 1862. Its colonel was David Wilson, a lawyer and Democratic politician from northern Iowa. Rotund, with an open and friendly personality, he was popular with the men. In April the 6th Iowa Cavalry started to arrive in Sioux City. The men of Company I, 7th Iowa Cavalry, were from the Sioux City area and were veterans of serving on the frontier. Sully would use them as his personal bodyguard during the expedition. Fearful of increased troubles with the Sioux, the territorial legislature of Nebraska asked the War Department for authorization to raise the 2nd Nebraska Cavalry. Colonel Robert W. Furnas, editor of the Brownsville *Nebraska Advertiser* and later governor of Nebraska, was appointed the regiment's colonel. The regiment arrived much later at Sioux City than the Iowa units.[1]

Unlike most of the soldiers from Minnesota, the men serving under Sully did not see the expedition's motive to be that of revenge and punishment, and they were far more negative about their participation. Although the 6th Iowa Cavalry was organized for frontier defense, someone forgot to inform the men enlisting in the unit of this fact. Recruiting officers for the regiment told would-be volunteers that the unit would serve in the South against those states rebelling against the government. Sergeant John Wright, a twenty-year-old Quaker, had joined not only because of patriotism but for his abolitionist beliefs. J. H. Drips, also a sergeant, believed the men had been lied to and "recruited under false pretenses." Drips enlisted to fight

Confederates and not American Indians. Frank Myers wrote, "These outbreaks [Dakota War of 1862] prevented our regiment from ever engaging in the war." Writing to the *Iowa City Register*, Henry Wieneke reported rumors of the regiment either joining an expedition against the Sioux or heading South, "pray it may be the latter," he concluded.[2] Although part of the Union Army involved in the Civil War, Wright, Drips, Myers, and the other men of the 6th Iowa Cavalry found themselves marginalized, sent to a backwater department to wage war on a completely different enemy from the one they had expected to fight.

In the writings of soldiers from Minnesota, a firm belief is expressed in a righteous cause against the Santees. The Santees had launched a surprise attack against their white neighbors, often marked by atrocities and death, and now needed to be punished. The men on Sibley's expedition viewed the campaign as a justified war against a people whose guilt had already been determined. There had been a specific threat to their homes and kin, and they now took defensive action to eliminate that threat. That the soldiers from Minnesota were suspicious of any and all Sioux and referred to them in racist terms was played out against the backdrop of the earlier events of the Dakota War.

The soldiers from Iowa and Nebraska, as well as their families, had not been so deeply affected by the uprising, although the war did cause an increase of alarm and fear along the frontier. Yet these men's views toward the Sioux were much more bitter and genocidal than the attitudes of the Minnesota troops. Lieutenant Colonel Samuel Pollock, 6th Iowa Cavalry, said that Cook had once told him that the general "had one infallible rule of ascertaining whether an Indian was hostile or not . . . to examine his liver." Pollock, very much a racist toward American Indians, embraced this sentiment, and these views were present as well among the enlisted men of the 6th Iowa Cavalry. "I wish they would all die," Wieneke wrote to his wife. "It would save us the trouble of killing them next summer." Wieneke also confided that the feeling among the regiment's men was one of "take no prisoners." Drips believed that "there was a romantic idea existing among a large number of men that the great majority of the Indians were the real nobility of the country. . . . But the first sight of a camp of friendly Indians . . . dispelled that romance, and every subsequent acquaintance with 'the noble red' went to emphasize the idea that 'the good Indian was the dead Indian.'"[3] With such attitudes, it is not surprising that members of the 6th Iowa Cavalry would be involved in several atrocities.

Those Sioux encountered by the soldiers were often described negatively. Siegmund Rothammer, a thirty-six-year-old German serving as a hospital steward for the 6th Iowa Cavalry, was a natural-science enthusiast, filling his diary and letters to his wife, Rosanah, with lengthy entries of information about the fauna, horticulture, soil, animals, and birds he experienced while in the West. In letters home he also wrote of the Sioux. "The Indians on this [side] of the river are iff anything, more degrading . . . with but one exception, and that the wife of a white man," Rothammer told Rosanah. He noted that some of the men were cohabitating with Sioux women even though "they are all a dirty, nasty set, and as yet I have not seen one who could offer efficient attractions to a white man to choose her for a companion, though all our men do not think so. Many are anxious of their company. They seem to be scant of provisions and a few crackers can buy most anything, of which many of our Boys take advantage."[4]

Only one band of the Sioux, the Yanktonais, met with favor by the Iowa soldiers, who were impressed by how the Yanktonais had refused to be drawn into the conflict and had worked to free white prisoners held by the Santees. Amos Cherry, 7th Iowa Cavalry, in a letter home discussed how the Lakotas had come to Fort Randall to encourage the Yanktonais there to drive the soldiers out of the fort: "The Yanktonais informed them they should leave and that they was going to stand by the traders who had befriended them and fed them all winter and that the soldiers had treated them well and they would fight with them and die all together." Pleased, Cherry stated, "Thus you will see the Yanktonais are on our side." Cherry went on to name several chiefs, including Bear's Rib, Drag the Rock, White Crane, and Crazy Dog, who had gone out to save white prisoners. "What do you think of that friends? Is not that a pattern of principle and feeling worthy of being imitated by white men?" Cherry queried. A letter to the *Iowa City Press* written by "Co B" spoke of a feast given at Fort Randall for sixteen chiefs of the Yanktonais who had supported the whites and saved white prisoners. "Never were a party of friends more welcome," stated the writer and called the Yanktonais "firm and abiding friends."[5] Sadly, these good feelings would not stop the Yanktonais from being slaughtered at Whitestone Hill by the very same soldiers who praised them months earlier.

Reasons for the expedition other than revenge and punishment emerged among Sully's troops. Settlement and expansion of the Dakota Territory and protection of steamboat travel up the Missouri to the mine fields in Montana were given as causes. Land companies were looking at high losses of money if the Sioux continued to prove a problem for settlers afraid to venture into the Dakota Territory. In 1862 gold was discovered at Bannack and Alder Gulch, and the following year in other areas of Montana. With the ever-increasing cost of the war back East, such gold resources were important to the government. The Sioux, not pleased with the steady flow of white settlers across their lands, were alarmed at the volume of steamboats carrying miners up the Missouri River. George Kingsnorth, twenty-five years old and serving in the 7th Iowa Cavalry along with his nineteen-year-old brother, Jesse, thought that all the Sioux had signed treaties placing them on reservations and the upcoming campaign was "to persuade the Indians, if possible, to return to their agency and cease their depredations" against the miners and Dakota Territory settlers.[6]

Like other Union soldiers, the troops preparing to depart on the expedition often thought of home and their loved ones. Again, the lack of letters from those at home was a constant complaint. Rothammer, who had enlisted with patriotic zeal, wrote Rosanah, "O Love! My country is dear to me, and my love for it . . . caused me to make the sacrifice." He chastised his wife, saying that the men received regular mail deliveries but he had lately found no letters from her. In one letter to his wife he had mentioned a woman named Nellie. Rosanah's next letter teased her husband about his fidelity. A very serious man, Rothammer quickly responded, "I have never given you any reason to doubt my veracity and fidelity to you, and you may rest assured, that I never will." With heartfelt passion Rothammer told Rosanah that he was looking at her picture as he wrote her: "I have you before me, and I can see in your Eies plainly, that you love me dearly and wish me to kiss you, and so I do so with my whole heart, and can only wish you were large enough, so I could put my arms around you, and press you to my true heart, and have the pleasure of feeling yours beat near mine, as I can feel my lips press the cold glass which covers yours so dearly loved features."[7]

Even Colonel David Wilson, commander of the 6th Iowa Cavalry, complained over the lack of correspondence. "I was quite disappointed in not receiving a letter from you today. All the officers heard from home but me. . . . Oh! If you only knew how much your letters were prized you certainly would write oftener," pleaded Wilson to his wife, Henrietta. Amos Cherry was not so concerned for himself but for another man in his company who rarely obtained mail. "Archie never hears from home at all never has had but 2 letters from home since he entered the service," Cherry informed some friends. "I know he is lonesome and anxious and would like to hear from them. . . . I do wish you would all write to him . . . . It would do him good I know."[8]

Growing tired of Sioux City, the soldiers were ready for the campaign to commence. During May and June the various elements of the expedition proceeded to leave Sioux City, marching first to Fort Reynolds and later to Fort Pierre, the forward base for the operation. The first troops to advance were from the 6th Iowa Cavalry, followed shortly by the rest of the expedition. On June 16, friction developed between the 6th Iowa Cavalry and 7th Iowa Cavalry over a fire set by members of the 2nd Battalion, 6th Iowa Cavalry. The incident occurred following a difficult day that had the thirsty horses of both regiments stampede down to the Little Missouri River. Soon after, for an unknown reason, men from the 2nd battalion started a fire that, with the dry conditions, quickly got out of hand and turned into a full-blown prairie fire that consumed all the grass the expedition needed to feed the horses. The fire continued into the next day before burning itself out. In a letter to his wife, a furious Henry Wieneke raged against the men who set the fire: "They are the meanest set of men taken them all together that I ever set my Eyes on. Some few of them are good but the greater part of them are Secessionists and jaolbirds—if the whole reg't are like the 2nd Batalion I would not give any thing for the fighting they will do."[9]

Other members of the 6th Iowa Cavalry caused controversy by their participation in an atrocity against friendly Lakotas at Ponca Creek. On June 12, while at Fort Randall, a Sergeant Neuman had gone looking for his horse, which had wandered away during the night. He had later returned to the fort and reported he had been fired upon by a small group of Sioux. A detachment of the 1st Dakota Cavalry under Sergeant Abner English was then sent out but could not locate the Sioux. The next day a Captain Moreland, with ten men from G Company, 6th Iowa Cavalry, and five men of Company H, 1st Dakota Cavalry, had taken up the pursuit. By then, any Sioux who may have fired at Sergeant Neuman were long gone from the area. However, other Sioux—eight male members of the Two Kettles band of the Lakotas, innocent of any wrong-doing—had been nearby, having just left the Yankton Agency. Their leader, named either Puffy Eyes or Pouting Eye, had been an elderly man who had recently been involved in saving white prisoners held by the Santee resisters, obtaining their release by giving ponies to their captors. Moreland and his patrol had discovered the Two Kettles group and surrounded them. The Lakotas had offered no resistance and had willingly turned their weapons over to the soldiers. Puffy Eyes had produced a letter, signed by General William Harney, proclaiming the chief to be a good man. Although there are different versions of what happened next, at some point the Sioux had been told they were free to leave. When the Lakotas started to depart, with their backs to the soldiers, they had been gunned down. Only one man had escaped the massacre.[10]

Reactions to the Ponca Creek Massacre and the way it was explained varied. Sergeant English later wrote that the Sioux were killed in battle, falling before a mounted charge of Moreland's men, "the entire party were left food for the coyotes." Drips reported that the Sioux were killed when they tried to escape. Writing to the *Iowa City Republican*, Wieneke stated that Captain Moreland "had a little brush in which seven Indians were killed none of our men were injured . . ." and added that the Sioux were "excellently armed with rifles and shotguns." Others, upon learning the truth, were shocked by the massacre. After some men tried to portray the massacre as a battle, Milton Spencer voiced his disapproval by writing, "I suppose the cowardly wretches who committed that cold blooded murder feel a little uneasy and so try to give the affair the appearance of a battle." Lieutenant Colonel John Pattee called the murdered men "the most loyal and friendly Indians that could be found in the whole country." Rothammer, writing to Rosanah, also declared the attack a "cruel wanton outrage" and then related his conversation with the sole survivor of the massacre. The survivor was the son of Puffy Eyes and wanted to know why they had been attacked. What had they done except always befriend the white man? He would not take revenge as his people were too few to fight the soldiers, and he was resigned to remain friends with the whites, wrote Rothammer.[11]

Local Sioux living on the reservation near Fort Randall responded to the massacre with deep mourning and resentment toward the army. Wieneke noted in his diary that the murdered men "all have relations here and these have commenced howling and crying already." Rothammer noted the absence of any Sioux in the soldiers' camp following the incident: "Heretofore plenty of Indians and Squaws would be all around the camplines trading moccasins and Bows . . . and other trinkets. . . . Today none are visible, and our men begin to think, that trouble may result from the . . . butchery." Pattee was concerned enough to go alone to a Sioux camp near Fort Pierre and apologize for the actions of the soldiers. Upon hearing of what became known as the Ponca Creek Massacre, Sully was furious, having Lieutenant Colonel Pollock, the bigoted commander of the 6th Iowa Cavalry, arrested and later setting up a board of investigation to look into the incident. Eventually the matter was dropped.[12]

The Ponca Creek Massacre was just a larger manifestation of the racist attitudes held by many of the soldiers. While at Fort Randall, a post Rothammer called "not worthy of the name, as it really is no fort at all, but only an assembly of loghouses," Henry Pierce related that, even after the massacre that had upset the Sioux, men broke into Sioux burial mounds: "Their curiosity also incites them to disturb their dead, a dangerous passion in indulge in, even among hostile or peaceful tribes." And Abner English still referred to the Sioux as "blood-thirsty savages." Camping near the Crow Creek Agency, the men of the 2nd Nebraska Cavalry received the attention of the near-starving women of the reservation who were willing to sell their bodies for food and goods. With no sympathy for their plight, Furnas dismissed the women's actions as "seeking substitutes of Bucks, I presume." Furnas was disgusted by the women, calling them "filthy hags whose ugliness was only equaled by their want of anything like modesty or virtue." At Fort Pierre, while soldiers unloaded supplies from steamboats on the Missouri River, several Sioux objected, demanding a portion of the supplies. Pattee gave them gifts of crackers and tobacco and defused the situation, to the frustration of Drips. Desiring conflict, Drips complained, "Here was lost one of the finest chances for an Indian fight we had on the whole expedition through the cowardice . . . of Col. Pattee."[13]

On July 4 most of the expedition was still at Fort Randall and able to celebrate Independence Day. The commander of the expedition rose to address the men. General Alfred Sully was a graduate of West Point and, at age forty-three, an experienced officer. Sully had fought in the Mexican-American War and served in the West prior to the Civil War, where he had come to respect and like the Sioux, who in some ways he found superior to whites. During the early part of the Civil War, Sully had been in the eastern theater, where he had participated in the battles of the Peninsular Campaign, Second Bull Run, Antietam, Fredericksburg, and Chancellorsville, earning a brevet rank of brigadier general. Sully was blunt, opinionated, hot tempered, and profane. He was a friend and supporter of the out-of-favor George McClellan; hated reporters as, he said, they distorted the facts; was openly critical of superior officers who, he felt, were incompetent; and already hated Pope, whom he found to be arrogant and a popinjay.[14]

On this Fourth of July, Sully, dressed as he always did in an old uniform with no markings of rank, spoke not of the upcoming campaign but rather of the men he had known while he had been stationed at Fort Randall years before. Many of these men currently served with the Confederacy and were "now in arms against their and his country." Rothammer was very disappointed: "We expected to hear some orations from our accomplished officers, but not a single sentence was uttered, and had not a half ration of whiskey been distributed, the men would not have known the difference of any other day."[15] Some men of the

6th Iowa Cavalry had obtained a few gallons of poor whiskey mixed with water from the Missouri River to celebrate what became a fairly lackluster event.

Rothammer soon perked up with news of the Union victories at Gettysburg and Vicksburg. "Glory had been won by our gallant armies," Rothammer proclaimed. "The heroes who by the shedding of their noble blood have won for it the liberties, which treacherous tyranny attempted to deprive them of. Thanks be to God." The report of eastern successes against the rebels led others to reflect on the current campaign against the Sioux. Henry Pierce was excited about the expedition, writing, "We expect to see something. All are anxious to smell the powder." Albert Childs wondered if the poor water levels of the Missouri River would cause the campaign to fail. "It appears to me, to be one of the most foolish things in the world, to take this expedition any further," he wrote his brother Ellsworth. Childs had heard rumors that Sibley had turned back, and if so, then he felt it was Sully's duty to also retire from the field.[16]

On July 25 the column reached Fort Pierre. Like Sibley's men, they had encountered the terrible conditions caused by the drought. "Creeks in this country are not streams of running water like you have in Iowa. . . . At this time they are nothing but deep ditches with here and there a small pool of water," reported Milton Spencer, a veteran of the Battle of Shiloh. Rothammer, the nature buff, was busy investigating a prairie dog community and "their little dens," observing rattlesnakes and going off on short mineralogical trips by himself. Pleased with his adventures, Rothammer still complained of the drought conditions, writing Rosanah, "We eat dirth, drink dirth, breath dirth, sleep in dirth and we are altogether a dirty sett." On July 1 Colonel Furnas, commander of the 2nd Nebraska Cavalry, jotted down only two words in his journal: "Day hot." Corporal Henry Pierce, also of the 2nd Nebraska Cavalry, was even more repulsed by the terrain, writing on June 27, "Left this miserable camp of sand and drought and parched fields. Traveled today over a district of country that would starve a forlorn hope of catapillers. . . . May God speed any man that deserts this part of the country for it is destitute of wood & water & destitute of grass, destitute of game." Although there was little game to be found, the soldiers did find numerous frogs. "Many suppers of frogs were ate . . . ," recalled Pierce, who initially refused to eat the reptiles but then discovered he loved the taste and "Whenever I can get frogs enough to eat I'm going to have them."[17]

Rothammer described Fort Pierre as "built in a square, and consisted of 4 log buildings with log towers, each of which is provided with loopholes for infantry. On one of these little towers, who like all the buildings in this fort are covered with shingles, is a small gallery for the accommodations of a Sentinel and lookout, and the whole is enclosed by a wall of logs sett perpendicular in the ground projecting about 12 feet out of it." After a dry, barren march to the post, Milton Spencer found the lands around Fort Pierre to be quite good: "This is a great country, wild and free, and will be so far a long time to come. Nearly 400 miles eastward to reach the advance guard of white civilization and this is the nearest white neighbors to have."[18] It was good the outpost met with overall approval, as the expedition would now spend weeks there waiting for steamboats to bring supplies up the low water levels of the Missouri River.

As the army waited for the necessary supplies in order to mount their operation against the Sioux, the Yanktonais were also making preparations for two important events—religious ceremonies and the summer buffalo hunts. During the early part of the summer, April and May, the various villages and bands would start to move across the prairie. If food was low following the winter, some hunting would take place; this was also the time for young men to mount raids against their people's enemies. By July, or the "Moon of Cherry Ripening," the various groups would begin to gather together for a variety of social and religious ceremonies. The Yanktonais met to deal with foreign and domestic issues facing the band, feast and spend time together, play sports, and hold religious rituals, such as the Sun Dance.[19]

The Sun Dance was a tribal affair that included a variety of rituals and ceremonies. Usually held in July, the event lasted for twelve days. The first four days were spent in preparation and reunions among the different villages and bands. During the next four days, the men who would partake in the dance were given instructions, and the final four days were devoted to the dance itself. Men volunteered to perform the ritual to show their devotion to the tribe, to fulfill a vow they had made earlier, for spiritual guidance, or to achieve a vision. Fasting and self-torture, such as cutting of one's skin, took place before a rawhide strap would be inserted through each breast and an area of the back. Black Elk, a Lakota holy man, described the process: "Then each would lie down beneath the tree as though he were dead, and the holy men would cut a place in his back or chest, so that a strip of rawhide, fastened to the top of the tree, could be pushed through the flesh and tied. Then the man would get up and dance to the drums, leaning on the rawhide strip as long as he could stand the pain or until the flesh tore loose." The Reverend Samuel Pond, a missionary to the Santees in Minnesota, witnessed a Sun Dance and observed, "The dancers danced with their faces towards the Sun, till their strength was exhausted." Many continued to dance until they could pull themselves off the rawhide strips; others required help to gain their release. Although of the highest importance to the Sioux, the Sun Dance was dismissed by Wieneke when he saw one performed, commenting that the dance was "to an unseen spirit."[20]

Thus, as the army prepared for war, the Yanktonais were carrying out important social and religious rituals. Although concerned over the events occurring around them involving the Santees and Lakotas, the Yanktonais went on with their day-to-day existence. They had not made war on the whites; in fact, a number of their leaders had aided the whites in obtaining the release of prisoners held by the Santee resisters fighting the army. Yet, as they moved across the plains in search of buffalo, they were approaching the very area into which Sully was intending to advance while looking for an enemy to engage.

Back at Fort Pierre, news of another Sioux raid incensed the soldiers gathered there. Life at the fort had become fairly relaxed. Rothammer wrote about how the men spent their off-duty time: "Some . . . by singing, some by telling stories, some by dancing, others by reading, playing cards swimming, wrestling, chumping, running, quarrelling, and a few by winning squaws. Whiskey is not among the soldiers, though most Officers have some." Then word arrived of what became known as the Wiseman Massacre.[21]

Henson and Phoebe Wiseman and their five children had a farm near St. James, Nebraska. Henson enlisted, joining Company I, 2nd Nebraska Cavalry, and was currently serving with the expedition. Wiseman had wanted his wife and children to move to St. James until he could return from the war, but Phoebe disagreed, wanting to remain in their home on the farm. On July 16 Phoebe went to town to obtain supplies, leaving her sixteen-year-old son, Arthur, in charge. After spending the night in St. James, Phoebe returned home to discover a grisly sight. Three of her children had been murdered by a Sioux raiding party, and the other two, Lauren and Hannah, were mortally wounded. Two detachments of the 1st Dakota Cavalry were sent to find the attackers but could not locate them. Rumors soon started that the massacre had been perpetrated by Inkpaduta, the leader responsible for the 1857 Spirit Lake Massacre. However, although it was common to blame Inkpaduta for any killings or raids occurring on the frontier during this time, he and his village were not responsible for the Wiseman murders. The perpetrators were discovered during a patrol by Yankton scouts Sully had hired to make raids against the hostile Sioux. During the patrol, a small

band of warriors was captured, and when their two leaders confessed to the Wiseman murders, they were executed by the scouts.[22]

The massacre had a deep impact on the soldiers, especially
those men who were married and worried about their own families and their safety. According to Albert Childs, "We have passed
by hundreds of Indians and left them unmolested because they
claim to be friendly. . . . We can not molest any of them, if they
claim to be friendly, till they have proved themselves hostiles,
and it is my candid opinion, that 99 out of 100 of them, would
profess friendship to your face . . . and as soon as they thought
you was in [their] power, would not hesitate to kill you." Henry
Pierce, who was from Nebraska, noted the effect the attack had
on the men in his regiment: "A great sensation prevails in the
reg't in regard to that locality. A majority of men in that part enlisted for patriotic motives & now they have been called away
from those homes that they desired to protect." Lashing out at
the current campaign, Pierce angrily wrote, "No greater abuse to
the territory of Nebraska never was offered in calling its own
reg't out of its own lines, to chase retreating Indians over a country that is cursed by drought & famine." He ended solemnly with
"May God forgive the man that called us hence."[23] Furious over
the massacre and being called away from Nebraska, even those
men who had enlisted to serve on the frontier against the Indians
now resented the expedition, although for the Nebraska troops,
the expedition also gave them a chance for revenge against any
Sioux they encountered.

The men of the 2nd Nebraska Cavalry were not the only ones
unhappy with the expedition. Sully was also under heavy pressure from Pope to find an enemy to engage. On August 5, after
informing Pope of the drought and difficulties he was encountering in getting supplies to his force in the field, Sully received an
unsympathetic and highly critical letter from Pope. "I have just
received your letter of 27th instant, and I assure you it both surprised and disappointed me," Pope stated. "I never had the slight

idea you could delay thus along the river, nor do I realize the necessity of such delay." Pope told Sully to simply load up 120 wagons with supplies and get going, adding, "Sibley has had equal difficulties with yourself." This was followed by a letter on August 25 that again criticized Sully for not reaching a position to block the Sioux being attacked by Sibley. "I am constrained to believe that with energy this much at least could have been accomplished," a chastising Pope wrote, adding, "Your movements have greatly disappointed me." Six days later Sully received another letter from the department commander that placed any failures of the campaign squarely upon him: "Your presence on the Upper Missouri in time to have co-operated with General Sibley would probably have ended Indian troubles, by destroying or capturing the whole body of Indians which fought General Sibley, but your failure to be in proper position, at the proper time, however unavoidable, renders it necessary that you should prosecute with all vigor and dispatch the campaign I have marked out for you."[24]

Well aware that Pope did not like him, Sully was convinced by Pope's communication of August 5 that he was being set up to take the blame if the campaign failed. Sully needed to prove his worth to Pope, and he could do that only by achieving a victory in the field. Pope wanted the Santees to be punished for the Dakota War of 1862, and Sully would do just that if he could find the Sioux, any Sioux, to fight.

Sully had been waiting for three steamboats—the *Alone*, *Shreveport*, and *Belle Peoria*—to arrive with his much-needed supplies. Only one, the *Alone*, finally managed to work its way up the Missouri River to Fort Pierre. Determined to move, Sully ordered that twenty-three days' worth of supplies be placed on mules and announced to the troops that the column would march on August 14. The news raised the morale of the soldiers, who grew more excited at the possibility of action. With military braggadocio, Furnas had earlier written, "We are approaching the region where cowards run and brave men prepare themselves for fighting." J. H. Drips called it "the great expedition." Hearing some say that certain men were afraid to face the Sioux in battle, Pierce rejected the rumor, believing the column made "a formidable appearance" and that they were "confident we can thrash any force of Indians we may meet." He concluded with the statement "We in this campaign are all bravados." Not everyone agreed with Pierce; the night before the expedition left Fort Pierre, six men deserted.[25]

On August 14 the column pulled out of Fort Pierre. The advance guard of one company went first, followed by Sully, his staff, Company I of the 7th Iowa Cavalry (Sully's bodyguard), and an artillery battery. The mule train, separated into two files, came next, with the 2nd Nebraska Cavalry on the left flank and the 6th Iowa cavalry on the right flank. Close behind followed the ambulance wagons and, finally, a rear guard of one company. The march ended that day on the bluffs of the Missouri River, with Drips commenting that the campsite had "no wood, no grass and very poor water."[26]

The march had started with cool weather, but within days this changed to ever-increasing warm temperatures. Sully, intending to travel light, ordered all spare equipment, along with the men's overcoats and extra luggage, sent back to the fort. August 18 opened with a violent windstorm. "Wind blew perfect hurricane," reported Furnas. "Horses stampeded, tents blew down, followed by the heaviest rain we have experienced." The next day the rain turned to hail. Milton Spencer recalled, "Men and horses quickly broke ranks for the shelter of brush . . . but horses could not stand such a pelting very quietly. Some threw their riders and themselves, others getting wild and crazy . . . ran across the flat about half a mile as fast as their legs could carry them." The hailstorm lasted twenty minutes, with hailstones as large as "hen eggs and the smallest were as large as hickory nuts," added Spencer.[27]

The storm resumed again on August 20. Private James Thomson, 6th Iowa Cavalry, called it "one of the hardest hail storms that ever I did see, the hail was as big as chicken eggs and it rained awful." Drips also described the coming of the storm: "The sky darken up and looked very portentous, indeed. It still came blacker and blacker, and louder and louder roared the thunder . . . the rain soon began to come, and come it did with a vengeance." It rained for an hour and was then followed by more hail. The camp was soon under anywhere from six inches to three feet of water, causing great confusion.[28]

Wet and discouraged by Mother Nature's recent assaults, Wieneke's thoughts turned to home and the war back East as he wrote in his diary, "Most of the boys gone . . . to hear a sermon. Very dull, and set me to thinking of home and of my family . . . just imagine myself in my dear old home on this day. . . . In such moments as these (sitting bored in camp) how sweet are the lines of that dear old song 'Home sweet home There is no place like home.'" Still, even with the bad weather, Wieneke would be satisfied to serve on the expedition "if my stay here were only doing my beloved country any good, but I would prefer serving in the southern fields where I could show that I were indeed a soldier."[29] As was true of many of the men serving against the Sioux, Wieneke did not deem the fighting to be as crucial as the war against the South. Union soldiers, even if they had enlisted for frontier defense, still wanted to prove their love of country by defeating the secession of the Confederacy.

On August 21 Sully left the Missouri River at the mouth of the Cheyenne River and headed toward Devil's Lake. The column was entering buffalo country. On August 25, after sighting buffalo several times, Sully decided to allow the men to go hunting. The men took to the hunt with a great glee but very little ability. "It was our first buffalo chase and all were greatly excited," wrote Abner English. Although he was not successful, "I kept after the herd until I had emptied my revolver, when I realized that I was

alone on the prairie without ammunition and no meat for supper." Between fifteen and twenty buffalo were brought down and
taken back to camp, with at least one man shooting his own
horse. Furnas was surprised that "many more were not as most of
them who went out were inexperienced." The meat was appreciated for supper that night, with Drips commenting, "We had a
pretty good feast. The meat was good." Still thinking of the war
back East, the men named the small stream where the buffalo
had been killed Bull Run, after the first battle of the conflict.[30]

The next day the hunt continued but quickly got out of hand.
In large numbers, green soldiers were riding and shooting at will,
many killing their own mounts. First Lieutenant James Brown,
6th Iowa Cavalry, a Lieutenant Stewart, 2nd Nebraska Cavalry,
and several enlisted men shot their horses while attempting to
bring down a buffalo. Private Jerry Pyles, 2nd Nebraska Cavalry,
rode off by himself without orders to hunt. The eighteen-year-
old Pyles attacked a bull, firing at him twice. The bull, angered
by the assault, turned and charged the surprised Pyles. Pyles's
horse panicked and threw its rider to the ground. Pyles would
have been killed if another hunter had not happened by and shot
the bull. Not only did Pyles fail to show much hunting prowess,
but he lost his horse and all his equipment, totaling some $150.
Pierce found this fair: "He left ranks without permission & this
was his penalty for not minding his own business." Sully, alarmed
by the damage to the horses of the column, called a halt to any
further hunting. Many of the buffalo already killed were simply
left to rot.[31]

As Sully's men fired clumsily at buffalo, the more experienced
Yanktonais were hunting in a manner quite different from that
of the soldiers. Hunting buffalo was both a religious and an economic undertaking for the Sioux. They attributed wisdom, a
spirit, and soul to animals. Animals were to be revered and ven-
erated. In particular, there was a strong relationship between
humanity, the buffalo, and the entire universe; a hunt was not

something done on a whim. To the Sioux, Wakan Tankahad, or "the Great Mystery," had given buffalo to mankind. If the buffalo were by a river, then the Sioux went to the river. When the buffalo moved, the Sioux also moved. The summer hunt, lasting for two months during June and July, brought the various villages and groups of the Yanktonais together. The massed camp could spread out for over a mile.[32]

The decision to hunt was made by the headmen of the tribe and was a communal event. The hunt needed to be well organized, controlled, and supported by the entire village. If it was critical to find buffalo, holy men would be called at the start of the hunt to find the buffalo through visions, dancing, making medicine, and other rituals. Scouts were sent out to locate a buffalo herd. Once buffalo were discovered, a crier went through the encampment, calling, "Many bison, I have heard; many bison, I have heard! Your children, you must take care of them." A warrior society was chosen to act as a police force to stop any individuals from leaving the camp early and possibly ruining the hunt.[33]

On the day of the hunt, the men chose a bow, preferring this to a gun or lance, with which to kill the buffalo. With a good, experienced horse the hunter would race to the side of a buffalo and fire one arrow into the animal, aiming for the heart. Black Elk described one hunt: "Then we had come near to where the bison were, the hunters circled around them. . . . then there was great dust and everyone shouted and all the hunters went in to kill—every man for himself. . . . they would ride right up to a bison and shoot him behind the left shoulder. Some of the arrows would go in up to the feathers and sometimes those that struck no bones went right straight through." Another account comes from Standing Bear: "One of them went down a draw and I raced after him on my pony. My first shot did not seem to hurt him at all; but my pony kept right after him, and the second arrow went in half way. I think I hit his heart, for he began to wobble as he ran and blood came out of his nose." The hunt was well organized and accomplished, with great skill shown, in comparison to that of the soldiers. Oscar One Bull remembered, "No one ever killed just for fun of killing, like so many whites did."[34]

Hunters would each kill one buffalo for their families and another for the helpless and poor of the village. The distribution of the meat was done by the leaders of the hunt, with the support of the policing society. The women took charge of handling the carcass. "When the butchering was all over, they hung the meat across the horses backs and fastened it with strips of fresh bison hide. On the way back to the village all the hunting ponies were loaded, and we little boys who could not wait for the feast helped ourselves to all the raw liver we wanted," recalled Black Elk. Once in camp, the women would cut long poles and make fork sticks to create drying racks for the meat. Black Elk continued, "The women were all busy cutting the meat into strips and hanging it on racks to dry. You could see red meat hanging everywhere."[35]

The Yanktonais were finishing their hunts and busily preparing the meat for winter as Sully's column marched closer. On August 26, the same day as the army's disastrous hunt, scouts brought into camp two Sioux women and their children who were on their way to the Crow Creek Agency. From them, Sully learned more about the earlier Sibley fights. Attempting to locate Sibley and any possible Sioux villages, Sully sent out on patrol Captain D. LaBoo and Company F, 6th Iowa Cavalry. The following day, August 27, Sully's men found a crippled, elderly Sioux man, whom the soldiers called Keg. Keg likely had become too much of a burden on his family and been left behind with some food and water. This practice of leaving the elderly behind was frowned upon by the Sioux but still occurred. This man gave more information about Sibley's battles with the Sioux and discussed an attack by the Sioux upon a small boat on the Missouri River. The boat's passengers had been ambushed and twenty-one men, three women, and some children had all been killed. Sully also learned that the Sioux had recrossed the Missouri after Sibley left; this fact was reinforced when the column found numerous signs of large numbers of Sioux in the area. Concerned for the safety of the fifty men under Captain LaBoo, whose patrol was overdue to return, Sully sent Major J. W. Pearman and five companies out to find the patrol. On August 29 LaBoo arrived back in camp, having traveled 187 miles without uncovering any sign of the Sioux other than ten abandoned lodges, which he burned. A second patrol also reported finding the site of the Big Mound fight, Doctor Weiser's grave site, and Sibley's trail that led back toward Minnesota. The trail was three to four weeks old; Sully was too late to rendezvous with Sibley.[36]

Sully was in the midst of his campaign, but for Sibley's men, their expedition was nearly over. Although the column had been placed on half rations for the return journey, morale among Sibley's troop was high. The joy of returning to Minnesota and the rumor that they would then be sent to serve in the South put the men in a positive mood. Anticipating that he soon would be seeing his family, Captain John Jones wrote a letter to his wife. His son George had requested that his father bring him a pony back from the expedition, but Jones wrote, "Tell George that the Indians ran to fast for me to capture him a pony." Tenderly, Duren Kelley wrote his young wife, "I never knew how much I loved you till now."[37]

Others took time to reflect on the merits of Sibley and the campaign. Eli Pickett, who in June had been very optimistic about the expedition, now was consumed with bitterness toward Sibley, who he felt had lacked enthusiasm for slaughtering the Sioux and actually supported them. Pickett regarded "every moment here as so much wasted time—wasted because we are neither benefiting our country or ourselves—most of us are men who left home not to better themselves or because they had a desire to go to war, but because they felt it to be a duty to lend a helping hand to sustain the cause of our country." As for the campaign itself, Pickett stated, "I have no interest in it. . . . I regard it as one of the greatest humbugs that was ever got up."[38]

Henry Hagadorn had become disillusioned with his fellow man. On August 9, after an illness, a man named Starbuck, 10th Minnesota Infantry, died in the hospital tent. Just feet away men were playing horseshoes, "swearing so loud that they can be heard all through the camp," stated Hagadorn. Even as the coffin was brought out containing Starbuck's remains, the profanity continued with no one chastising the men, not even a chaplain who "passes them time after time without a word of advice." Hagadorn confessed "that I have seen but little of the wickedness and depravity of man until I joined the army." In a letter to Mariette, George Clapp acknowledged to his wife that many of the men had seemed to have lost their patriotism and would not reenlist. Yet, he did not share these feelings, maintaining, "I don't see that I feel any different or have any less patriotic zeal in the cause then when I first enlisted."[39]

On August 11 the column reached Camp Atchison, where the men discovered the truth about Chaska's faithfulness. Two days later the Cheyenne River was crossed. Fort Abercrombie was reached on August 21, Hagadorn calling the post "a beautiful place and the Prairie about it is as pretty as any in the world." Four days later the eastward march continued with Arthur Daniels writing in his diary, "Homeward bound again, and in MINNESOTA!" On September 12 the 6th Minnesota arrived at Fort Snelling, their part of the Punitive Expedition of 1863 at an end.[40]

Meanwhile, Sully's column had encountered the remains of the battle at Big Mound. Not only were the carcasses of a number of mules and horses located, but also the bodies of several Sioux believed to have been wounded and left to die alone. Frank Myers, 6th Iowa Cavalry, believed they had "crawled off to die" as would an injured animal. Sully's scouts had informed him that if the Sioux had recrossed the Missouri River, they were likely camping around the Coteau or Missouri Coteau region, areas of small rolling hills, ravines, and numerous small lakes. The Coteau region was thirty miles east of the James River and eighty-five miles west of the Missouri River. Here the Sioux could find good grass, fish in the lakes, and many buffalo. From here they would then move back to the Missouri, crossing over before the winter.[41] Smarting from Pope's criticisms, wanting a victory to redeem his professional honor, Sully decided to march to the region, still hoping to gain something positive for the campaign. Although some of the resister groups had recrossed the Missouri River after the departure of Sibley, the Sioux did not come back in great numbers. The majority of the Sioux present in the area now being entered by Sully were the Yanktonais, just ending their summer buffalo hunt and unaware of the disaster they were soon to face.

CHAPTER 7

Whitestone Hill

"THE PRAIRIE WAS COVERED WITH WHITE WARRIORS"

On September 3, at seven A.M., the Sully column started marching as the weather turned cooler. After an eighteen- to twenty-mile advance over a level prairie covered with numerous lakes filled with geese and ducks, the soldiers reached a small lake containing poor water. Here they discovered the carcasses of some fifteen to twenty-five buffalo killed within the last two to three days. The Sioux were nearby and still involved in hunting. At two P.M. Sully ordered the army to encamp.[1]

At five-thirty A.M., prior to the departure of the main body that morning, Sully had ordered Major Albert E. House and Companies C, F, H and I, 6th Iowa Cavalry, to scout ahead for any sign of the Sioux. According to Elkanah Richards, Company F, 6th Iowa Cavalry, the men were excited, as they believed they were close to those who "so savagely massacred the citizens, men, women and children at New Ulm, Minnesota." The main body headed in a southerly direction. Five miles in front of the patrol rode the scout Frank La Framboise; two miles behind La Framboise came another scout, Crazy Dog. Around noon, having found a spring with good water, House called a halt to water and feed the horses and for the men to eat a brief lunch of raw pork and hard tack. The soldiers were relaxing when La Framboise came racing back to the patrol, shouting that he had stumbled upon twenty lodges located five miles ahead. Richards wrote that the men nervously loaded their pistols as "we knew that we were not in Dixie where the enemy took prisoners, but hundreds of miles from civilization where the savages took no prisoners." With wishful thinking, some men thought that La Fromboise, although an experienced frontiersman, had actually seen Sully's camp. Advancing five miles soon relieved everyone of that idea. Reaching a small rise, "We suddenly came upon a whole Indian city of tepees," recalled J. C. Luse, 6th Iowa Cavalry.[2]

Luse estimated that there were between five to eight thousand people in the village, with House reporting that the camp contained some four to six hundred lodges with a potential fighting force of twelve to fifteen hundred men. The camp was located at Whitestone Hill, near the headwaters of Elm Creek, fifteen miles west of the James River. The Sioux, mainly Yanktonais but also some Lakotas and several small groups of resister Santees, were in the midst of performing the Buffalo Call Ceremony, since they were still hunting buffalo even as fall approached. Luse acknowledged, "The ground was covered with Buffalo skins which were drying and curing. The women were scraping them and drying the meat." The village was in a region where, traditionally, the various bands of Sioux gathered to trade, hunt, and hold ceremonies. Reacting quickly to his discovery, House sent La Fromboise and two soldiers, Whitcomb Moon and W. C. Evans, back to report their discovery to Sully. Another soldier, James Thomson stated, "We seen there was more indians than we could easy handle so we dispatched to the main body of the brigade."[3]

As with many aspects of what occurred at Whitestone Hill, there was disagreement between the army and the Sioux over the makeup of the camp at the time of House's arrival. The soldiers who gazed upon the large village of some thirty-five hundred people believed that these were the Sioux who had perpetrated the atrocities in Minnesota and engaged Sibley's troops in combat. In their reports after the fight, Sully and Furnas stated that the village consisted of a large number of Lakotas—mainly Brules, Blackfeet, and Hunkpapas—resister Santees, and, finally, Yanktonais. The Sioux maintained that although there were some Lakotas and resisters, the camp was largely Yanktonais and pro-peace Santees, neither group having played a part in the earlier fighting in Minnesota. Known definitely to have been present were the Hunkpapa chieftain Black Moon; the small resister groups led by White Lodge, Lean Bear, and Inkpaduta; and various Yanktonais leaders, including Two Bears and Little Soldier, both supporters of peace, and Turning Thunder, Chasing Bear, Big Head, and Medicine Bear.[4]

Although the village did contain resisters who had fought against the whites in Minnesota and certain Lakotas who may have participated in the skirmishes against Sibley, the camp overall was a peaceful one, focused on hunting buffalo and not prepared to make war against the soldiers who were now overlooking the camp. Historically, it was not uncommon for the Santees to join with the Yanktonais for a tribal hunt. Further, in their traditional role as mediators for the larger Sioux confederation and practicing the important kinship roles, the Yanktonais had allowed the Lakotas and Santees, regardless of their position on the Dakota War of 1862, to be present among their camps. To the Yanktonais, this arrangement did not change their peaceful relations with the army, and they did not appreciate that the soldiers might see this differently.

Direct accounts from the Yanktonais on what transpired at Whitestone Hill are few in comparison to those of the soldiers. The Reverend Aaron McGaffey Beede was a missionary to the Yanktonais many years after the events at Whitestone Hill. Beede had the opportunity to get to know many of the Sioux survivors of the engagement, and based on the information he had gathered from them, wrote the play *Heart-in-the-Lodge: All a Mistake*, about the Yanktonais' experiences. Although the play cannot be taken as a primary or completely accurate source, it can still be used to ascertain how the Yanktonais remembered what occurred. In the play, Beede writes that the Yanktonais "had no part in the 'Minnesota Massacre' in 62. They were at home planting and harvesting and hunting meat and wild fruits by the Missouri River." When House's men appear, a messenger runs through the camp yelling, "The enemy! The enemy!" But an old man responds, "We have no enemies. They are white people always friendly to our people." Chief Two Bears then announces that he will send messengers to meet with the soldiers and says, "We can make peace with them, if we are hearty and careful." Soon, an army captain enters the camp inquiring if there are any Santees present and calling upon the Yanktonais to surrender.[5]

Over time, a totally different interpretation of House's contact with the Yanktonais emerged from white writers. In those accounts, House confronted a hostile village ready for war; he was soon surrounded and faced with an overwhelming assault that would wipe out his command. Fortunately, Inkpaduta, the overall leader of the villages, decided, arrogantly, to wait before attacking, either to allow the men to ritualistically prepare themselves for battle or because he was in a sweat lodge purifying himself and could not be disturbed. One historian of the battle declared that "heavily outnumbered and quickly outflanked by the Indians, the troopers prepared to make a stand—most probably their last one." A biographer of Pope wrote that House "stumbled upon a warparty of 1,500 warriors . . . and after surrounding House, haunted the trapped Iowans and prepared for a ceremonial slaughter."[6]

In reality, there was no overall commanding chieftain; the Sioux had no such tradition of placing one man over a collection of villages or bands such as those that gathered at Whitestone

Hill. Nor was Inkpaduta even present at that time, being away
hunting buffalo with his sons. He had placed one of his wives
and two of his smaller children who were in the village under
the care and protection of the Yanktonais' leader, Medicine
Bear.[7]

House's situation was never as threatening as later accounts
have implied. Spreading his men out, with Company I in the
center, Companies F and H on the flanks, and Company C in
reserve, House waited for Sully's main body to arrive. The appearance of the soldiers did not cause a panic in the village or an
attack by the warriors, as could have been expected if the village
were as hostile as believed. A group of young men did start putting on war paint. According to Elkanah Richards, "With a wild
yell that still lingers in my ears, the young warriors rushed to a
little lake and taking up some of the blue clay they daubed it over
their bodies, marking themselves hideously, as they did not have
time to get the regular war paint." However, the leaders of the
camp sent out embassies under a flag of truce to meet with the
soldiers. House responded by coming out with four other officers
to parley. The Sioux wanted to smoke pipes and discuss what the
soldiers wanted. Several of the Sioux delegation spoke English,
and during the parley it became clear to the Sioux that House
was there looking for Santee resisters. The offer by the delegation to turn over certain resister leaders was rejected by House,
as was the willingness of the Sioux to turn over hostages to
the army, who now demanded that the entire camp surrender.
The Sioux declined to do this, and the embassies returned to the
camp, nervous and alarmed at what was happening. Only now
did the women start to take down the lodges and prepare to leave
the area. "All this time the Indians were busy backing up and
getting ready to leave," recalled James Thomson. Seeing this
movement, House tried to spread his command out even farther
in an attempt to surround the village, but warriors blocked his
efforts.[8]

Meanwhile, La Fromboise and the soldiers with him were riding back to find Sully. La Fromboise later claimed that along the way several young warriors approached, shouting that they had fought Sibley and "they could not see why the whites wanted to come and fight them unless they were tired of living and wanted to die." If true, it was empty bravado, as the warriors did not attempt to stop the three men. The messengers covered more than ten miles before seeing Sully's camp. "We discovered a man on horseback coming towards our camp at full speed," Corwin Lee, 6th Iowa Cavalry, remembered. To Henry Pierce, "the scouts came in at full rate under the whip stating the Indians were camped within eight ms of us!" La Fromboise arrived at four P.M. and informed Sully that House had "surprised and surrounded a large camp of Indians" some ten miles away.[9] Nothing in La Fromboise's report implied that House was in danger or was himself surrounded. Also, there is no evidence that Sully inquired if the camp was hostile or to what Sioux bands the camp belonged. Now the desire was for battle; Pope had demanded action from him, and Sully was going to comply.

Sully ordered the column to break camp, and the news met with cheers from the men. "I carefully finished my supper, and took out a supply of hard bread in my saddle-pockets, in case of an emergency," a thoughtful Lee wrote. In less than an hour, the 6th Iowa and 2nd Nebraska Cavalries were on the march. "Everyone seemed eager for the Fray and in a few minutes the forces were galloping to the scene of action," Siegmund Rothammer wrote to Rosanah. The horses were not, at first, ready for the advance. They had been ready for a rest and did not appreciate the new movement. To Lee, the advance looked more like a rout, with some of the horses "rearing, kicking and plunging, and putting forth their best endeavors to dislodge their riders . . . hats, caps, haversacks and picket-ropes strewed the way."[10]

Sully left camp with the 2nd Nebraska Cavalry to the right and the 6th Iowa Cavalry on the left. Sully, with his bodyguard of the 7th Iowa Cavalry and the artillery, remained in the center. The column rode at a full gallop, with the men from the 2nd Nebraska Cavalry yelling, "Remember New Ulm," and "Don't take prisoners." Many years after Whitestone Hill, Joseph S. Phebus, a Nebraska soldier, stated that Sully had told the men they were fighting under a "black flag," a reference to Confederate guerilla fighters in Missouri, and to take no prisoners. This may have been how the soldiers from Nebraska felt about the upcoming action, recalling the Wiseman Massacre, but given that Sully took prisoners during the action, it is unlikely he made this statement.[11]

As the soldiers drew near, Sioux scouts from the village rode in to warn the camp of the approaching troops. One scout yelled, "The soldiers are coming out of the ground!" while another shouted that "the prairie was covered with White warriors." The news sent a wave of panic throughout the camp. The women were in the process of taking down the lodges and packing up all the goods and supplies, but the village was immense; J. C. Luse estimated that it numbered between three and four hundred lodges spread out over one mile. With successful hunts there likely would have been over 200,000 pounds of dried buffalo meat to recover. Watching from the hill, Luse could see that "the Squaws made big packages of all this meat and the skins about two feet wide and three feet thick and about five feet long, each weighing three or four hundred pounds. . . . They tied several long poles together which they call a traviox [*sic*] and upon this they carry the package of skin and meat."[12]

Sully's force reached the camp near sundown. Many, but not all, of the lodges had been taken down, and grabbing their most necessary or valuable possessions, the Sioux were "moving slowly toward the south," recalled Lee. In his report, Sully later stated that it was not supplies or possessions being removed by the Sioux but plunder taken from whites. Sully was determined to strike the village although it was offering no resistance, had not attacked House, and was attempting to leave. Acting quickly, Sully ordered the 2nd Nebraska Cavalry to attack from the right and the 6th Iowa Cavalry to charge from the left, while Sully, the artillery, and three companies struck in the center. The 2nd Nebraska Cavalry under Furnas "took to the right of the camp and soon lost in a cloud of dust over the hills," wrote Sully. Frank Myers, 6th Iowa Cavalry, recalled "the superior speed of our horses over the Indian ponies, soon placed us in a position to flank them and bring the reds between the fire of the divided command." Reaching House's command, Colonel David Wilson, 6th Iowa Cavalry, ordered House to mount his men and prepare for an advance on the camp.[13]

Outmaneuvered by the swiftly moving cavalry, the Sioux were forced to retreat into a ravine approximately one half mile from the village. Richards wrote, "We drove them into a deep ravine where there were thousands of men, women and children, ponies and dogs and they were a hard looking lot of humanity, I can assure you, after they were surrounded." The ravine had jutted sides and a deep hollow in the center that now sheltered the women and children. Fearing the worse, many of those trapped in the ravine started to sing their death songs while warriors, including the members of the Brave Heart Society charged with the protection of the helpless, along with others, prepared for the coming assault. Two chiefs did not take their people into the ravine but surrendered as the army entered the abandoned village. Little Soldier, a Lower Yanktonais deemed a "good Indian" by Sully, with a few followers, and Big Head, an Upper Yanktonais who Sully viewed as "notorious," and 120 people surrendered. These Sioux were taken prisoner and removed to the rear.[14]

The 2nd Nebraska Cavalry dismounted and was preparing to advance on the ravine when Sully ordered a halt as he met with Little Soldier and Big Head. Frustrated by the delay, a Captain Bayne addressed the men: "Boys, we have come a long way to fight the Indians, and now that we have got them, I am in favor of whaling them. Shall we advance?" According to George Belden, the men responded with a hearty "Yes! Yes!" Moving forward, Pierce believed that "never could I have supposed that 9 months men, raw recruits, wholly unused to fire, could advance with such coolness & steady." Still attempting to avoid bloodshed, a man stepped out of the ravine wrapped in a U.S. garrison flag. He gestured to the Nebraska men that he wanted to talk by moving his hands up and down in a shaking hands motion. "The Indian in the flag continued to advance, and when he was close to our line, a little Dutchman on the left fired and killed him, he gathered the flag about him as he fell . . . ," acknowledged Belden. One hundred yards from the ravine, the regiment commenced firing, "which they did with precision and effect, creating quite a confusion in the enemy ranks," reported Furnas.[15]

To the left of the 2nd Nebraska Cavalry position, House's battalion had been steadily approaching the ravine. "They were now completely in our control," recalled Milton Spencer, "and everyone supposed they would surrender, or else be obliged to fight us at a great disadvantage." One hundred fifty yards from the ravine, the Sioux opened fire on the Iowa men. The 6th Iowa Cavalry returned fire, Lee recording that the men "fired their guns and revolvers among the Indians who lined the ravine as thick as they could stand, and among whom our Minnie balls told with fearful effect, and the Nebraska boys were pitching into them from the opposite side." Firing from both sides of the ravine proved dangerous to the soldiers, who soon came under friendly fire. John Wright, 6th Iowa Cavalry, was hit in the left leg, and at one point the Nebraska soldiers were ordered to cease fire for fear of hitting the Iowa troops.

The fighting was intense and lasted from twenty minutes to half an hour. Captain Lewis Wolfe, 6th Iowa Cavalry, wrote to the *Iowa City Press* that he believed it a miracle more soldiers weren't killed, as "we were very close to them and the bullets and arrows flew about us like hail." To Pierce, the Sioux "fought like enraged men that had nothing but their lives to lose or a victory to gain. Volley after volley flew the leadened hail from our enraged fire." Earlier, the men from Nebraska had declared that they were fighting for the protection of their homes and families. Pierce failed to understand that now it was the Yanktonais warriors who died to defend their loved ones. He was disappointed that the troops were unable to drive the Sioux around a small hill and into the fire of the waiting artillery, which "would have poured their grape & shell, till that ravine would have run blood. Infants & innocent children & women alike shared the fate of their guilty fathers."[16]

The nighttime combat was confusing for the men, having to fire at close range, and a nightmare for the soldier's horses. With "such a storm of bullets and arrows . . . the horses became unmanageable . . . the horses could not be persuaded to go in amongst the yelling, screeching crowd . . . ," wrote David Wilson. Sensing the troubles, the Sioux attempted a breakout of the slaughter pit. "The Indians charged right at us, shooting, firing arrows and hurling weapons at us," stated Luse. Wilson's horse was hit, throwing the officer to the ground. The attack by the Sioux warriors was both desperate and heroic: even Pierce was impressed, calling the warriors men and saying that they fought well. As the warriors opened a hole in the soldier's line, the women and children poured out and ran for safety. Prior to the breakout, parents had tied their small children to the backs of dogs and ponies and sent them through the broken lines, scattering them out onto the prairie and hoping they could find them at a later time.[17]

During the night, the soldiers started to regroup and determine their losses. David Wilson reported one officer and ten enlisted men killed and eleven wounded, including one who shortly thereafter died. Sergeant Drips noted that the officer was Lieutenant T. J. Leavitt of Company B, adding, "He was a noble man, a good and brave soldier," and one of the enlisted men was Elder

Clark of Company C, whom J. H. Drips thought "one of the best men in the regiment." Clark had been shot through the head and died instantly. The 2nd Nebraska's losses were less than those of the 6th Iowa Cavalry, two men killed and thirteen wounded. The 6th Iowa Cavalry suffered higher casualties because the desperate breakout of the Sioux had struck their lines.[18]

Losses for the Sioux were harder to determine. The Sioux claimed that 300 men, women, and children died in the fighting. Prisoners taken during the engagement, all Yanktonais, numbered 32 men and 124 women. How many other Sioux, now retreating from the village, were wounded or later died is not known. In his play, Beede has an unnamed woman lament, "Yes, yes a lot were killed, men, women and children . . . an iron hammer went through my little boy's head and split it wide open . . . oh, oh, they chased us so fast I couldn't pick up his body." Nape Hote Win (Gray Hand Woman), later known as Mary Big Moccasin, was nine years old when the soldiers attacked the village. She became separated from her family and was shot in the leg. She dragged herself into a small ravine and hid there for days until family members located her. The shock of the events of that day never left her; as an elderly woman, she would still awake at night, crying out, "They are coming, run, run!"[19] For the Yanktonais, Whitestone Hill was not a battle but an unprovoked slaughter. It is their Pearl Harbor or 9/11, something that changed their history forever and is still remembered today with sadness.

For the soldiers at Whitestone Hill, the opinions on the fight were mixed. Drips felt "the defeat of the Indians was the worse from the fact that they had made this camp on purpose to put up their winter's meat and the season being well over they had a very large quantity on hand, all which was destroyed." With the usual Civil War bravado expressed by many soldiers after any combat, Pierce announced, "I don't think there had been a battle so fierce & destructive to any one tribe as this." Rothammer started a letter to his wife about the fight with "Ever memorable to all our forces." Sully's only regret was that he did not have more daylight, for if he had, "I feel sure . . . I could have annihilated the enemy. As it was, I believe I can safely say I gave them one of the most severe punishments that the Indians have ever received." Others were not so positive about the engagement. Joseph Phebus, reflecting on the events of the expedition, stated, "There was no glory in this whole campaign." Nineteen-year-old Sam Brown, the mixed-blood son of Joseph Brown, a former Indian agent for the Santee reservation in Minnesota, was present at the camp when the soldiers came. He denounced the actions of the army, claiming that some of House's men were shaking hands and speaking of peace with the Sioux when Sully's troops arrived and attacked the village. Brown observed that it was mainly women and children who were killed that day.[20]

Sully was sure he had struck the main group of hostiles who had fought with Sibley and later recrossed the Missouri. He claimed to have found proof, letters and papers, from the massacre of the miners whose boat had been attacked on the river. As time passed, the soldiers began to believe that the village had been hostile. La Fromboise spoke of encountering Sioux warriors on his ride back to Sully who confessed their involvement in the Sibley fights. J. C. Luse, writing long after the fight, maintained that when the Sioux delegation rode out to speak with House's battalion, one hundred warriors had appeared, each holding a lance with a white scalp, and "some of them had as many as a half dozen" attached to it.[21] Given that the Yanktonais had not participated in the Minnesota uprising, had helped in the release of white captives, and had told House that they were peaceful and did not want to fight, it is highly unlikely that the leaders of the camp would have been so foolish as to send out envoys with white scalps on their lances. Later writers and historians added the myth of House being surrounded and the Sioux preparing to assault his outnumbered command, even though none of this had been reported by House or the other key officers on the expedition. These later accounts also claimed that Inkpaduta, not present that day, was the evil commander of the hostile Sioux ready to devour House's troops. In truth, the Yanktonais were hunting buffalo and not involved in any hostile actions against the army. The Lakotas may have fought against Sibley, and there were resister and pro-peace Santees in the camp. However, the numbers of the Lakotas and Santees were minor compared to the Yanktonais present at Whitestone Hill.

The night following the end of the fighting was a difficult one. The men were told to sleep with their rifles handy, but "such an awful noise as was kept up during the night, the dogs howling, and the squaws squalling, there was not much chance to sleep," a tired Drips wrote. Many of the wounded soldiers lay where they fell on the field, waiting to be found in the morning light. One soldier from Company E, 2nd Nebraska Cavalry, had been hit in the ankle and spent the night in the cold, chilled and suffering from his wound. More alarming was the return of some Sioux women to the camp. Likely they were looking for loved ones and food, but when they came upon the dead and wounded soldiers they attacked them with a vengeance. As Lee recalled, "Our dead that were left upon the ground over night were invariably toma-hawked but not scalped. Some of them had arrows driven into them so that their points protruded on the opposite side." Belden remembered that the women also assaulted the wounded, "beat their brains out, after which they took a butcher-knife and cut out their tongues." Lieutenant Leavitt was one of those wounded and attacked by Sioux women. Using his saber, he fought them off but was stabbed three or four times. The next day, Leavitt died from his wounds.[22]

With the start of the next day, the devastation was even more apparent to the men in the occupied Sioux camp. According to Furnas, "The whole country for miles was covered with roving howling dogs and ponies. The Indians fled leaving everything, tents, meats, cooking utensils." Lee walked to the ravine, the site of the heaviest fighting. "In the ravine the Indians plunder lay the thickest, literally covering the ground, showing unmistakable evidence of the severity of our fire. Dead and crippled ponies, squaws, papooses and Indians lay in confusion and blood scattered on all sides," he reported. The men were allowed to loot whatever they found and took leggings, mittens, horse bridles, cooking utensils and kettles.[23]

Most troubling for the soldiers were the children. "We saw a little Indian boy on the field, naked and crying; no one paid any attention to him," remembered Lee. "There were eight or ten little children scattered around. They were collected together and put with the prisoners. At one place there lay two papooses; one of them four or five years old, the other only a few months. A dead squaw probably their mother, lay by them; the elder would insist on keeping covered saying 'shoot, shoot' whenever uncovered. Another was crying 'Mamma! Mamma!' as pitifully as any white child could." Not all the soldiers were as sympathetic as Lee; Joseph Phebus and a squad of troops were sent out to find meat. When eight children were discovered, Phebus was sure that the men with him were intent on murdering them. Speaking with a light tone, he announced, "We were sent out for meat, these babies are meat, we will take them in." Collecting up the children before anyone could protest, Phebus likely saved their lives. Pierce mentioned a little boy who had been shot through the head. Still alive, "he has never cried or appeared to suffer pain."[24]

Most shocking was the sighting of children tied to dogs who wandered back into the camp. F. E. Caldwell, 2nd Nebraska Cavalry, wrote of dogs pulling packs on small poles fastened to a collar, "in one instance a young baby" attached. Belden, who saw a number of children pulled by dogs, remembered "the little babies that the dogs were dragging about on their travoises, never cried, but lay perfectly still though the dogs galloped over the ditches and gullies." The dogs would not let the soldiers get close enough to release the children; the only way to try to save the babies was to shoot the dogs. However, when the soldiers attempted to do so, several children were hit and many of the dogs ran away with their passengers. "Poor little creatures, however much we pitied them we could not help them," Belden recalled with regret.[25]

Warriors were also encountered in the village. One wounded man, with a bow and arrows, lay hidden in some tall grass. Firing two arrows at a time, he wounded two soldiers before a bugler and a sergeant finally shot him with their revolvers. Lee observed that "the bugler scalped him before he ceased kicking." Lee further witnessed an unarmed warrior who rose up from the ground after being discovered, shaking a clenched fist in helpless rage at the destroyers of his village before being shot and killed. Lee dismissed the actions of the man, stating he was "savage to the last."[26]

Sully ordered the destruction of the lodges, materials, and the massive amount of buffalo meat. Drips wrote that it took a hundred men two full days to burn all the items in the village. Twelve wagonloads of buffalo meat were packed up for the use of the expedition. An estimated 400,000 to 500,000 pounds of dried meat and 300 lodges were destroyed. The human and economic loss to the Yanktonais was overwhelming. The home was the center of Sioux life, and the loss of the lodges, their possessions, and meat for the winter, coupled with the large loss of life, crippled the Yanktonais' society.[27]

On September 5 Sully sent out several patrols to reconnoiter the area and engage any Sioux that were found. Lieutenant Charles Hill, 2nd Nebraska Cavalry, and thirty men were tasked with finding the doctor, Bowen, and a small group of soldiers who had left camp to bring back ambulances for the wounded men. They had not yet returned to camp, and Sully, worried about their safety, sent Hill to locate them. Dr. Bowen's party soon arrived at the village, but Hill's patrol ran into a large Sioux war party. In a running fight back to the camp, Hill lost six men killed. Sully ordered Furnas and the 2nd Nebraska Cavalry to find the responsible war party. Furnas later reported that he only "founded 4 straggling Indians who I killed and brought in one small Indian prisoner." Another patrol brought in a further 130 women, children, and elderly men as prisoners. One other patrol made contact with the Sioux. Sixty men under a Lieutenant Bayne spotted two Sioux on foot and wounded. Bayne ordered a charge even though the white scout with the patrol proclaimed it a trap. The soldiers charged into a canyon that contained 300 to 400 warriors, who ambushed the troopers. When Bayne panicked, a Sergeant Bain took over and ordered the men to charge through the Sioux lines to safety. As the soldiers fled toward the camp, Bain's horse was killed. No one stopped to help the sergeant, who died fighting, alone and abandoned by the men his bravery had saved.[28]

Having completed his mission, Sully started his return march to Fort Pierre. The Indian prisoners were loaded into wagons for the journey. On September 11 the Missouri River and Fort Pierre came into sight. "I tell you the faces of the soldiers brightened up when the familiar scenery of the old Missouri once more loomed into view and we saw one of our steamboats lying at the bank with supplies," wrote a happy Drips. Soon after their arrival funeral services were held for the men who had died at Whitestone Hill. Drips recorded, "The Chaplain had regular religious services today. He preached a funeral discourse on Elder Clark's death. He had a large and attentive audience."[29]

At Fort Pierre the expedition was broken up, with some troops remaining at the post, five companies of the 6th Iowa Cavalry under Lieutenant Colonel Pollack ordered to build a new post called Fort Sully eight miles below Fort Pierre, and another company of the regiment sent to Fort Randall. Sully and his headquarters traveled back to Sioux City. The Sioux prisoners were sent to the Crow Creek Reservation. The journey was difficult for the prisoners, and the Yanktonais still refer to it today as a death march. Once at Crow Creek, the prisoners joined the other Sioux there for a brutal winter of near starvation. The Sioux were fed a watery gruel of flour, beans, pork, and some beef poured into a vat. The smell was horrendous, with Dr. S. C. Haynes, a medical surgeon, remarking that "the settlings smelt like carrion—like decomposed meat." Some Sioux chopped wood to exchange for flour, others stole horse feed to eat, and women once again prostituted themselves to obtain food.[30]

The winter was equally hard on those Sioux who had survived the assaults of the Sibley and Sully expeditions but had not been taken prisoner. Standing Buffalo and his people encamped at Dog's Lodge, where were gathered a number of Sissetons, Wahpetons, Mdewakantons, Yanktonais, and a few Lakotas. They were in hiding; most had lost their homes and supplies for the winter. Temperatures fell to thirty-five below. Unable to locate food, the villages began to disperse. Other Santees, those not in Standing Buffalo's group, went to Devil's Lake. Here too the biting cold and lack of food made living difficult, and many decided to flee to Canada. As they made their way north, the refugees were attacked by enemy tribes. According to Charles Eastman, "We were harassed by them almost daily and nightly. Only the strictest vigilance saved us." Even worse was a blizzard that lasted for a full day and night. Fortunately, when the storm ceased, a small herd of buffalo was located close by. A brief hunt provided everyone with a warm, filling meal. Once in Canada, the Sissetons wintered on the Upper Assiniboine River and the Mdewakantons at Turtle Mountain.[31]

Having been chastised often by Pope for his lack of offensive spirit, it was with great satisfaction that Sully received a letter from Pope on October 5 that congratulated him on his victory at Whitestone Hill and warmly praised the field commander. Pope was pleased with the results of his campaigns against the Sioux. Following Sibley's three battles, Pope wrote Halleck with vindication, saying, "The results of this expedition furnish a sufficient commentary upon the representation and recommendations made to you and the secretary of war by irresponsible persons concerning the organization and conduct of this expedition and the condition of Indian affairs in Minnesota." Pope added that he believed that all the American Indians in the region had been "reduced to a style of quiet." Not only did Pope appear to be the military victor, but by the fall of 1863 he had clearly won the political war as well. Alexander Ramsey had defeated Henry Rice, Sibley's and the punitive expeditions' harshest critic, for the United States Senate, and Stephen Miller, a pro-Sibley man, was elected governor of Minnesota.[32]

Pope may have celebrated this victory, but not everyone agreed with the outcome of the campaigns. Corporal Albert Childs, 30th Wisconsin Infantry, had been sent to the West with his regiment to garrison the new posts being built. Writing his brother Ellsworth, Albert discussed the recent expedition: "Well what has your expedition accomplished? It has enabled several individuals to obtain fortunes by defrauding the government, and although it has cost thousands upon thousands of dollars, not a cents worth of benefit has the government received from it." Milton Spencer agreed with Childs. Hearing a rumor that another expedition was planned for 1864, Spencer believed it would be good for "those that is speculating out of it" and would not be pleasant "for the poor soldier" who would have to serve on it. He observed that "some one is making a good thing of" providing supplies and materials to the army for offensives against the Sioux. For most soldiers, interest in a new expedition was not high. Arthur Daniels of the 6th Minnesota Infantry declared the entire expedition a "wild goose chase." The 10th Minnesota, upon hearing they had been ordered South, went "wild with joy," as this was why the men had enlisted, having no interest in serving further in the West.[33]

Most critical of the operations were various editors of regional newspapers. Sibley's battles were viewed as inconclusive and his expedition a failure to annihilate the Santee menace. Sibley "is not a soldier," determined one Republican newspaper, while the *Minneapolis State Atlas* declared, "The hour for striking the avenging blow had arrived, but the blow was not struck." The paper also focused on the reason why—the treason and cowardice of General Sibley—and called for another expedition, set for 1864, to finish off the Sioux once and for all. "They must be conquered," also insisted the *Yankton Dakotian*, and the *St. Paul Weekly Press* agreed: "It will require another season of vigorous and active operations to reduce the fierce and haughty tribes of the Missouri Valley to submission."[34] Regardless of the reality, many in Minnesota and living along the frontier believed that hostile Sioux were still a threat and had to be dealt with before they could strike again.

The true results of the campaigns are mixed. There is no doubt that those resister Santees who engaged Sibley or Sully suffered grave losses in personal lives and materials. Yet Sibley's blow fell hardest upon the peace faction of the Santees, destroying their efforts to remain out of the conflict and scattering them across the plains and into Canada, often homeless, without food, and in mourning for the deaths of loved ones. The Yanktonais had not participated in the Dakota War of 1862 but received a devastating attack by Sully that inflicted tremendous losses, while the Lakotas were also drawn into the conflict. Instead of ending hostilities, the army had enlarged the war, as many Yanktonais and Lakotas now advocated for revenge against the whites.

With the expeditions over, Pope proceeded to organize for frontier defense and where best to station the troops under his command. Part of Sibley's force was sent to the South to feed a growing need for troops to fight the Confederacy, while three companies of infantry and one hundred cavalry were posted to Forts Abercrombie and Ripley. Fort Ridgely, key to the line of defensive posts, received ten companies of infantry and one hundred cavalry, and other infantry and cavalry companies occupied a series of smaller outposts. Pope believed that this defensive system, based on smaller outposts constantly patrolling, would check any further Sioux raids into Minnesota. To break up any large-scale operations by the Sioux, Pope considered the creation of forts at Devil's Lake and on the James and Missouri Rivers. He also considered having Sully lead a column through the Black Hills and establish a fourth post on the upper Yellowstone River.[35]

There was no doubt that the military presence in Minnesota was of considerable importance to the state's economy. "Mankato is emphatically a military community," noted the editor of the *Mankato Semi-Weekly Record*. "Our male population is composed of at least two-thirds soldiers." The army was everywhere. "Along the whole frontier from Iowa to Fort Ridgely, 300 miles, there is camps fortified and garrisoned . . . every ten or fifteen miles," wrote Robert Perry of the 1st Minnesota Mounted Rangers.[36] The needs of thousands of soldiers had to be met, and the government contracts to accomplish this caused many to achieve financial success. Local merchants and farmers vied for the contracts. Some farmers started to raise cattle, while others ceased to plant crops and went entirely into ranching. Steamboat travel increased at a rapid rate across the region and into the Upper Missouri River area.

For the soldiers and officers back from the campaign in the West, it was a time for reflection and the continuous desire for letters. Siegmund Rothammer missed his wife and was tired of the vastness of the plains: "Perhaps never in my life before have I felt so lonely, so much like a shipwrecked mariner cast on some lonely Isle as at that moment," he confessed to Rosanah. Having complained often to his mother over her lack of letter writing, Hubert Eggleston, 6th Minnesota Infantry, finally received an answer. Calling Hubert her "absent son," his guilt-ridden mother wrote, "I have taken my long neglected pen to try and write a few words to you as you say you will not excuse me any longer. I do not blame you for I think it quite to bad that your father and I have not so much as answered one of your letters." She assured her son that "you must not say Mother has forgotten me . . . you know not the many anxious feelings that I have while thinking of the many hardships and dangers you are exposed to."[37]

The coming of winter found the soldiers established in posts from Minnesota across the Northern Plains. The campaign season was over, but the year ended with another atrocity committed by the soldiers. The Dakotas were not the victims this time; rather they were the Poncas, a small, peaceful tribe. On December 3 a small group of Poncas was returning from Omaha to their reservation. The party consisted of four men, six women, and five children. At midnight, near Niobrara, Nebraska, some thirty miles from Fort Randall, a group of drunken soldiers from Company B, 7th Iowa Cavalry, came across the encamped Poncas. The friendly Poncas greeted the soldiers warmly. The soldiers immediately rushed upon the women demanding sex, some offering to pay and others pulling their revolvers. The Poncas ran from the camp, while behind them the intoxicated troopers burned their tents. After a cold, frightening night, the Poncas were resting when the soldiers encountered them again and this time opened fire. One woman and the baby on her back were wounded as the Poncas again fled the scene. Unfortunately, three women and a girl who had tried to hide were discovered and murdered. Outraged by this atrocity, the Ponca agent, J. B. Hoffman, contacted Governor Edmunds of the Dakota Territory, insisting the soldiers responsible be punished, bluntly admitting, "I call this murder." Army officials promised the Poncas that the soldiers would be punished, but no action was ever taken.[38]

Charles Eastman. Eastman was a boy during the expeditions and later wrote about "up Dakota." Minnesota Historical Society.

Frank Griswold. During the expeditions, Sergeant Griswold served with the 1st Minnesota Mounted Rangers. Joel Emmons Whitney, Minnesota Historical Society.

John Jones. An experienced artillery officer, Jones's major problem was dealing with his wife's loneliness. Minnesota Historical Society.

Gabriel Renville. Of mixed heritage, Renville supported the army and served as a scout on the 1863 expedition. Minnesota Historical Society.

Standing Buffalo. A leader of the Sissetons, Standing Buffalo tried to keep his people out of the conflict but failed. Whitney's Gallery, Minnesota Historical Society.

CHAPTER 8

Sully's 1864 Expedition

"GENERALS POPE AND SULLY ARE
ANXIOUS FOR ANOTHER CAMPAIGN"

With the campaigns of 1863 over, Pope immediately started planning for new expeditions to commence in the spring of 1864. During the winter, Pope, Sully, and Sibley met to discuss the upcoming operations. Pope found no opposition for his intentions from Halleck, who, on January 17 asked Pope to submit his plan, including troop numbers and supply needs, but did insist that "as the demands of the principal armies in the field for reinforcements are pressing, these proposed Indian expeditions should be made as small as possible." But "small" was not what Pope had in mind; what he proposed would be the largest campaign against American Indians ever launched by the army.[1]

He informed Sibley that "it is my purpose that the whole cavalry force in your district shall be massed, with two or three pieces of field artillery, to take the field as early as spring." Sully was to organize a similar force of manpower. Four new forts were to be constructed, at Devil's Lake, the James River, the Upper Missouri River, and the Yellowstone River. The garrisons of the posts would consist of three or four infantry companies and three to five cavalry companies.[2]

Secretary of War Stanton was not in favor of new operations against the Sioux, believing that "if we want war in the spring a few traders can get one up on the shortest notice." However, Commissioner of Indian Affairs William Dole endorsed Pope's desire for offensive actions. Finally, on February 14, having read over Pope's plans, Halleck wrote, "Your plan of an Indian campaign is approved, subject to such modifications experience may suggest."[3] Pope's war with the Sioux would continue for another year.

The 1864 expeditions set to commence in the spring would be quite different from those of the previous year in both rationale and opponent. In 1863 the reasoning behind the campaigns was revenge for the uprising in Minnesota, directed specifically against the Santees, although the Lakotas and Yanktonais were drawn into the conflict. Sibley, in a letter to certain Minnesota newspaper editors, laid out the reasons for the expeditions: "The chastisement and subjection of the bands of savages on the both sides of the Missouri River"; to protect the overland route to the Idaho and Montana gold fields by building posts along the route; and finally, "the security of the Minnesota and Iowa frontier against hostile raids." In other words, gold was the chief motivator for a new round of conflict. In 1861 gold had been discovered at the headwaters of the Missouri River, setting off a rush to the new fields, and by 1864 Montana's population had reached 30,000. The Civil War did not curtail the arrival of more miners and settlers, many coming up the Missouri River or overland through Sioux territory. The vast cost of the war also made gold mining extremely important to the Lincoln government. As the mine camps needed supplies, large amounts of money were to be made in the carrying of supplies and goods to the fields. Minnesota became a key starting point for wagon trains heading west to the mining camps, as well a main source of trade with the miners.[4]

Standing in the way of this new encroachment by white settlers were the Sioux. The Lakotas in particular opposed the flow of miners across their territory, and in the spring of 1864 bands of the Lakota were willing to fight to stop the invasion. The Sioux intended that steamboat travel up the Missouri would be stopped and the overland trails blocked. If the army tried to intervene, the Sioux believed, then let them start a war. The Sioux did not consider themselves to be the aggressors; once again, their war would be a defensive affair. Standing with the Lakotas would be over seven hundred lodges of the Yanktonais, driven to fight by Sully's unprovoked assault at Whitestone Hill, as well as the remaining Santees still willing to continue the struggle. Although it was a popular belief that the Sioux mainly made war with war parties and raids, the nation could, at times, rally together to make war on a larger scale. This occurred after the Sand Creek Massacre, during Red Cloud's War, and again with the Sioux War of 1876–77. In 1864 elements of the Lakotas and Dakotas were joining in a united effort to deny further white encroachment.

Pope was quite aware of this massing of the Sioux. Various reports had arrived at his headquarters during the early spring. A mixed-blood scout informed the commanding officer at Fort Abercrombie that the Yanktonais were "decided in their hostility." Sibley wrote, "The Yanktonais have invited the disaffected of the other bands of Sioux to join them, and are determined to attack any boats or parties found within the limits of their country." Sully added that "the Indians have a piece of artillery with which they intend to stop boats going up the river." Other information stated that the Hunkpapas and other Lakota bands had crossed to the east side of the Missouri River, intending to link up with the Yanktonais near the James River.[5] The enemy was no longer just those Santees who had participated in the Dakota War of 1862; instead, Pope and the army faced a Sioux alliance of far greater strength and willingness to engage in combat.

This information only reaffirmed the reasons the expeditions needed to go forth. Major Edwin Hatch, serving on the frontier during the winter, received a dispatch reporting that "General Sibley has positive and detailed information from the Missouri of the existence of a formidable combination of the several bands of Sioux on both sides of the river, to hermetically seal their country against further intrusions by emigrants to the gold mines." Pope wrote Halleck of the Sioux alliance, stating that its purpose was to "give battle to General Sully, to obstruct the navigation of the [Missouri] river, and to resist the passage of emigrants across the upper plains." Yet Pope also assured Dakota Territory governor Newton Edmunds, who was concerned that the expeditions would leave his territory unprotected, that "the sole object of his expedition is to accomplish this purpose," the defense of the frontier settlements. To do this, Pope argued, "the power of the Yanktonais and Teton bands of Sioux must be broken to pieces."[6]

The commanders of the expeditions may have seen the upcoming operations from a political/economic "big picture," but for the common soldiers and civilians the reasons for the coming campaign were more basic. Punishment of the Santees was still the main focus, coupled with protection of the frontier from further attacks. To Frank Myers, 6th Iowa Cavalry, stationed at Sioux City, Iowa, the chief cause for the new operations was protection of the frontier. Lieutenant David Kingsbury, 8th Minnesota Infantry, later wrote that the expedition's purpose was to further chastise the Sioux who had committed the massacres in Minnesota and compel them to surrender, if possible. Kingsbury's commanding officer, Colonel Minor Thomas, agreed, stating that although the 1863 campaign had "freed all of Minnesota and most of Dakota of their terrifying presence," the Sioux were "still strong and defiant, and openly boasted that the white soldiers dare not follow them further." Thus the army had to "follow the Indians west of the Missouri, and fight and conquer them if possible." Isaac Heard, whose book on the Dakota War of 1862 was issued before the 1864 expeditions, thought that "in the spring another expedition should be fitted out to inflict further chastisement upon all wrong-doers and enforce security."[7]

There was disagreement among the enlisted men over the necessity of a new campaign. Sergeant Major Eugene Marshall, Brackett's Cavalry Battalion, was a twenty-nine-year-old farmer from Caledonia, Minnesota; to him, "these Indian Wars are a great humbug. I expect that for the next few months after [the] grass starts we shall go on some wild goose chase across the plains. . . . I am not much elated at the prospect before me, and on many accounts would prefer being in the South." Milton Spencer, spending the winter stationed at Fort Randall, clearly understood what motivated the new campaign: "Generals Pope and Sully are anxious for another campaign in the indian country, while all the Bobs and Nabobs in the territory are using all the influence they posses [sic] to get the government to send out another expedition. I fear they will get the thing to work." Unlike many, Spencer did not blame the Sioux for fighting back: "I do not blame them much. . . . They have had provocation enough for a few months past to make milder tempered people than they are think of murder."[8]

Other men were less concerned about a possible Indian war and more focused on events dealing with the defeat of the Confederacy. Albert Childs, 30th Wisconsin Infantry, fumed over the lack of good patriotic officers to command the army. Criticizing the running of the war, Childs complained to his brother, "First, if our government had good officers this rebellion would be crushed long ago." He deemed their failures were caused by a lack of patriotic blood, and if pressed together they "would not get as much true patriotic blood as flowed in George Washington's vanes." If officers were not paid, "they would quit" the service, Childs surmised. For James Thomson, the results of the fighting back East were very personal. His April 27 entry in his diary was direct and painful: "i received a letter stating that William and

Alexander was dead." He never mentioned his feelings on the upcoming operation versus the Sioux.[9]

Other soldiers greeted the news of new campaigns with anticipation. For Kingsbury it was a desire for revenge, even though the expeditions would not be directed at the Santees: "Every soldier had witnessed scenes to arouse the uttermost bitterness toward those who seemed destitute of any sentiment of humanity, and all were filled with an insatiable desire for revenge." Corporal John Robinson, 2nd Minnesota Cavalry, also desired vengeance, writing his wife, Libbie, that when he thought of what the Sioux did in the uprising, "my blood would boil and I would almost ache to send a bullet through their hearts." Benjamin Brunson received a commission as a first lieutenant in a colored regiment, but as it had yet to be organized, and being bored with camp life, he volunteered to accompany his former regiment, the 8th Minnesota, saying, "I preferred the active duty in the field." Those soldiers coming from the Dakota Territory were ready for action. "We were ordered to hold ourselves in readiness to join the expedition against the Sioux," wrote Abner English. "This we hailed with delight, as we thought it would give us an opportunity to meet the savages in battle."[10]

Just as soldiers disagreed over the coming warfare, there was disunity among the Sioux over the conflict. As some Sioux came together in a pro-war alliance, others surrendered or did not join in order to avoid further violence. During the winter, 91 Santees came down from Canada to Pembina and surrendered to Major Hatch. They were sent to Fort Snelling. Farther west, in February, Yanktonais leaders Bone Necklace, White Bear, and Buck, along with 280 of their people, came to Fort Sully asking for peace. They were soon joined by 500 to 700 more Yanktonais and Lakotas, who then encamped around the fort. At Fort Wadsworth another seven chiefs desiring no further conflict met with the post commander. On April 20, 200 lodges of Sisseton followers of Scarlet Plume, Big Ribs, Sweet Corn, and other leaders surrendered at Fort Abercrombie.[11]

Surrendering caused new problems for those Santees still out on the plains. There were those who had participated in the Dakota War and felt they could not surrender, others who feared a massacre if they gave up, and some who did not want to be sent to the Crow Creek Reservation. Not wanting to make peace, they put pressure on those Santees who wanted nothing more than to end the hardships they had been enduring for more than a year and a half. Santee women who had mixed-blood children were concerned that the disagreement would lead to bloodshed and their children would be killed. Frank Jetty was a six-year-old mixed-blood. At Pleasant Lake his people met up with some Métis from Canada. Jetty's mother and other women pleaded with the Métis to take their mixed-blood children and raise them so they would remain alive. Jetty and thirteen other boys and girls were accepted by the Métis; Jetty would not see his mother for the next thirty-one years.[12]

The Santees, especially those who had fought in the Dakota War, had a right to feel concerned over what would happen if they surrendered. At the start of the new year, American agents had led a covert operation into Canada to capture two resister leaders, Shakopee and Medicine Bottle, who were wanted for war crimes. The chiefs were drugged with opium and chloroform, tied to sleds, and taken out of the country by a Lieutenant Cochrane, part of the military garrison stationed at Pembina. After a trial, the two men were sentenced to death and later hanged, on November 11, 1864. The violation of an international border did not seem to bother Pope or Sibley; both had been requesting permission from the federal government to cross the border to attack those Santees who had taken refuge there. Sibley argued that the Santees being fed and cared for by the British government would, in the spring, cross back into the United States following the buffalo and soon after start raiding into Minnesota. In January Seward again asked the British for permission to enter Canada, only to be once more refused.[13]

As winter gave way to spring, the organization of the expeditions was completed. Sully's column, from Sioux City, referred to as the 1st Brigade, would consist of eleven companies of the 6th Iowa Cavalry, three companies of the 7th Iowa Cavalry, two companies of the 1st Dakota Cavalry Regiment, Major Alfred Brackett's Minnesota Cavalry Battalion of four companies, a company of scouts, and an artillery battery commanded by Captain Nathaniel Pope, the nephew of the general. Sibley's force, leaving from Fort Ridgley, was comprised of the 8th Minnesota Infantry Regiment (mounted for the expedition), six companies of the 2nd Minnesota Cavalry, 3rd Minnesota Artillery Battery, scouts, and the 30th Wisconsin Infantry Regiment, who were to man the soon-to-be constructed Fort Rice. Sibley, however, soon begged off leading this new expedition, and Colonel Minor Thomas, 8th Minnesota Infantry, was designated the new commander of the Second Brigade, also called the Minnesota Brigade. Sully, the overall commander of the expedition, had a powerful offensive weapon at his disposal: a strike force of divisional strength consisting of some thirty-five hundred well-armed and mounted men.

Of the forces being sent on the expedition, few had seen service in the 1863 campaigns. The 8th Minnesota Infantry, organized in 1862, had, because of the needs of the Sioux Uprising, never served together as a regiment prior to the expedition; they had been scattered out across the frontier, doing duty at small posts and garrisons. The regiment would not be brought together until May 1864. In 1862 the 30th Wisconsin Infantry had also been organized but had yet to see any combat. It was first used to oversee draft inductions into the army before being ordered to proceed to the West to build and garrison the new posts authorized by Pope's department. Two companies were sent to construct Fort Sully, while two other companies, under Colonel

Daniel Dill—an officer Pope found to be "a poor soldier, though otherwise a clever, respectable man"—were sent to build Fort Rice. Brackett's Minnesota Cavalry were veteran troops. Organized in 1861, the three Minnesota companies had been assigned to various larger units, the last being the 5th Iowa Cavalry. Brackett's men had seen action in Missouri and Kentucky and were present for Grant's capture of Forts Henry and Donelson and the Battle of Shiloh. While on furlough in Minnesota, Pope requested that the battalion be transferred to his department for use on the expeditions. His requested was granted, even though the men of the battalion preferred to fight in the South and saw their new assignment as a lesser affair.[14]

Creating such a large force had not been without problems for Pope. The demands of the Civil War were great, and Pope was under pressure to scale back his offensive. In February Halleck wrote Pope that members of Congress had gone to the Secretary of War to request that the 30th Wisconsin Infantry be released for service in the South, and he wished to know if they could be spared. Pope responded firmly that no regiment could "be spared from this department." The following month Pope tried to obtain the 2nd Nebraska or 7th Iowa Cavalry from Major General Samuel R. Curtis's department. Like Pope, Curtis insisted, "I could not spare a man," but Pope did receive part of the 7th Iowa Cavalry. He further retained the 6th Iowa Cavalry, even after Grant wanted the regiment for other service. Pope, however, failed to retain the 6th Minnesota Infantry. In March, Halleck wanted that regiment for the Southern campaigns. Pope blamed the request upon "agents, Indian traders, whiskey sellers, contractors etc." who did not want to see his expedition successful in the Indian War with the Sioux; he assumed they wanted the conflict to continue as it involved "the payment from the government of large sums of money." The thirty-eight hundred men of the expedition, Pope maintained, could win his war while doing little to change the odds in the South. Halleck, briefly, rescinded the orders to remove the 6th Minnesota Infantry, but in May, with the growing needs of the Red River Campaign, the regiment was ordered to Helena, Arkansas.[15]

Under mounting political pressure from certain congressmen complaining that Pope's department was too overmanned, coupled with the Red River debacle and Sherman's manpower needs for his offensive against Atlanta, Grant finally sent Lieutenant Colonel W. L. Duff of the Inspector General's Office to investigate. Duff reported that many leaders in the area felt that Pope's war was overblown and that "the whole thing was a humbug," yet he himself felt that those opposed to the expeditions had a secret agenda; many of Pope's critics were making large sums of money from the troops garrisoned in the department. Grant allowed Pope to keep his troops.[16]

The need for troops and the upcoming campaign caused friction between Pope and Sibley. Hearing a rumor that the 2nd Minnesota Cavalry was to be sent south to join the Red River Campaign, Sibley wrote Pope that this must not happen, as "there will not be left in the district a force sufficient to effectively protect the frontier against the powerful bands of savages who inhabit the prairies within 200 or 300 miles." The removal of the 2nd Minnesota Cavalry was a mistake, although Pope did intend to use these men on the expedition, and Pope responded to Sibley's statement with annoyance. Sibley was advocating for a stronger force to remain on the frontier instead of serving in the campaign, something Pope strongly opposed. "I think you entirely over-estimate the danger from the Indians, as well as the amount needed in Minnesota," he wrote Sibley, then followed up with a personal swipe: "If there be the danger you seem to apprehend, surely it may fairly be said that your campaign of last summer accomplished very little."[17]

The exchange did little to change Sibley's mind that Pope was dangerously reducing the number of men needed to protect the frontier regions of Minnesota. Sibley opposed Pope's desire to establish posts at Devil's Lake and on the James River. Pope's expedition would involve so many troops that, as Sibley argued, "I shall then be left without any infantry force to establish the two posts in the interior," let alone to garrison Forts Ripley, Ridgely, and Abercrombie. Sibley further observed that if soldiers were not kept back, there would be trouble with the draft in Minnesota because "in some localities in this state there will be resistance unless there is a military force on hand to compel submission." But Sibley's main concern still was the fear of new raids into the state from "the very scum of the Isanti [Santees]" who were "imbued with a spirit of bitter hostility to the government and unless they shall be effectually chastised during the present summer there will be accumulated numbers to meet hereafter."[18] It is unclear whether Sibley truly believed the frontier was in imminent danger, was supporting those political interests that wanted to see the war continue for economic profit, or desired to maintain the importance of his district by retaining as many soldiers as possible. As with other officers and politicians that had opposed Pope, Sibley's efforts to rein in the size of the coming campaign failed.

The raids that Sibley feared did occur that summer in Minnesota and Iowa, but were far fewer than in the previous year. In May, a war party killed two soldiers at Spirit Lake, Iowa; another soldier died while fishing at Lake Hanska, Minnesota; and sixteen-year-old Ole Moss was killed near Madelia, Minnesota. Sibley reported the attacks to Pope, who dismissed them and informed Sibley not to report "small raids." He claimed they were to be expected and instructed Sibley not to release the information to the public, as it would only create "unnecessary and injurious alarm and excitement on the frontier."[19]

While Pope dealt with the larger strategy and kept the campaign moving forward, the common soldiers who were soon to march westward focused on the basic issues confronting them. Gathering at Sioux City and Fort Ridgely, the men expressed their views on the Sioux and their commanding officer, Sully. A. N. Judd, 6th Iowa Cavalry, called the Sioux "the fiend incarnate" and believed them to be "great cowards but very cunning." Of all the Indians with whom he was familiar, Judd wrote, "I despise the Sioux the most." John Robinson described the Sioux to his wife as "a miserable race of beings."[20] After nearly two years of war, the racism of the soldiers toward the Sioux, and especially their military prowess, had not diminished. Where Union soldiers, after several years of warfare, had come to respect the Confederate soldiers as opponents, the Northern troops facing the Sioux, for the most part, maintained a deep hatred toward their foes.

If the Sioux had the soldiers' contempt, Sully as a commander had their admiration. According to Milton Spencer, "Although his name is not known as far over the world as some other men, [Sully] is a very good officer, and for myself, would rather go into battle under his command than that of many whose names are trumpeted over the states." And according to A. P. Connelly, Sully was unpretentious and experienced, had a genial temperament, and was an agreeable commander. George Doud, 8th Minnesota Infantry, did not recognize Sully when he first saw him and "would not have known him from a common plug had it not been for [the] star on his shoulder." "No one can question Genl Sully's fighting qualities," G. Merrill Dwelle, 3rd Minnesota Artillery Battery, wrote his sister Carrie.[21]

As time grew short before the start of the expeditions, soldiers took time to write home and reach out to loved ones. Albert Childs, 30th Wisconsin Infantry, wrote often to his brother Ellsworth on a wide range of topics. One important concern was the conduct of their father. Their father was an alcoholic and deeply in debt. When Ellsworth wrote Albert of the passing of their father, Albert responded by warning his brother, "May it prove a warning to you . . . to keep clear of the influence of the intoxicating cup, and shun it even as would Satan himself. God only knows

how I hate the death dealing soul damning poison." Albert sent
sixty dollars to aid their mother, who was in danger of losing her
home to creditors. Worried about his brother, Ellsworth wanted
to know how Albert's spiritual life in the army was. "I am sorry
that my letters have given you any reason to suppose for one moment that I had given up my hope in Christ . . . ," replied Albert,
but he reassured his brother that he never touched tobacco and
had only drunk one beer since enlisting. Eugene Ware, 7th Iowa
Cavalry, wanted everyone to know that the men were not afraid
of the coming danger, as "the men had no lack of courage, nor of
will to go into any fight, or into any dangerous place, or to do any
valiant military act." Henry Wieneke's letter to his wife did not
contain such deep issues as those of the Childs brothers or in
Ware's correspondence; he complained only of doing his laundry,
"an ugly job no wonder that you women always are cross washdays
it is enough to make any one cross."[22]

Although not serving in the field on this campaign, Sibley was
still concerned with the well-being of the Minnesota troops heading into the West. Ever the cautious commander, Sibley met with
Colonel Thomas and encouraged him repeatedly to be careful
and put safety first. Growing tired of the interference, Thomas
responded bluntly, "General, I am going to hunt for the Indians,
and if they will hunt for and find me it will save me a heap of
trouble." On June 5, with the band playing "The Girl I Left Behind Me," Thomas and the Minnesota Brigade marched out of
Fort Ridgely. For David Kingsbury it was a glorious event: "I must
confess that to me . . . this seemed more like war than anything
we had previously experienced." Nine days later, Sully and the
1st Brigade left Sioux City.[23] The new campaign had begun.

Thomas had received orders to unite with Sully's 1st Brigade
at Bordache Creek by June 20. He was to be careful with his
horses and prepare defensive camps each night. Similar to the
1863 expeditions, the new offensive was challenged by rough terrain, oppressive heat, and the lack of good water; the region was

still held in the clutches of a drought. Still, Lieutenant Colonel
Robert McLaren, commander of the 2nd Minnesota Cavalry,
found the march compelling: "One feels as though he was setting
out on a long sea voyage when he starts on an Indian summer
campaign. . . . Before us all is uncertain; behind us near and dear
friends. God grant that we may all live to see each other in the
land of the living." For Charles Hughes, the commencement of
the expedition was not so exciting. Hughes had served in the 1st
Minnesota Infantry before being mustered out. He signed on to
be a mule herder for the campaign and quickly came to regret
his decision: "This is a miserable low dirty life it is my opinion
that I am about as low as a man can get that is in regard to the
labor I perform."[24]

As with the 1863 expedition, the first few days of marching
took the column past the sites of the Dakota War and invoked
strong memories of the massacres. "Sad evidence of the Indian
barbarity of 1862 are visible all around," a solemn Ebenezer Rice,
2nd Minnesota Cavalry, noted in his diary. "The ashes of many
houses is all that remain of a once happy family . . . Father,
Mother, Babe youth and manhood gone." Finding Sioux graves,
some soldiers defiled them, an act that George Doud did not con-
done: "Thay Dug up the bodies of the red man and woman and
kicked them around just as thay pleased and left them above the
ground," and their commanding officer did not put a stop to
"their horrid acts." The next day the column reached the abandoned Lower Sioux Agency, The place, according to Doud,
"showed the effects of the horrid massacre of 62." Here soldiers
proceeded to burn down nearby Sioux lodges. This time the soldiers were arrested, and Doud's company captain congratulated
his men for not participating in the burnings. On June 8, while
marching by the site of the Battle of Wood Lake, First Lieutenant
Lewis Paxton, 8th Minnesota Infantry, discovered the skulls of
three Sioux warriors. "I got two teeth from one of them as trophies," he recorded in his diary.[25]

Also on June 8, the column was joined by an emigrant train headed for the mining camps in Idaho. The leader of the civilians was Thomas Holmes, and the train consisted of 123 wagons and 250 people. Neither Sibley or Pope had favored civilian travel through the Dakota Territory during the summer because of the coming Indian war. Sibley believed "it would not be imprudent to attempt the trip until the route has been rendered safe by the troops," while Pope sent out a circular entitled "Notice to Emigrants by way of the Missouri River and Upper Plains to the Idaho Mines." In it Pope reported that strong forces of Yanktonais and Lakotas planned to block passage on the Missouri River and harass any travel overland. He encouraged all civilians to wait until Sully's campaign against the Sioux had concluded. Holmes and other wagon train bosses would not heed the warning; the allure of gold was too powerful.[26]

Moving westward, soldiers kept record of the temperature and number of miles marched daily. The heat increased rapidly, from 76 degrees to 90 degrees in two days, and remained firmly in the 80s until the later part of June, when the temperature soared to over 100 degrees. With the sun beating down on them, the soldiers averaged marches of sixteen to twenty miles a day. Sundays were a day of rest and worship, something that McLaren firmly supported: "We can hope for success when we recognize Him, and not otherwise."[27]

As few men currently on the expedition had served during the 1863 campaign, lessons had to be relearned, and finding good water was a high priority for the men. According to Kingsbury, "Water was very scarce and when found was vile." He insisted that "water from the streets of St. Paul would have been better, for it would have lacked the alkali." The presence of alkali, which burned the tongue and could cause dysentery, bothered John Robinson. He explained to his wife that alkali was "something I suppose you never saw and tasted, and I hope you may be never obliged to drink." What small lakes they encountered were foul.

"The proper name would be stinking lakes thay smelt very bad and mudy," observed Doud. The heat and lack of drinkable water led Thomas Hodgson, 8th Minnesota Infantry, to later note, "I . . . conceived such a strong dislike for Dakota that, I have never had a desire to live there or own any of it." John Robinson concurred with Hodgson, telling his wife, "I used to think, when a boy, that I would like to roam over the vast prairies of the west and see the wild animals and hear the wolves howl, but I believe I have had enough of it."[28]

Finding no wood on the prairie, soldiers turned to collecting buffalo chips. The chips, which were plentiful, were collected by being pierced with a ramrod and placed in piles. Kingsbury wrote, "These chips make an intensive fire and were far preferable to wood, requiring less labor to secure."[29]

Overall the march was not difficult, and the Minnesota Brigade made good time as it approached the rendezvous point with Sully's forces. On June 29 Thomas's scouts encountered ten scouts from the Sully column, and the next day contact was made with a cavalry patrol sent out by Sully and the unification of the two columns achieved at three P.M. the same day.[30]

Sully's march up the Missouri River went far better than that of the previous year. For a week, the column averaged eighteen miles a day before reaching Fort Sully on June 24. Along the way the men had been serenaded by two bands accompanying the expedition. "I think I never heard music so clear and beautiful as it did on those prairies," recalled Frank Myers. At Fort Sully, Sully found waiting two to three hundred lodges of Lakotas and Yanktonais who wanted peace with the army. These Sioux informed Sully that a large encampment of hostile Sioux were on the Heart River, preparing for battle with the soldiers. Sully greatly overestimated their numbers in his report to Pope, claiming that six thousand warriors were massed to fight him.[31]

On June 26, after two days of rest, Sully marched out once more, covering twenty-five miles and camping on Okoboji Creek.

Two days later came the first skirmish of the campaign and an incident that outraged the Sioux.

Captain John Fielner was a forty-year-old German topographical engineer and naturalist assigned to the expedition by Pope. Pope, a natural science buff, had given him precise orders on his duties; Fielner was to make "as full a report as possible upon the geology, botany, natural history, and physical character . . . of the region. . . . I need not remind you of the important results to science which will ensue from even a partial success in these observations," Pope stressed.[32]

On June 28 Fielner, with a sergeant and private from the 6th Iowa Cavalry, rode out to inspect a rock formation and collect insects. Sully, an experienced frontiersman, warned Fielner to be careful, but Fielner simply laughed off his concerns. Later in the day, Fielner was returning towards the camp when he and his escort stopped near the Little Cheyenne River for water. Fielner was reaching into the water with his cup when a shot rang out and he was shot through his lungs. Three Yanktonais warriors emerged from the bushes to try and capture the soldiers' horses, but the horses bolted and the attackers soon fled the scene. Fielner lived until ten o'clock that night, and Siegmund Rothammer was moved enough by the loss to write, "By his death the country lost a brave, efficient & accomplished officer, our command a gentleman, who . . . commanded the respect of all, who knew him."[33]

Sully ordered an immediate pursuit of the warriors. Three groups rode out of the camp: the Dakota scouts, elements of the 6th Iowa Cavalry, and Company A, known as the Coyotes, 1st Dakota Cavalry. There is confusion over who made contact with the Sioux. Two soldiers, Sylvester Campbell and James Thomson, wrote in their diaries that the Dakota scouts with the column hunted down the warriors. "The scouts followed them and killed 3 of them," recorded Campbell. Henry Wieneke, who was with the 6th Iowa Cavalry, stated that his company went in pursuit but "we were put on the wrong track and missed them," adding that the Company A, 1st Dakota Cavalry, fought the Sioux.[34]

Company A and its captain, Nelson Minor, were experienced soldiers. Lieutenant Colonel John Pattee, 6th Iowa Cavalry, remembered, "In this company there were many excellent men, most young men but old in experience as frontiersmen." Minor ordered his company to mount, and they raced to the site of the attack. Ole Oland, a member of the Coyotes, stated, "Our company was called on to kill his murderers." Once at the site, they followed the trail of the Yanktonais, the company spreading out as they rode. Fifteen miles from the ambush site, Minor spotted three warriors ducking into a nearby ravine. As the soldiers grew closer, the Sioux opened fire. Dismounting, the soldiers advanced and a lively skirmish ensued. The Sioux put breechcloths on their ramrods and waved them to draw the soldiers' fire, but the Coyotes were too experienced to fall for the trick. One warrior was shot in the head as the troopers came within twenty feet of the ravine. With loud war cries the other two men, outnumbered and knowing they would die, charged the soldiers bravely before being shot and killed.[35]

However, A. N. Judd claimed that it was his company, the 6th Iowa Calvary, who had killed the Yanktonais. Judd was part of the thirty-man detachment sent after the ambushers. According to Judd, "We had gone but a mile or a little more when we sighted them on their ponies, going at a stiff gait." After a four-mile chase, "they deserted their horses, as our long range guns were knocking the dust out of their hair. They took refuge in a dry creek bottom but were too slow to get away." Judd reported that there were five warriors in the ravine and the Iowa soldiers killed only three, the other two escaping.[36]

J. H. Drips, another member of the 6th Iowa Cavalry, gave the credit to Minor and Company A. "Had it not been for Capt Minor's men, who are Indian hunters, and Indian haters too," the Sioux would not have been apprehended. As Sergeant Abner

English rounded up the scattered men from Company A, Minor returned to camp to report on the skirmish. Sully was pleased with the report and sent to join the troops a Lieutenant Bacon, 1st Dakota cavalry, with a keg of water and some whiskey for the men in the field. Bacon was accompanied by an ambulance and had orders from Sully to cut off the heads of the three dead Sioux and bring them back to camp. This order was popular with the men, who saw the Sioux action as murder rather than what it was—a legitimate act of war. George Northrup, a scout with the column, cut off a partial scalp from one of the bodies and sent it back East to his brother with a note: "I enclose a lock of hair from one of the heads, it is yet bloody, but if you wish to preserve it you can wash it out."[37] The Sioux, when hearing of the beheadings, had an opposite reaction: the news was met with shock and outrage. Furious at the soldiers, the Sioux became even more desirous of fighting them.

The following day, Sully had rockets fired to alert Thomas and the Minnesota Brigade that he was nearby, and on June 30 the two columns were joined. To Sully's surprise and dismay, Thomas informed him of the civilian wagon train accompanying his column. Later, in a report to Pope, Sully vented over the presence of emigrants in a war zone. "Why will our government continue to act so foolishly, sending out emigrant trains at a great expense?" Sully fumed, maintaining that the civilians encouraged desertion and "curse and ridicule the expedition and officers in command." Still, Sully did his best to provide for the emigrants as his command rested, waiting for the arrival of more supplies being brought up the Missouri River on a steamboat and then overland by wagon train.[38]

On July 3, resupplied, Sully continued his advance on a pleasant day that caused Eli Williamson, 2nd Minnesota Cavalry, to remark, "All is well. The Lord rules. I'm satisfied." The Fourth of July was celebrated with a twenty-mile march; not until after the expedition had encamped was any attention paid

to Independence Day. Lieutenant Colonel Samuel Pollock, commander of the 6th Iowa Cavalry, gave a short address to his
men, "assuring us that if we had a fight it would be within thirty
days, we gave him three rousing cheers and adjourned," wrote
Drips. The mood in the camp was less festive than in the previous year; Williamson noted, "Not one gun has been fired today
to commemorate the day our forefathers declared they would be
free. Far different than the one a year ago." Captain Minor
brought his men in Company A, 1st Dakota Cavalry, cans of
peaches in celebration of the day. "I ate mine with some hardtack
out on the picket that was the whole of my supper," a glum Ole
Oland stated, adding, "I felt bad here."[39]

Once incident that day highlighted the racism that was a com-
ponent of the expedition. In his diary, Thomas Hodgson reported on a sermon delivered by a soldier from his regiment
named Harris, who was an Adventist minister. Harris first spoke
of the flag, Constitution, and certain religious themes, but it was
not until "the speaker turned upon the Sioux Indians that he
completely captivated the boys," related Hodgson. Harris "gave
the redskins such a roasting . . . the more barbarous the speech
became the more the boys applauded. There were to be no prisoners taken—even children or women were to be butchered if we
ever got at them." Sitting in the audience was another soldier
who was a minister in civilian life. When Harris finished speaking, this minster approached him and "severely rebuked Harris
for his unchristian speech." Unfazed by the criticism, Harris responded that Christians, when fighting savages, must use the Old
Testament method. He quoted from the Bible, "Destroy them utterly, root and branch. They had forfeited their right to life."
Hodgson believed that the more humane minister was thoroughly
vanquished in his debate with Harris and that most of the men
listening agreed with Harris.[40]

The following day the column passed between Beaver and
Little Beaver Creeks. The Sioux called one prominent butte the

Thunder Nest. It was said to be the home of the mythical Thunderbirds and where they hatched their eggs. The birth of a Thunderbird was marked by thunder and lightning. Once, according to legend, the noise awoke the Grizzly Bear spirit, who went to destroy the eggs. This led to a combat between the spirit and Thunderbirds that shook the entire earth.[41]

July 6 found the expedition one mile from the Missouri River and the soldiers annoyed with their officers. The officers had been pushing the march, and the horses were worn down. According to Doud, "Horses faged out, and some of the men. Officers have no mercy on the horses." Making matters worse, once camp was reached that day the officers "then lay in thair tents and drink the best of brandy & some very drunk," Doud reported. Upon reaching the Missouri River the next day, Sully decided that the new post, Fort Rice—named for General Clay Rice—would be built there. Rothammer approved of the location, as it had "an abundance of heavy timber & excellent grazing—lands accompanied by a good boat-landing & ferry-site." Abner English also praised the site as "the finest I have seen on the Missouri River." The construction of the fort commenced on the west bank of the river.[42]

The materials and supplies needed to establish the post were brought up the river by the steamboats *Peoria*, *Isabella*, *New Gaty*, *General Grant*, *Tempest*, and *Island City*. Doing most of the building were the four companies of the 30th Wisconsin Infantry, who would remain to garrison the fort. Pattee admired the Wisconsin men as good axmen and also for their pie-baking skills: "They had lots of pies ready to sell us after we got across the river." Fort Rice took two weeks to construct, with Pattee describing the new post as "log building—general 80 feet long—erected 24 feet apart around a square that measured 400 feet on each side. The 24 feet between buildings was filled in with a stockade with a gate near the center of the east, west and north site large enough to drive a wagon through."[43]

While at Fort Rice, three men—Frank Femmone, Richard Clayton, and Ben Wallace, 2nd Minnesota Cavalry—deserted. A patrol of six men was sent after them, but they made their escape. Sully published an order that any further deserters were to be shot. Soon after came word of the death of Andrew Doud. The twenty-two-year-old Doud was a veteran of the Siege of Vicksburg, where he had been wounded. He had joined the 8th Minnesota Infantry only to die at Fort Rice of "bilious Colick." More positive news was the arrival of mail from home. John Strong, 8th Minnesota Cavalry, wrote about the effect it had on the men: "Mail day is of all others the liveliest . . . in the faces of the men you can see a smile upon their faces, and a sorrowfull countenance if bad news is received, and if the orderly says all done . . . a bewildered blank look as if they thought they were forgotten by those that they left behind them." Taking time to write his brother Joseph, Leonard Aldrich, 8th Minnesota Infantry, agreed with Strong that "the worst thing about it will be the lack of mail. It has been three weeks since we had any . . . ," and mourned the failure of his wife and children to correspond: "I wish Martha and the girls would write." Frustrated with the campaign and homesick, Aldrich complained, "We find no sign of Indians yet. They are something like going to the place where a rain bow comes to the earth. I don't believe we shall be able to find any that will fight. This whole thing is a confound humbug."[44]

On July 17, a day that Amos Cherry, 7th Iowa Cavalry, found "awful hot," Sully held a review of his army. Afterward Williamson wrote that "Isaac, Cory & myself went out into the woods & had a pray meeting. The Lord met us there—Bless His holy name." Two days later, on July 19, Sully marched the column out of the post. Sully had planned on using pack mules for the supplies, but a stampede occurred that "scattered boxes of hard tack boiled sowbelly ect [sic] over miles of plains" and changed his mind. One wagon per company, each carrying fifteen hundred pounds of supplies, was kept with the expedition instead. Coming with them were the emigrants, to Judd's disgust. Judd disliked the fact that among them were men "who were trying, as some of them said, to 'shunt the draft.' . . . It went against the grain some, as the majority of them were Southern sympathizers."[45]

Marching along the Cannon Ball River, Frank Myers noted, "We entered a very different country from that on the east side of the river." Describing the region, Myers wrote, "The grass was all buffalo, scenery the wonderful and fantastical shaped buttes . . . the buttes were apparently piled up across the prairie, from one to five hundred feet high in all manners of shapes."[46] The anticipation that the army would soon be in action against the Sioux had everyone excited. Oland noted, "Rumors are afloat of large bands of Indians a short distance in our advance." The pressure perhaps led Sully to become intoxicated, as Captain William Silvis, 8th Minnesota Infantry, tersely recorded in his diary, "Sully drunk." At midnight on July 22, two messengers arrived from Fort Rice with news that the Sioux, estimated at eighteen hundred lodges, were camped on the Knife River and ready for a battle. The next day the column crossed the Cannon Ball River and marched toward the Knife River.[47]

July 24 proved a hard day's march. The weather was brutally hot. "I never experienced such a hot day in all my travels. Men were sun-struck, dogs died by the roadside, and oxen were left to die," remembered Robert McLaren. Hoping for good water, the men were disappointed when the Heart River was reached. A thirsty Myers found the "river contained very poor water for drinking, strongly impregnated with coal and minerals."[48]

Knowing he was closing in on his opponents, Sully decided to strip down his command for action. At the Heart River he left behind the civilian wagon train, a strong military guard, and many of his supplies. On July 26, with a force of some twenty-two hundred men and forty-five light wagons each loaded with less than a thousand pounds of supplies, Sully continued toward the Knife River.[49] He made contact with the Sioux that same day.

Out in front of the column was the Nebraska scout company. It encountered a Sioux war party of some thirty to forty men. The party had been on a raid against the traditional enemies of the Sioux, the Crows. Successful in their efforts, they were returning to their people with two Crow prisoners. Upon encountering the war party, the captain of the scouts, Christian Stufft, who was drunk, panicked and ordered his men to retreat. His lieutenant refused the order and called for an attack. Pulling his pistol, Stufft insisted on a retreat as most of the company broke for the rear, including him. Stufft raced back to camp, screaming that the scouts had been cut to pieces by the Sioux. Sully ordered Major Brackett to ride to the aid of those scouts who were still fighting. As Brackett rode out, furious at Stufft's cowardice, he took a swipe at Stufft with his saber. Arriving on the battle scene, Brackett found the skirmish over. During the fight, the Sioux had shot several horses and wounded one scout in the knee, while the scouts killed three men and saved one of the two Crow prisoners, the other having died during the fighting. Back in camp, aware of Stufft's condition, Sully placed the man under arrest and removed him from command.[50]

Any hope of a surprise attack upon the Sioux village was now gone. Both sides were aware of each other and preparing for combat. Every night Sioux scouts signaled the movements of the expedition by attaching burning twists of grass to arrows and shooting them up into the sky from some piece of high ground. Sully ordered the men to keep their horses saddled at night and to sleep with their weapons in hand. At ten A.M. on July 28, scouts for the army discovered the Sioux camp at a place called Killdeer Mountain.[51] The largest battle of the Indian Wars was about to begin.

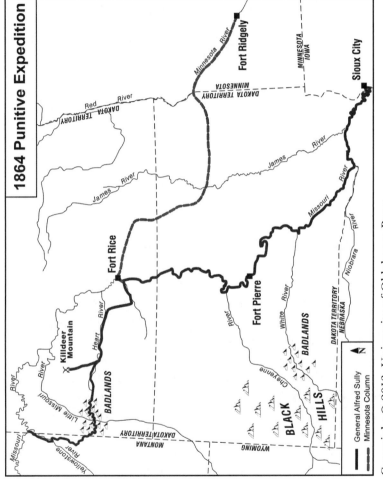

1864 Punitive Expedition

Fort Ridgely

Sioux City

MINNESOTA
IOWA

DAKOTA TERRITORY
MINNESOTA

DAKOTA TERRITORY

Red River

Minnesota River

James River

James River

Missouri River

Fort Rice

Killdeer Mountain

Heart River

BADLANDS

Little Missouri River

Missouri River

Yellowstone River

MONTANA
DAKOTA TERRITORY

WYOMING

Fort Pierre

BADLANDS

White River

Cheyenne River

River

BLACK HILLS

DAKOTA TERRITORY
NEBRASKA

Niobrara River

N

General Alfred Sully
Minnesota Column

Copyright © 2013, University of Oklahoma Press.

201

CHAPTER 9

The Battle of Killdeer Mountain

"THE PRAIRIE SEEMED ALIVE WITH INDIANS"

At midnight on July 28, bugles sounded across the camp awakening the troops for a new day. Yawning and stretching, the men readied themselves and their mounts and proceeded to march at three-thirty A.M. Already it was proving to be a warm day; by midafternoon the temperature would reach 96 degrees. After advancing fifteen miles, the column stopped near a small lake for a quick breakfast of coffee and hardtack at nine A.M. Resuming the march, the column again stopped at noon to eat. During this noon rest, scouts raced into the camp at noon to announce their discovery of the Sioux encampment a few miles ahead. The Sioux scouts went to the headquarters wagon and changed into the blue uniforms of the soldiers in order to not be confused with the enemy in the upcoming battle.[1]

The reaction to the news of the village was mixed. Colonel Samuel Pollock, commander of the 6th Iowa Cavalry, turned to a nearby captain and exclaimed excitedly, "Well, captain, we have found the Sons of Bitches at last!" as the men around him responded with a yell. Realizing it would be a hard fight, men in

Company B, 6th Iowa Cavalry gave their watches, pictures, and other valuables to the regimental saddler, Dwight F. House, for safekeeping. "A few hurriedly scratched off a farewell letter to loved ones, if they should fall in the battle," remembered Frank Myers. Some men started to drink, but when John Robinson was offered some alcohol he refused. Robinson admitted that he was "a little excited" but wanted to rely on his "native courage." John Wright was more confident about the engagement: "We go to battle feeling right and justice is on our side and we resolved to conquer or die." However, Corporal Seth Eastwood, 3rd Artillery Battery, a good, reliable soldier, was not so sure. Eastwood went to Captain John Jones and requested a pair of spurs. When Jones asked why, Eastwood responded truthfully: "Well sir, I might want to run." Lieutenant G. Merrill Dwelle believed that a number of men in the battery felt the same way.[2]

The soldiers were still advancing across a rolling prairie that had little grass because of the drought. "The day was very hot and the boys sweat as they toiled steadily on over the dusty plain and suffered much for want of water," wrote John Pattee. Reaching a small creek, the thirsty men found some water, but it was too alkali to drink. Crossing the creek and moving up a steep rise, they soon witnessed the Sioux village for the first time. Although both sides knew that the enemy was near, it appears that the army still took the encampment by surprise. Not until the soldiers were within two or three miles did the Sioux see the approaching danger.[3]

In their letters and diaries the soldiers offered a variety of spelling for the Sioux pronunciation of the region. "Toc-Sha-O-Wa-Coo-Ta" was how Pattee wrote it, meaning "the place where they kill deer," or Killdeer Mountain. The location, with its rugged terrain, provided a good defensive position. The ground was uneven and rose gradually into broken hills. Abner English described the area this way: "The mountains were in full succession of ridges and buttes, each one rising above the other, broken by ravines, gulches and canyons . . . the whole rising several hundred feet about the surrounding plains." The hills ranged from four hundred to eight hundred feet high, Pollock stating that "deep, wooded ravines almost inaccessible to cavalry protected nearly the whole front of these buttes." David Kingsbury could see that the difficult ground made "the chance of flanking them and meeting them when they emerged near the timber . . . equally impractical and in fact, almost impossible." At the base of these formidable hills was the Sioux village.[4]

The Hunkpapas of the Lakotas had been the first to arrive at Killdeer Mountain. Among them were twenty-four-year-old Gall, a rising leader, and Sitting Bull, who was likely thirty years old. According to Ernie LaPointe, Sitting Bull's great-grandson, Sitting Bull had come out of curiosity. He wanted to observe how the white soldiers fought, and he later stated that he had not wanted to fight but "still just wanted to be left alone." According to him, "Our Hunkpapa tribe was peacefully camped above the mouth of the Little Missouri in the Killdeer Mountains." Here they were joined by the Lakota bands of Sans Arcs, Miniconjous, and Blackfeet. Yanktonais, upset over Whitestone Hill, also gathered at the growing camp, and on July 26 Inkpaduta and his band of resister Santees arrived. An experienced and well-respected warrior, Inkpaduta suggested the camp be moved up the mountain, and according to Sitting Bull, "selected a flat at the mouth canyon that was surrounded with wooded ravines and breaks, where he felt we could best avoid, or fight against the whites . . . if necessary." Eventually some sixteen hundred lodges, occupied by eight thousand people, of whom two thousand would have been men of military age, settled at the base of the mountain.[5]

Sitting Bull's fourteen-year-old nephew, White Bull, was watering the family horses when a group of young hunters brought word of the approach of the army. Sitting Bull, White Bull, and Sitting Bull's uncle Four Horns mounted their horses and rode out to a high hill. From there White Bull saw "a whole string of soldiers coming a whole bunch of infantry [Sully had dismounted part of his command]—long string mile wide and companies on horses ride in bunches back of them."[6]

At first, neither side made much noise as both groups went about preparing for combat. Sully placed the 1st Brigade on the right and the 2nd Brigade on the left side of the line. Three companies of the 7th Iowa cavalry were ordered to dismount and were sent out along the entire front of the line as skirmishers. Sully also had six companies of the 8th Minnesota Infantry, who had been mounted for the campaign, on his left and six companies of the 6th Iowa Cavalry on his right dismount as well. The 2nd Minnesota Cavalry were left mounted to support the 8th Minnesota Infantry, as was Brackett's Battalion, who would support the 6th Iowa Cavalry. In the center of the line, Sully placed Nathaniel Pope's artillery battery supported by the two companies of the 1st Dakota Cavalry. Behind the front line came the wagon train and ambulances, defended by John Jones's artillery battery and several companies from the 6th Iowa Cavalry, 8th Minnesota Infantry, and 2nd Minnesota Cavalry. Quietly, a number of the Sioux scouts slipped away to fight alongside their people, loyalty to their kin being more important than serving the whites.[7]

The Sioux took time to apply their war paint and go through the various rituals before entering combat. Slowly they rode out to meet the soldiers. It was an intimidating sight. The "Indians appeared covering [the] plains 6 miles or more front and back to the hills as far as you could see was Indians & ponies," an impressed Henry Wieneke wrote, adding that the Sioux were "showing some very good horsemanship and defying us to come on." James Fisk, 2nd Minnesota Cavalry, recalled that the soldiers could "see them by the thousands in their camp, mounting their horses and getting ready for battle." According to twenty-year-old Harlen Bruch, 8th Minnesota Infantry, "The Indians gathered on their horses, stripped for battle, and began to leisurely ride out towards us, first a few fine looking fellows rode up nearly within gunshot to reconnoiter and then little bands would leave the camp and advance."[8]

In awe of this display of military might, numerous reports from soldiers present that day overestimated the numbers the army faced. A. N. Judd claimed that there were eight thousand warriors prepared to attack the column. Most other accounts, including the reports of Sully and Pattee, stated they were opposed by a force of five to six thousand men.[9] Sully, an experienced veteran of the plains, likely knew that the figure was too high, but as was a common occurrence with reports during the Civil War, wanted to impress Pope and others, in order to show the seriousness of the fighting at Killdeer.

Killdeer was the first battle in which the army faced a sizable portion of the Lakotas' military power. The fight started in a very traditional Lakota fashion. Lakota warriors were known for their flamboyant and courageous behavior. Personal honor being extremely important, warriors tried to draw attention to themselves on the battlefield, so witnesses would later give them praise and recognition for their military accomplishments. As the soldiers approached, one Lakota man, Lone Dog, announced that he would ride close to the soldier's front line to see if they would shoot at him, then "we will then all shoot at the soldiers." White Bull states that Lone Dog was charmed: "He ran close to the soldiers. When they came and gave them the chance to shoot first . . . ," the soldiers fired but missed. Lone Dog once more rode along the soldier's line, again returning unharmed. Impressed by Lone Dog's bravery, the young White Bull could not resist joining on his third run toward the soldiers. "They all took a shot at us and we weren't hit and returned to the hill . . . ," White Bull remembered. Sitting Bull was pleased with White Bull: "I was glad my nephew had taken this opportunity to show such courage in his first battle."[10]

Not as pleased with a performance that showed the poor marksmanship of the army were the soldiers trying to kill Lone Dog. Benjamin Brunson, 8th Minnesota Infantry, assumed Lone Dog was a chief, writing that "at this point their apparent leader would ride out in advance of his line, waving his banner of eagle feathers, then wheeling around give instructions to his forces." Pattee also remembered Lone Dog: "About this time an Indian very gaily dressed, carrying a large war club gorgeously ornamented appeared out front of the 6th Iowa Cavalry and called loudly to us and gesticulated wildly about one-half mile away." Three men fired at Lone Dog but could not bring him down. Even Sully grew angry at the affair, sending Pattee an order: "The general sends his compliments and wishes you to kill that Indian for God's sake." Taking his two best marksmen, Pattee had them fire at Lone Dog, only to once more miss. Then Lone Dog "immediately stretched himself out flat along the horse's back and plied his left heel vigorously against the flank of his pony and disappeared from my sight over the hill," recorded Pattee.[11] Few men gained the honor that Lone Dog did that day.

Sully ordered an advance toward the village that Thomas Hodgson referred to as "slow and majestic." Sent out front of their regiment as skirmishers were five companies of the 8th Minnesota Infantry, spaced some twelve feet apart, and according to Colonel Minor Thomas, "There was a determined look on the faces of the men that indicated that they now had a chance to get satisfaction from the redskins." There may have been a number of reasons for the 1864 expedition, but for the men on that expedition there was still only one reason: revenge. At twelve-forty-five P.M. the first shots rang out, starting the battle, and for Thomas, "Everything changed." The Sioux opened fire on the skirmishers and then charged.[12]

More than one soldier remembered that first charge and the powerful psychological impact it had on them. "It looked awful," wrote Fisk. "Thousands of Indians were rushing down on us, in a dead run. It looked to me as though they couldn't stop if they wanted to, and that we would be run over and have a hand to hand fighting with the savages. There's no use denying it—I was badly scared." Kingsbury also was shaken by the assault: "To soldiers, or others, who have not seen or heard an Indian charge, it cannot be described. It is calculated to strike terror into the hearts of the bravest. I have not the command of words to attempt to give any proper description of it." He could only compare the charge to "the imps of Hell let loose." Impressive as it might have been, a mounted charge could not withstand the volley of long-range rifle fire. The attack was halted and driven back as the soldiers continued marching forward. "We gave it to them good," a satisfied Fisk wrote. The Sioux responded with more charges that Harlan Bruch reported followed a similar pattern: "The bands concentrated and, uttering their war cries, they dashed towards our lines. Riding at full speed they would fire their guns and wheel and disappear to load and come again."[13]

The firepower of the troopers was something the Sioux could not compete with. The Hunkpapas were poorly armed with old flintlock muskets and little ammunition, and it is unlikely that the other bands were better armed. For Sitting Bull, "I had never seen white troops fight before. The number of guns and the amount of shooting was much more than I had ever expected." During their attacks, the warriors were suffering losses. Although they boldly advanced at first, John Strong soon noted that "they discovered that our guns were long range and in the hands of men capable of making a good shot." The reluctance of the Sioux to push home a charge frustrated John Richardson, 2nd Minnesota Cavalry: "They came pretty near us once or twice but not never enough for to scare us much or fight much either." To the soldiers the Sioux seemed to "all set up the war hoop and commenced to circle us around, each vying with the other to see which could make the most noise." Stymied in their frontal attacks, the Sioux spread out all along the line, moving to attack the flanks, looking for an opening.[14]

As the battle expanded, the Sioux recorded an act of bravery. During the fighting, a group of men emerged from the encampment singing and dragging a travois bearing a crippled man. The forty-year-old Man-Who-Never-Walked had been crippled from birth and now wanted to die a heroic death "as he cannot be of use." His friends honored his request, giving him weapons, and as the man sang his death song, the horse pulling the travois was whipped and sent directly into the path of the oncoming soldiers. The horse was hit first and went down; shortly afterward Man-Who-Never-Walked was shot to death. Proud of how their friend died, the Sioux renamed him Bear's Heart.[15]

Soon after, Sitting Bull's uncle, Four Horns, was wounded. Sitting Bull had been engaged in the fighting, mounted on a fast sorrel he had purchased from some Canadian Indians for several buffalo robes. He was well armed with a good rifle and a bow. Observing the battle, Sitting Bull was shocked by the lack of personal honor and bravery shown by the soldiers. When a Sioux warrior was wounded or killed, other men worked in pairs to rescue the wounded man, taking him to safety, or to throw a lariat around a dead man to save his body from the enemy. Sitting Bull did not see the soldiers doing these things and concluded, "They seem to have no hearts . . . when a white soldier gets killed, nobody cries, nobody cares; they go right on shooting and let him lie there." During one of the many charges on the troopers, Four Horn was struck "in the back of the ribs." Sitting Bull and White Bull raced to his side when Four Horns shouted, "I am shot." The two men led Four Horn's horse back to the village, where Sitting Bull took care of the wounded man. White Bull stated that Sitting Bull had "medicines on hand at all times and put some on the sore—gave him some to drink then bandaged the hole." For Sitting Bull, the battle was over as he cared for his relative.[16]

Moving toward the flanks of the army lines, the Sioux were starting to adapt to the soldiers' fighting style. To overcome the soldiers' firepower, the Sioux would start firing at one point of the line, diverting the attention of the soldiers, and then charge at another point. Their skills as horsemen further reduced casualties. As Robinson recalled, "The Indians are fine horsemen, that is expert riders, when they saw that one of our men was going to fire at them they would drop upon the side of their horse in an instant."[17] Using these tactics, the Sioux struck at the left flank of the army.

To counter the attack, Major Ebenezer Rice and Companies A and D, 2nd Minnesota Cavalry, were ordered to the extreme left of the line. The cavalry raced "at a gallop for about one mile when we wheeled into line and dismounted," according to Rice. For the next two hours they engaged the Sioux. Rice was almost killed, noting, "I saw the Indian when he came up and took aim but not supposing him in the act of firing upon me I felt no alarm . . . but I soon found that I was his man . . . in a twinkling a ball came hissing by my head." Three other Sioux also tried, and failed, to shoot Rice. During the action, John Wright, 8th Minnesota Infantry, saw three soldiers advancing up a hill while several Sioux warriors were coming up from the other side. The two groups clashed, and one warrior was killed as the others retreated. Wright noted that soon "two Indians swooped back side by side and reached down gathered their dead companion and was back over the ridge before our men recovered sufficient to give them another shot." When joined by two more companies of the 2nd Minnesota Cavalry, Rice mounted his command and charged the Sioux, driving them back nearly eight miles.[18]

Another factor in the defeat of the Sioux assaults was Sully's use of artillery. Sully was a strong supporter of the effect of artillery on Indians on the battlefield. At the start of the engagement he had placed his artillery on high hills, giving them a wide range of fire. During the Sioux frontal assaults, their charges were met by artillery firing canister. When the Sioux moved to challenge the flanks, Sully maneuvered his artillery into positions that gave him an enfilade fire that again swept the Sioux lines. "The cannons were a revelation to these Sioux," Kingsbury maintained. "They had probably never seen, much less heard, one before." Sitting Bull commented on the use of the artillery: "The cannon which shot so loud and so far and so often was a big surprise." Once more, however, the warriors learned to adapt. Thomas Hodgson observed that when the artillery fired at a group of Sioux, they would quickly scatter, thus lessening the impact of the shells as they arrived. By doing this, Hodgson believed, the Sioux did not suffer the high casualties often claimed in the army reports of the battle.[19]

Sully found a further use for the artillery, one that was not used in any other theater of the Civil War. Approaching the village, about a mile from the encampment, soldiers noticed hundreds of women, children, and elderly on a butte watching the progress of the battle. Sully ordered eight artillery pieces to open fire on them. The first volley of shells fell short, but the second and following volleys were on target. Periodically, citizens during the Civil War would come under artillery fire. However, no officer intentionally fired artillery upon noncombatants; to do so would have been met with shock and censorship. Yet, at Killdeer, Minor Thomas not only approved of the act but called it "a magnificent sight," remembering, "1,600 lodges filled with women and children, dogs, horses and all paraphernalia of their homes, and their attempting to save them with the shells bursting about them, carrying destruction in their path."[20]

During the fighting on the left flank, the Sioux did force elements of the 8th Minnesota Infantry to fall back, opening a hole in the line. With this, several hundred Sioux made a major effort to strike into the rear of the army in an attempt to reach the wagon train. "A horde of Indians tried to come up behind and take the batteries" was how Sylvester Campbell viewed the attack.

Alarmed, Myers believed that "the prairie seemed alive with Indians bent on our immediate destruction." Sully saw the threat and ordered Jones's battery and Company A, 1st Dakota Cavalry, to plug the hole. The Sioux charge was "met by a steady fire of our boys," reported Abner English. Meeting in a ravine, the two sides fought it out at close range, including a hand-to-hand melee. The Sioux fired arrows that "swished by our heads with great force," stated English, as the soldiers replied with their pistols. "The steady fire . . . and the shells of Jones guns made sad havoc in their ranks." Supported by the artillery, the Dakota troopers broke the attack, and the Sioux "never succeed in piercing that line of blue," boasted a proud English.[21]

Relentlessly, although the soldiers were suffering from the heat and lack of water, the army came ever closer to the village; the warriors were unable to stop the advance. A tired Sergeant Drips wrote, "All this time our column was advancing, sometimes on the double-quick, under a scorching July sun and hardly any water fit to drink." The men fought well; Henry Wieneke told his wife that "most of the boys stood right up to the work and never flinched." Fighting alongside the soldiers were mixed-blood and full-blood scouts, a number of whom were Sioux. Milton Spencer believed the scouts "fought like tigers" and were often taunted by the Sioux, who "abused them terribly" for being traitors to their people.[22]

Defeated in their efforts to break the soldier's lines on the front, flanks, and rear, the Sioux grew alarmed at the obvious threat to their loved ones and homes in the village. All hopes of winning the battle were gone, and the only thing the warriors could do was try to hold back the troopers to give their families time to escape the coming destruction. Excelling as a good defensive fighter, Inkpaduta rose to the occasion, rallying his men for one more effort to hold the Sioux's left flank, the closest to the panicking village.

Inkpaduta's Santee and Yanktonai forces charged out of the ravine and into the right flank of Sully's line. "They massed their forces between our lines and their village, and made one final and desperate charge on our right, which was within a short distance of their camp," observed Kingsbury. Brackett's Battalion of mounted cavalry counterattacked this new Sioux offensive. Brackett's men had been doing good service during the day, blocking Sioux assaults on the right. At one point, Brackett had sent out a decoy of ten to fifteen troopers to an exposed hill. Watching the move, Myers thought the men would be slaughtered. As the Sioux attacked the soldiers, the troopers fled, leading their pursuers into an ambush prepared by Brackett. Now, faced with Inkpaduta's advance, Brackett ordered a saber charge into the flank of the Sioux. "No more welcome order could have been given," recalled Sergeant Isaac Botsford. "With a yell, they swept down the hillside, across a ravine and up the opposite sloop and in a moment were upon them."[23]

The struggle was fierce, with neither side giving ground. Sitting Bull, watching the fight, remembered, "We pulled some of the troopers from their saddles, counting coup on them." Revenge was again a motivating influence on the actions of the soldiers. Most of the men in Brackett's Battalion had lost loved ones in the Dakota War of 1862. Corporal James Edwards's father had been murdered by the Sioux at Butternut, a small town near Mankato, Minnesota. The twenty-three-year-old Welshman had learned of the death while serving with the 5th Iowa Cavalry. He swore revenge, and now seeing a warrior on foot, drew his saber and charged him, yelling, "Now is the time for revenge!" The Sioux warrior calmly watched Edwards advance upon him, aimed his rifle, and fired, killing Edwards's horse. Both men now on foot, the warrior swung his empty gun at Edwards, who parried with his saber before killing his opponent with a lunge. A sergeant, who Judd believed to be deranged, also rushed ahead in vengeance for his murdered wife, Bella, who had died at New Ulm. Charging into a mass of Sioux warriors, the trooper slashed with his saber as the warriors tried to pull him from his horse. By the time other soldiers reached his side, the sergeant had been pierced with arrows, his horse killed, and his saber broken. "Tell the folks I am satisfied," the dying man panted. "They paid a good price for Bella."[24]

The fighting was hand to hand. A sixteen-year-old trooper fought with a powerful, experienced warrior. The terrified boy shot off all the rounds from his pistol and finally killed the man with his saber. Later, after taking the dead man's scalp, the scared trooper, half laughing and half crying, shared his story with his comrades. John Strong remembered that "for a few minutes the fighting was desperate," before the Sioux were driven back. Once more, Inkpaduta gathered his men for another attack, only to see this one dispersed by the effective use of artillery. Having bought what time he could, he called upon his followers to retreat. Behind him were left the bodies of twenty-seven Sioux. Brackett, wounded in the hand during the fighting, had lost two men killed, one being Sergeant George Northrup, the well-known frontiersman, who was struck by between eight and ten arrows. Brackett also had eight men wounded, one who later died.[25]

Supporting Brackett was Lieutenant G. Merrill Dwelle and a section of the 3rd Artillery Battery. Shells from Dwelle's artillery dispersed Inkpaduta's final attempt at a counterattack, and once the Sioux had retreated, Dwelle continued to fire rounds into the wooded butte near the village. He was soon joined by other artillery, which commenced to bombard the encampment. Strong could see the village, noticing that "a large part of their force were busy in taking down tepees, hiding their property and getting the women and children out of the way." With the arrival of the artillery, Strong said, "the batteries were brought up and planted on another hill with in reach of them. Now commenced the work of death among the Indians. Shells were thrown into the timber, driving them out of it, then others would be thrown among them, till they broke and ran for the top of the mountain."[26]

Even as the soldiers were on the verge of entering the village, which was in panic with people desperate to escape, some warriors continued to risk their lives to defend the encampment. White Bull remembered that shortly after Inkpaduta's clash with Brackett's men, another group of soldiers charged some Sioux who had taken shelter behind a hill. Noticing the attack, some warriors rode to their defense, and White Bull saw the soldiers "turn around and run and [Indians] whip their horses and catch up and pull some [soldiers] off horses and kill some [soldiers] . . . and rest [soldiers] run clear back." It was the last success the Sioux gained that day.[27]

Entering the village, the soldiers seemed to be consumed by a bloodlust. Soldiers from the 8th Minnesota Infantry found a helpless old man, whom "our boys dispatched to the happy hunting ground with as little compunction as if he had been a tiger," wrote Hodgson bluntly. A major in the regiment tried to regain control of the situation as the men chased the Sioux into the foothills and timber behind the village, ordering them to cease fire, but Hodgson remarked that the men would not listen: "We were after redskins and didn't propose to lose a good chance." Captain Christian Stufft, reinstated to the command of the scouts following his disgraceful performance in the skirmish prior to Killdeer Mountain, proudly reported that finding three Sioux, one of whom was wounded, "my Winnebago boys afterwards killed, scalped and beheaded."[28]

The Sioux scattered into the deep ravines and woods behind the village, hounded by the artillery shells. The cannons kept firing until darkness fell, ending the ability to find further targets. Myers found the action humorous: "It was amusing to see the desperate efforts made by the Indians to get out of reach of the cannon." Four companies of the 8th Minnesota Infantry kept up a pursuit until reaching a deep canyon, "which the Indians had crossed by some path known only to themselves," wrote Kingsbury. "Beyond this canyon the Indians, with their squaws, could still be seen retreating, but they were out of reach of our guns." Kingsbury noted that, again, several warriors fought until killed to gain time for their people to flee. Eventually, the Sioux made good their escape and the pursuing soldiers were called back.[29] The battle of Killdeer was over.

The battle lasted anywhere from six to eight hours, depending on the accounts of the soldiers present. The numbers of casualties for both sides are confusing. Amos Cherry, 7th Iowa Cavalry, placed Sioux losses at 150, as did Kingsbury, while Abner English estimated the number to be closer to 200. Judd, later involved in the destruction of the village, claimed the troops buried 208 bodies, while Wieneke stated that 1,000 bodies were burned along with the village. On one point all accounts agree: no prisoners were taken the day of the battle. Two young boys were found and placed on a blanket by troopers, who gave them hardtack to eat, "which the little fellows ate with avidity and relish," wrote one of the soldier who was present. When Sioux scouts rode up, they "struck their tomahawks into their brains . . . ," killing the boys. Kingsbury recalled finding a baby who was only a few months old; since the soldiers were unable to care for the infant, the child was shot, "by, or possibly without an order, but it could not be helped." Estimates on the army losses also vary, but it is likely five men died and ten more were wounded in the fighting.[30]

The soldiers were pleased with their victory, although unaware of the magnitude of the battle itself. English wrote that the army "had been engaged in one of the most hotly contested battles ever fought with Indians." Wieneke commented to his wife, "I guess our Indian fighting is over as they got so badly drubbed that they will not let us get at them again. It is more fun to fight Indians they cannot do anything against our drilled troops with our arms. Besides that they are too great a set of cowards to come up to us."[31]

The night of the battle, the soldiers—hot, thirsty, and tired—discovered a mud hole with water half a mile from the village. Myer followed a line of men to the hole, where the men "filled our camp kettle and returned to strain the stuff through a towel, which, by the way, had not been to the laundry lately." Later the exhausted soldiers slept in the captured lodges of the Sioux. At four the next morning, Sully ordered a pursuit of the Sioux.[32]

The army marched six miles from the village before giving up the pursuit. The terrain was simply too rugged and rough for the wagons, and Sully ordered a return to the camp. Upon their arrival the soldiers encountered Sioux who had come back to the camp looking for supplies, materials, and lost loved ones. After a brief skirmish the Sioux were driven away. Later another group of Dakotas approached the soldiers, bearing a white flag. The men ignored the peace delegation, and it is unknown why the Sioux wanted to speak with the soldiers.[33]

The rest of the day was spent in the burning and destruction of the village. Fourteen companies from the various regiments were assigned the duty of destroying the encampment. The work began at seven A.M. and continued until three P.M. More than sixteen hundred lodges were burned, and "buffalo robes, dried buffalo meat, dried berries, numberless camp kettles and other utensils were piled on their lodge poles, the match applied and all went up in smoke," reported English. Cherry also noted the burning of fifty tons of dried meat, after the men took what food they could carry, and that "many dogs [were] shot." Admiring the Indian robes, Hodgson remembered that "some of the robes were beautifully beaded and worked and many of us boys coveted them so much" that men appropriated them "by using them for saddle blankets by day and bed blankets by night." After hours of destruction, Kingsbury was satisfied with what had been accomplished, believing that the annihilation of the camp and its supplies "was a greater blow to the Indians than the loss of the braves who were killed."[34] He was most likely correct in his analysis.

While in the midst of burning the camp, the men encountered Sioux survivors of the attack. In his diary Wieneke notes that "they also killed ten more Indians that were found in the brush." Myers recorded the Sioux scouts' discovery of one wounded warrior hiding in a small clump of bushes. They set the man up on one side of the brush, mounted their ponies, and rode past the brush in single file, each then "shooting the poor wretch every time they came around." This was the second act committed by the Sioux scouts upon defenseless members of their own people, but no motive for their actions was provided. For Dwelle, the discovery of the bodies of two dead babies and a young teenage girl was regretful. "Is it not sad . . . such children never did us any harm," he wrote his sister Carrie.[35]

At four P.M. Sully started his march back to the Heart River and the base camp. After marching six miles, the column made camp for the night. The evening proved a harsh one for the soldiers, leading to losses almost rivaling those of the battle at Killdeer. While on guard duty, a nervous sentry shot and killed Sergeant Isaac Winget of the 6th Iowa Cavalry. He thought the sergeant, who was checking the lines, was an Indian approaching the camp. Soon after, the Sioux did strike the camp, chasing off some horses. Successful, the Sioux, likely young warriors engaged in the long-time practice of horse stealing, attacked again. The pickets were driven in and more horses captured. Two of the pickets were wounded and two others, privates David LaPlante and Anton Holzgen, 2nd Minnesota Cavalry, were reported missing.[36]

The next day, July 30, the column marched thirty-six miles, and along the way the bodies of the two missing pickets were recovered. "The bodies of the two piquets were found this A.M. Each had about ten or twelve arrows in it . . . ," wrote Wieneke. The dead men's weapons, horses, and equipment had all been taken. LaPlante and Holzgen were buried where they were found, and the column marched over the graves to cover them. Riding to the top of a nearby hill, the warriors who had staged two successful raids on the army showed off their captured horses to the soldiers. "They made great sport of us, dancing and hooting like demons," a bitter Hodgson wrote. The warriors also taunted the Sioux scouts, claiming that the soldiers had not fought fairly at Killdeer and that the Sioux would fight them again. The scouts answered that if there were another battle all the Sioux would be killed.[37]

On July 31 the column reached the base camp, where the remaining soldiers with their supplies and the emigrant wagon train awaited. David Jenkins was sick of the campaign and wished it would end: "The boys want to start home having had enough of this kind of sport."[38] Jenkins did not realize that the worse part of the expedition was yet to come, as the army would retire through the Badlands. Here the Dakotas were gathering for retaliation for Killdeer.

CHAPTER 10

The Fight in the Badlands

"THE INDIANS WERE ALL AROUND US TRYING TO BREAK IN"

Having won his engagement with the Sioux, Sully now planned to finish off the campaign by advancing westward to the Yellowstone River. This would allow him to end his obligation to protect the emigrant wagon train, to build a fort on the river, and to link up with steamboats loaded with much-needed supplies. Sully's column was down to less than a week's worth of provisions. However, for Sully to reach the Yellowstone River and make contact with the steamboats before running out of supplies, the army would have to cross the Badlands—an area so rugged and desolate that it was believed to be impassable by wagons. Faced with few options, the column started toward the Badlands on August 3.

It was a difficult journey. The heat was oppressive, and there was little good water available for the suffering soldiers and civilians. The men's tongues became so swollen that no verbal commands could be given. To counter the heat, the men rose at three A.M., started marching by five A.M., and camped by three P.M. Grasshoppers had consumed all the grass, forcing soldiers to feed their horses bare limbs of trees and bushes. So exhausting were the days that entries in diaries were only a few words. Ending the first day's march, Amos Cherry could only write, "Day hot. Water very scarce indeed."[1]

The party reached the outskirts of the Badlands two days later. Concerns over water and feed for the horses and livestock only increased. Cherry recorded that some water was found at the bottom of a steep hill and that he was "on watter squad to night, good joke on me." Writing what was on the mind of many of the soldiers, Henry Wieneke stated bluntly, "Halted on edge of roughest country. Ahead no water except what stood in pools or depressions of ground accumulation of heavy shower. No feed for horses and no fuel except Buffalo Chips." Even more troubling to some of the travelers was their first view of the Badlands. "Nature seems to have tried her hand at freaks, as if to see into how many shapes she could pile molten clay and rock," observed Lieutenant Colonel Robert McLaren. John Wright, intimidated by the scenery, claimed it "would take an abler pen than mine to describe and do it justice." Adding to his concern was that "at first sight one would think no sane man would attempt to pass [through]." The day ended on a solemn note. While halted on a high bluff, a trooper became confused by the darkness and campfires and fell off the embankment, plunging more than two hundred feet. The next morning his body was found, "an unrecognizable mangled, mass of broken bones and bloody flesh," according to Nicholas Hilger.[2]

Confronted by this seemingly impassable barrier, Sully was counting on one man, an American Indian scout, to get the expedition through the Badlands. In his report, Sully stated that the scout was a Yanktonai, while other accounts say the guide was an eighteen-year-old Blackfoot man who had once traveled through the area with his people. A. N. Judd claimed the guide was the Crow man saved from the Sioux war party in the skirmish prior to Killdeer Mountain.[3] Perhaps more than one scout stepped up to aid the struggling column as it maneuvered its way through the Badlands, but what is important is that without assistance from American Indian scouts, the column may not have gotten through the region, especially as the Sioux gathered to oppose its march.

The Sans Arc band of the Lakotas was the first to become aware of the army's attempt to travel through the Badlands. Accounts of the fighting that was to come there often argue that the Sioux were trying to overwhelm and annihilate the entire expedition. When considering the dwindling supply situation and the Badlands' difficult terrain, which made the standard defensive formation of the army—with flanking units—almost impossible, it is easy to understand how this conclusion could be reached. However, it is unlikely that the Sioux had formulated such a strategic plan when they first learned of the column's approach. Two more traditional forms of Sioux warfare did come into play. Although the Sioux preferred an open battle with their enemies, the use of ambush was acceptable, and the Badlands made ambush an effective weapon against the superior weaponry of the soldiers. Secondly, when encountering a superior force, the Sioux would harass the enemy until it was forced to retire from the territory. Such harassment had already started, with horse raids and attacks upon pickets; now, with the terrain as an ally, the Sioux could mount a massive harassment campaign. Upon discovery of the column, the Sans Arcs sent messengers to the various nearby bands and villages, calling upon them to once more resist the soldiers in battle—a battle in the Badlands they would call Waps-Chon-Choka.[4]

One of the villages found by the messengers was Sitting Bull's. They "asked me if our tribe would help them fight the soldiers of General Sully," he recalled. Although not enthusiastic about fighting the soldiers again, Sitting Bull had learned much about the whites' style of warfare at Killdeer. After some time for reflection, he realized the military advantage the Badlands gave to a defending force and agreed to support the other bands.[5]

In his report on the fighting in the Badlands, Sully stated that he faced the Lakota bands he fought at Killdeer Mountain and the Brules.[6] If this report is accurate, the war had changed once more. The Santees and Yanktonais were absent, and the sole force the army was now engaging was the Lakotas. In all prior battles with the Sioux, the soldiers had justified the warfare by the need for revenge, punishment, and defense of the border against those who had participated in the uprising in Minnesota. Now it was the Lakotas, who had in no way been involved in the Dakota War of 1862, who sought revenge, for the losses suffered at Killdeer Mountain. For them, fighting the soldiers in the Badlands was clearly justifiable.

On August 6 the army moved into the Badlands. Overwhelmed by the incredible terrain, soldiers were moved to write vivid descriptions, and the scenery of the Badlands became the single most written-about subject of the entire expedition. A. P. Connelly wrote, "The body of the earth had been rent and torn a sunder, as though giant demons, in their infuriated defeat, had sought to disembowel the earth." For Judd, the Badlands "are like a vast desolate city, made of scoria, mostly spires and domes, made up of all shades of red and brown, now and then as undisturbed strata of schist and grey sandstone." Far more briefly, Abner English described the region as "a terrible desolate world." More concerned with the army's need to march through it, David Kingsbury offered his view of the Badlands: "They consist of a depression or basin, covering an extent of about forty miles, having an average depth of some six hundred feet below the level of the surrounding country. . . . There are many deep and numerous canons, having no confirmed general direction and forming a bewildering labyrinth, in which one not familiar with the country must inevitably soon be lost."[7]

The march on August 6 started at five A.M. Sully, gravely ill from a bout of rheumatism and dysentery, ordered 150 pioneers with picks and shovels and seven companies of cavalry under Lieutenant Colonel John Pattee to carve out a road for the wagons ahead of the column. Following close behind were individual soldiers who wanted to explore the area. The soldiers were amazed to discover petrified wood and images of plants, fish, and reptiles embedded in the rock formations. To Hilger, the region was like a park "of circular stone monuments of columns, that varied in size from three to eight feet in diameter and from ten to fifty feet in height, and which were of an equal thickness from base to summit." The formations had flat tops or caps that Hilger described as looking like "a crop of giant mushrooms." J. H. Drips also found the formations fascinating: "We found here petrifaction in every variety, from what had been a tree of six or seven feet in circumference down to the merest atom, all hard as the granite rock."[8]

Slowly, the column moved forward twelve miles through the wasteland, reaching the Little Missouri River. The drought had reduced the river to a trickle. The soldiers marched along the river for a mile, fording the stream twice before entering a narrow, deep crevasse that Hilger described as "barely wide enough for the wagons to pass through." The crevasse zigzagged for three miles before opening onto a high bluff.[9]

Still out in front of the column, Pattee's men worked to open up a roadway through the crevasse. At one point a grizzly burst out from cover and ran off two companies' horses, and it wasn't until eleven A.M. that the dismounted men were able to retrieve all their mounts. Later in the day, Pattee ordered an end to their labors and a return to the camp, but Company K, 6th Iowa Cavalry, failed to receive the order and was to be left behind. Meanwhile, the main column made camp for the day. Looking for feed and water for their horses, the men arrived at a stand of timber next to the Little Missouri River and placed pickets to guard the animals.[10] Then the Sioux struck.

A war party drove the pickets back and seized a number of the horses. Quickly mounting, another cavalry force chased after the raiders and retrieved most of the horses. Judd had climbed up on some rocks and was busily carving his name and date into the soft rock. He had carved "A.N.J. Aug 7th 186–" when the attack on the camp commenced. He saw naked men, who had been bathing in the Little Missouri River, grab pistols and fire at the Sioux. One serious loss came with the death of the Crow scout who had led the expedition to the waters of the Little Missouri.[11]

Concerned with the attack and realizing that Company K had been left behind, Pattee saddled up his command and rode back to find the missing company. It was not long after leaving camp that Pattee saw Company K "coming out of the hills, while thousands of Indians, as if by magic, appeared all over the hills on the west side of the river." The soldiers fought their way back to camp, where the Sioux were driven off by the artillery.[12]

The fighting became general as "from every point, cliff, hole or cave, the Indians fired upon us. Our parties of explorers rushed in from all directions . . . ," recalled Hilger. Earlier, Sully had referred to the Badlands as "Hell with the fires put out," but with the sudden Sioux onslaught, one chaplain declared that it was really "Hell alive" with "his Satanic majesty's forces welcoming their new guests on Judgment Day." The Sioux occupied the surrounding buttes, close enough to shower the camp with arrows. When possible, given the lack of room, the artillery was placed to fire back at the buttes. As at Killdeer Mountain, the superiority of the soldiers' weapons made the difference. "Owing to the inferiority of their arms we could keep the savages at a tolerably safe distance with our long range guns and the artillery; otherwise there might not have been a man of us left alive, so numerous were they and so persistent in their attacks," wrote Hilger.[13]

All through the night the Lakotas kept up their assault on the camp, with the twelve pieces of artillery responding with solid shot, shell, and canister. According to Hilger, the camp was in confusion; "Such running and scrambling . . . many dismounted and bloody, and by riderless horses and ponies that went dashing in all directions . . . the noise of the guns and their roaring echoes made the hills almost shake." Judd remembered there was "skirmishing all night; some of it quite heavy." The wagons were placed in a single column, flanked on both sides by "a thin line of platoons, ready for any emergency." Trying to capture a wagon or two, the Sioux made swift, constant attacks, and the emigrants huddled in terror.[14] For the Sioux, the day was successful: a number of horses had been taken, several of their enemies had been killed or wounded, avenging the losses the Sioux had suffered earlier in battle, and the soldiers clearly had been harassed.

The morning of August 7 started with a small group of young warriors attempting to steal more horses. Slipping past the pickets, they rushed the horse herd. The half-asleep sentries panicked, running for the camp, all except John Beltz, 1st Dakota Cavalry. Beltz charged the Sioux, firing his carbine and pistol as he ran, and his courageous stand caused the warriors to retreat without achieving their goal.[15]

Still ill, Sully turned command of the column over to Colonel Minor Thomas. Thomas repeated the previous day's march, sending six to seven hundred men ahead to create a road for the wagons, while part of the 6th Iowa Cavalry went to the bluffs west of the Little Missouri River to guard those men. The pioneers cut open a road "through a strip of brush and timber that skirted the banks of a stream" for most of the morning. At ten A.M. a large body of Sioux appeared, resuming the fight and forcing the road builders to retreat to the main body.[16] If the column was to advance, it would have to fight its way through.

Milton Spencer described the formation of the expedition as it moved forward: "The heavy guns, supported by skirmishers on each flank, would go to the front of the column and clear away the Indians for half a mile in front. When the column would move forward . . . guns would be posted on either side of the road to protect the whole column." With the narrow confines of the canyons, the flankers could not continue mounted but dismounted, with every fourth man acting as a horse holder. Covering the front of the column was Brackett's Battalion and three companies from the 6th Iowa and 1st Dakota Cavalries, supported by Pope's artillery battery. The 6th Iowa Cavalry, dismounted, was on the right flank, and the 7th Iowa Cavalry, also dismounted, protected the left flank. With the bands ordered to play marches and polkas, the army advanced ten miles. Charles Hughes wrote that the army was "fighting the Indians all the way. . . . The Indians are plenty all around us."[17]

Warfare for the Sioux was often individualistic, with young men trying to obtain honor and status by acts of bravery, such as the counting of coup on an enemy and the taking of horses. The ownership of horses gave one status and wealth and allowed a young man to secure a wife. To steal horses from an armed enemy was also a matter of great personal bravery and skill—something that would bring approval from the young man's community.

At one point, sections of the 6th Iowa Cavalry dismounted and led their horses to the Little Missouri River for water. A sudden rush from cover allowed a Sioux party to strike the soldiers and stampede the horses, "creating a big racket, quite a number of horses being captured by the reds," as witnessed by Wieneke. Later in the day the Sioux made another attempt, hitting the column from multiple locations. In confusion, the troopers ran to grab their horses, firing their pistols as the warriors raced in, screaming their war cries. One soldier was leading his horse by a picket rope when a warrior ran up on foot, cut the rope, and seized the horse by jumping on its back and racing off. Bullets "whistling around him," the skilled raider got away, leaving the stunned soldier holding a piece of rope.[18]

The fighting was constant for most of the day. When the column passed through a narrow canyon, the Sioux attacked in force. A shower of arrows from the surrounding buttes caused panic among the emigrants, and the soldiers were unable to respond with artillery, since the canyon would not allow for movement and elevation. The American Indian scouts with the army were nearly routed. Hilger forced his way to the leader of the scouts, who was perhaps the incompetent Captain Stufft, pulled his pistol, thrust it into the face of the leader, and told him to stop the rout or he would kill him. With Hilger's threat, order was quickly restored, and the army fought its way out of the canyon, a harrowing experience. Later Sergeant Eli Williamson, 2nd Minnesota Cavalry, reflected on his role in the action and found that "I have stood the fight well."[19]

Almost worse than the struggle with the Sioux was the lack of water; this, combined with the heat and their reduced food rations, nearly defeated the soldiers and emigrants. According to Judd, "By eight o'clock we are strung out, the wounded and children are moaning for water. Some begin to talk thick from swelling of the tongue." One of Judd's squad mates, Charlie Griffith, thought he saw a small pool of water a quarter of a mile to the left of the column, in an amphitheater. Friends warned that it was a warrior flashing a piece of glass. Undeterred, Griffith and Judd grabbed canteens and rode to the spot, finding water. Filling the canteens, they soon noticed Sioux breaking cover. The "reds fairly swarmed from the rocks, then came a race for life," wrote Judd. Dismounting, Judd led his horse over an outcrop of rocks. Griffith, remaining mounted, chose a different route, splitting up the two men. Half a dozen Sioux chased Judd on foot while he fired his pistol back at them. As the Sioux returned fire, Judd could see that Griffith had also dismounted and was under fire. Hearing the shots, soldiers from the rear guard came to the rescue. Judd returned unharmed, but Griffith had been hit through his lungs and later died, on August 13. "I never see a canteen but what I think of him," Judd stated with sadness.[20]

At two P.M. a stagnant pool, roughly fifty feet in circumference, four inches deep, and filled with deep mud, was located. The water was of poor quality and tasted terrible, but people offered a dollar for a canteen of the muddy mixture.[21] For most, the day ended with a desperate need for water still a priority.

The fighting continued during the evening and all through the night. Having finished their work on preparing a road, six companies of the 6th Iowa Cavalry retired back to the camp. Company M was the last company in line, and as it passed through a narrow ravine, Sioux from atop the bluffs, three hundred feet above the soldiers, rolled stones down on the mounted troops until they were driven off by artillery fire. During the night, the camp was attacked three times, and at one point the pickets were driven in as the Sioux, to increase the fear factor among the whites, howled like wolves. Pattee recalled, "Pandemonium seemed to have broken loose—wolves howling and guns being fired in every direction." During the firefight, one soldier shot another soldier through his jaw.[22]

After a rough night with little sleep, an exhausted Frank Myers and the men of his company awoke to find a Lakota warrior on a butte only a short distance from the northeastern corner of the camp. Commencing fire, the soldiers with artillery support drove the Sioux off and the battle resumed for a third day. Too ill to command, Sully had spoken with Thomas during the evening about the coming day. "Meet them and you will then have the biggest Indian fight that will ever happen on this continent," Sully advised, adding, "You must make history today."[23]

With Sully riding in an ambulance in the rear, Thomas ordered Major Ebenezer Rice to take command of the advance guard, consisting of Company D, 8th Minnesota Infantry, and Companies C and H, 2nd Minnesota Cavalry. Part of the 6th Iowa, dismounted, formed the right flank guard, and the 7th Iowa Cavalry, also dismounted, protected the left flank. The 1st Dakota Cavalry and the remainder of the 6th Iowa Cavalry provided the rear guard.

At five A.M. the advance started, with eerie silence. The Sioux had faded away from the fight. "The advance seemed tedious; not a sound disturbed the progress," noted Hilger. For three miles the column marched through the Badlands, following a dry creek bed up a canyon. As the soldiers emerged from the canyon, they started climbing up onto a high, wide plateau—which is when the Lakotas ambushed the column. Knowing they were outmatched when it came to weaponry, the Sioux had made brilliant use of the terrain. "The sharp crack of guns was heard in all directions every peak in sight was covered with Indians" was how John Strong remembered the attack. To Thomas, "The advance guard was enveloped by the Indians, and on either flank their bands were chasing, yelling and fighting." "The Indians were all around us trying to break in on every side," wrote Drips, "but the Minnesota battery was mowing them in front and scattering them in all directions."[24]

It was the most intense fighting seen so far in the Badlands. The well-laid trap so concerned Sully that he mounted a horse and rode to the front. During the struggle, the Blackfoot scout now leading the column through the Badlands was shot in the breast, the ball passing out of his body beneath the shoulder blade. Richard Hobrack, 8th Minnesota Infantry, carried the wounded man, whom the army was counting on to see them out of the region, to the surgeon, and the scout's wound was treated as the soldiers fought off the attack. Once again, the Sioux simply lacked the firepower to make the ambush effective. Thomas reported that the warriors were "poorly armed, bows and arrows being the best weapon many had." The Sioux mounted serious attacks, admitted Drips, "but the potency of the old muskets and Minnie rifles assisted when practicable by Capt. Pope's battery, was a little too much lead for the great braves."[25]

Breaking out of the ambush, the troopers pushed the Sioux back several miles before stopping at noon to rest. Regrouping, the Sioux massed in front of the column to block any further advance. The artillery was brought up and opened fire, to the pleasure of Judd: "These stands became amusing at times; they would come out of cover, their naked bodies glistening with war-paint and perspiration making the most grotesque contortions and all kinds of threatening and insulting gestures, but one or two cases of grape or canister and a carbine volley or two from the advance guard, and every one of them was out of sight like so many prairie dogs or ground squirrels."[26] In truth, the Sioux had no response to the power of the artillery that proved a decisive factor in the battle. Still, the main goal of harassing the enemy until they left the territory was proving successful. The soldiers were wearing down, and the desire to escape from the Badlands was mounting. Keeping up the pressure, the Sioux launched a new attack at the rear guard, hoping to break through to the emigrant wagon train.

Company H, 6th Iowa Cavalry, and Company A, 1st Dakota Cavalry, were among those protecting the rear of the column when the Sioux focused their efforts there. The rearguard had just entered a particularly rough section of country when from "every rock or possible cover on both flanks of the rearguard gave up what seemed to be thousands of yelling, whooping and shooting red-skins, swinging buffalo robes and blankets," wrote Judd. To him nothing could cause a horse or mule to stampede as quickly as "a naked, yelling Sioux in full war paint, swinging an old smoky, greasy buffalo robe in his face." Struggling to control his mount, Judd wished that "for a few minutes . . . you had no horse." Fighting dismounted, the troopers faced multiple attacks, usually by groups of warriors numbering between thirty-five and forty men. "The bullets zipped past our heads thick and fast, and the swish of the deadly arrow was terrible to our ears," recorded English.[27]

The well-mounted Sioux moved quickly to engage the soldiers and made it difficult for the troopers to find good targets. "I presume forty of us fired at them without apparent success," admitted George Campbell, 8th Minnesota Infantry. "All I saw of the Indian I fired at was his leg hanging over the back of his horse; but, as I had my horse's bridle over my right arm and when I pulled the trigger the horse pulled back." Campbell's shot was sent straight up into the air. One group of thirty-five warriors broke through the lines and got among the wagon train. One rider crashed into an ambulance, between the mules and wagon. The warrior ended up in the lap of the driver, who shot him under the armpit. With aid from the 7th Iowa Cavalry, the Sioux were slowly driven back from the wagons and finally retreated. Drips praised the Dakota troopers for a stout defense, with the Sioux finding "a little more then their match in Capt. Miner and his little band." Still, the attacks had had success for the Sioux. One soldier had been killed and eleven more wounded, the last fourteen wagons had suffered damage, and five had been turned over.[28]

For the rest of the day, fighting was general all along the length of the column. To English, "it seemed as though for every Indian killed, ten more sprang up in his place." During one skirmish, English and his platoon were ordered to occupy a hill overlooking the column. "We soon found ourselves commanding the area," wrote English, but they were surrounded by five hundred warriors until a charge by the rest of Company A, 1st Dakota Cavalry, came to their rescue.[29]

On another part of the field, Company G, 2nd Minnesota Cavalry, was ordered to drive forty or fifty Sioux from a ravine near a high hill on the column's left flank. The men of Company G were German-American and from New Ulm, a town devastated during the Dakota War of 1862. Leading their horses, the company advanced until they reached a perpendicular rock formation blocking the way. Leaving the horses and guard, Captain

Jacob Nix and eighteen men proceeded another five hundred yards toward the ravine. Nearing the ravine, Nix was ambushed by a force of four to five hundred men. Under a hail of bullets and arrows, Nix and Sergeant F. Brandt rallied the company and fell back into a good defensive position before driving the Sioux back with good marksmanship. The Sioux rallied and attacked again. "Our position, however, was so strong that we could repulse all attacks," wrote Sergeant Major W. H. Meyer. Needing support, Nix sent Meyer back to the column. However, either Thomas or Sully refused to send out any rescuers, believing it impossible to reach the trapped men. Refusing to leave troopers from his regiment behind, McLaren, without orders, took twelve men from Company H and moved to help Nix, only to become surrounded themselves. McLaren was close enough to Nix to provide covering fire, and with this the two groups of soldiers first linked up and then fell back successfully to safety.[30]

Not so fortunate was Private Alfred Nicholson, Company H, 6th Iowa Cavalry. Heeding nature's call, Nicholson dropped out of the column to find a spot to relieve himself. While squatting with his pants down, Nicholson was hit in the rear by an arrow. The wound was painful but not dangerous, and Nicholson went screaming for help, leaving his weapons behind. Members of the 2nd Minnesota Cavalry rode back for Nicholson, driving off his attackers, but the wounded trooper's weapons—rifle, pistol, and saber—along with his horse, were taken. The warrior who had successfully acquired Nicholson's horse and gear rode to the top of a high butte, where he taunted the soldiers by swinging his loot in the air and proclaiming his deeds. English wrote, "There was probably a hundred shots fired at him, but none of them hit him."[31] It was another example of personal victory for the Sioux.

The Sioux tactic of harassment, greatly aided by the terrible terrain and hot weather, was working. During one action, the Sioux scouts started to yell over to the Lakotas. They said they were Yanktonais and one of them, Stuck-In-The-Mud, had been wounded in the arm. The Scouts wanted to know whom they were facing, and Sitting Bull, who was one of the warriors present, replied that it was the Sans Arcs, Hunkpapas, and Miniconjous, among others, fighting the soldiers. The scouts encouraged the Lakotas to keep fighting, as "most white boys are starving and thirsty to death, so just stay around and they will be dead." Sitting Bull wanted to know why the scouts were fighting with the soldiers. By the scouts doing so, "we have to kill you," stated Sitting Bull, adding, "You have no business with the soldiers."[32] This exchange brings into question the role of the Sioux scouts on the expedition. Given that the Badlands were in lands controlled and traveled over by the Sioux, and that the Lakotas had no problems maneuvering through the Badlands to give battle to the army, it is odd that not one of the Sioux scouts knew a route through the difficult terrain. Some had deserted at Killdeer Mountain and others were now encouraging the Lakotas to fight on, while at other times the scouts had brutally killed prisoners who fell into their hands. Likely it is an example of the deep divisions and conflicts the warfare had caused for the entire Sioux nation.

If the soldiers were worn down and the harassment of the Sioux was having an effect, Sitting Bull also knew that the Lakotas were low on food and ammunition. Never having wanted to participate in the Badlands fight, he advocated letting the troopers go and promised, "We will go home." Sitting Bull had yet to become an influential leader and his plea was not heeded, but the next day he and his village of two hundred people left the area.[33]

The need for water was of mounting urgency for the soldiers. The mules, oxen, and horses were starting to suffer, and a number were left behind. One soldier from Company F, 8th Minnesota Infantry, followed a gully to where a waterfall of fifteen to twenty feet had made a basin of water. After he informed his comrades of his discovery, half the company went down and got water while the other half kept guard, then switched places. Hodgson and Elijah Houck were sent across a small valley to a hill to be lookouts for any possible Indian threat, and they soon discovered an approaching force of Sioux. They raced back to warn the company, only to find that the men had gotten their water and left, forgetting all about Hodgson and Houck. Fighting for their lives, the two men were retreating when, realizing their mistake, men from their company came to their aid and drove off the attackers.[34]

Toward the end of the day, and with relief, the expedition started to leave the Badlands behind. Judd noted that "the country was getting open and good charging ground, with plenty of good grass and good water, a stranger to us since we crossed the Little Missouri." The Sioux broke off the attack, ending the fighting for the day. Thomas was convinced the army had faced eight thousand warriors, killing or wounding close to a thousand of them. In his diary, David Jenkins briefly acknowledged, "A good many were killed," mirrored closed by Amos Cherry's diary entry of "Many Indians killed to day." The Sioux were not present in those numbers, and it is highly unlikely they suffered anywhere near those high figures of causalities. Hodgson was much more realistic, writing, "Whether we killed or hurt any Indians was probably never known. It was nigh impossible to know." The column suffered nine men killed and one hundred men wounded, which was roughly 4 percent of the army—a not insignificant number for combat during the Civil War.[35]

The exhausted soldiers and emigrants made camp an hour before sundown. Myers stated that the men "were tired and hungry, having had nothing to eat since early in the morning and no water except what we had in our canteens in the morning." The animals were badly in need of water and feed: they put up "pitiful cries" for water, and the civilians fed them flour, bread, and anything else they could use to keep the beasts alive. Having barely settled in, the soldiers and emigrants were faced with the

Sioux, who once more returned to harass the camp. The emigrant train was close to the 6th Iowa Cavalry when the Sioux massed and charged over a ridge toward the civilians. "The women and children belonging to the immigrant train came rushing and screaming to our camp," recalled Myers. The soldiers ran quickly to defend them, and the artillery opened up on the attackers—"The shells singing through the air and bursting in front or among them," wrote Myers—breaking the assault.[36]

With sniping and brief assaults, which included firing fire arrows among the horses to create a stampede, the Sioux kept the whites awake and fearful and away from any source of water that evening. A difficult night was passed, with men afraid to fall asleep for fear of being killed by stealthy warriors. It was with relief that Judd greeted the dawn: "How thankful for daylight! It cannot have the sufferings of the last eight hours. Even the thirst, which is harder to endure than starvation, is condoned by the light of the east."[37]

On August 9, even before daylight, the expedition was again moving forward and still under attack by the Sioux. By five A.M. fighting was general and involved the entire length of the three-to-four-mile-long column. Wieneke wrote, "Indians thick on all sides of us." In contrast to the Badlands, this terrain, open and more level, favored the soldiers. The Sioux continued "whooping and shooting" but could not close against the superior weaponry of the army. Sioux struck again at the right flank and the rear of the column, both times engaging the 6th Iowa Cavalry, who, according to Drips, "drove the Indians back with a vengeance." By two P.M. the Sioux broke off their attack, leaving the soldiers in peace after days of conflict.[38]

Advancing twenty miles, the army came across the remains of the large abandoned campsite of the Sioux. It was so massive that Sully commented, "I should judge all the Indians in the country had assembled there. The space they occupied was over one mile long and half a mile wide."[39] One enemy had disappeared, but the soldiers still faced the problem of food and water.

According to English, the troopers were living on "one hard-tack a day, although we had plenty of bacon; but that without vegetables or bread; is a poor diet." Water was a greater issue. Horses were dying from the lack of it. One hundred horses were shot that day by the rear guard because the animals were unable to continue. Wieneke was one soldier who found water: "I had dismounted and passing around an immense rock discovered a depression of the rock enough clean cool rain water to supply our company with good drinking & cooking water enough for supper & coffee next morning."[40]

The fight in the Badlands is often interpreted from a Western military tradition. It is viewed as a loss for the Lakotas, as they were unable to surround Sully's forces and annihilate them in the dangerous terrain of the Badlands. Based on Civil War engagements where one army faced another with the ultimate, albeit not often achieved, goal of destroying the opposing force, the Union soldiers did defeat the Sioux, again through the use of better weaponry and tactics. In simple terms, the Lakotas were outfought and thus failed in their objective.

However, this is a narrow, Eurocentric approach to warfare, an approach not followed by the Sioux. Never in the history of the Lakotas had they fought a war with the intended eradication of an entire tribe or nation. The destruction of Sully's army—numbering close to three thousand people, the size of a small Plains tribe—would have been such an event. The purpose of fighting the army in the Badlands was threefold: personal honor, revenge for the defeat at Killdeer Mountain, and driving the army out of their territory. The Badlands were chosen as the location for this effort as the area mitigated the effectiveness of the rifles and artillery of the soldiers, proving that the Sioux were already adapting to military lessons learned at Killdeer Mountain.

During the course of the fighting, certain warriors did achieve personal honor by capturing horses, taking soldier's weapons, and counting coup. Revenge was always a major reason for war: if an enemy attacks your people and inflicts losses, you must strike them back. The losses of each side need not be equal, but revenge must occur. The Sioux did cause the army to suffer casualties, thus making the attempts at revenge successful. Finally, the army was driven out of the area low on food, desperately in need of water, and with many horses and mules succumbing to the conditions.

True, the expedition was nearly at an end, and Sully was not intending to continue his operations against the Sioux. But the Lakotas would not have known this; to them, it was their harassment that had forced the enemy to retire, a success that would be followed up by a positive new war with the whites starting later that year, following the Sand Creek Massacre in November, and then with the equally victorious Red Cloud's War starting in 1866.

Regardless of the military outcome, there was little doubt that the expedition was in serious physical straits from the lack of provisions and water. By August 10 the animals had gone without water for thirty-six hours and were starving from the lack of grass, and soldiers and civilians suffered from swollen tongues and cracked lips. By noon of that day the line of march was marked for miles with dead horses and abandoned wagons. Walking their horses, the men staggered along, barely able to continue. Reaching a dry creek bed ten to twelve feet deep, they constructed a bridge in order for the wagons to pass over in a single column. Late in the day the column came to the Beaver River, which offered good water and grass. Water may have been an issue, but Amos Cherry recorded that that evening "orderly Berry Lee & Hull got quite happy to night. Very well educated indeed." Where the two men found alcohol is not known, but the next morning Lee endured a chewing-out from his captain for not being prepared when the order to move out came. Cherry noted, "Orderly tight night before."[41]

The Beaver River proved only a brief respite for the army. August 11 again found the column marching through a hostile environment. "Marched . . . over the most barren part of the country that we have ever seen," wrote Drips. "Not anything growing but wild sage, when we came to a stream. When we tasted the water we found it to be alkali: or salt water, worse than any we had yet had." Sixty-three horses and mules died, and George Doud wrote, "Most of the boys on foot to favor thair horses."[42] Fortunately, the next day brought relief.

According to Myers, on the morning of August 12, the army awoke next to a "beautiful spring of water gushing out of the side of a bluff. It was strongly impregnated with minerals, but pure and cold and was accepted by man and beast as a precious boon from a kind Providence." Also discovered was an area of dry grass for the horses. Reflecting on the prior few days, Myers stated, "I never knew until after I had been through the year, what men or horses could endure and live through." The expedition rested until ten A.M. before marching away from their little oasis. At noon the column reached the Yellowstone River, where steamboats were to meet them with supplies. Captain Nelson Minor was sent out to scout the river in search of the steamboats. Minor soon located the light-draft steamboats *Alone* and *Chippewa Falls*, and the trials and hardships of the expedition were now over. On board the ships were supplies for the soldiers and grain for the horses. The area was teeming with buffalo, elk, and deer, and wild berries grew along the river.[43]

Upon reaching the river, Harlen Bruch observed, "All discipline was forgotten; men and animals rushed into the stream and swallowed life inspiring fluid and joy and happy shouts took the place of misery. With food from the ships and the hunting of game." Wieneke wrote, "By 10 o'clock P.M. we were feasting." At peace with the world, most of the men would have agreed with

John Strong's view of the country they had passed through: "The country taken as a whole is only fit for the Indian and they had ought . . . to posses[s] it, they and their children forever."[44]

During the next two days, the army and emigrant wagon train crossed over the river. It was a difficult passing, and several people and dozens of mules drowned. "Genl curses terribly because the Boats were so slow. Very much mixed up. Many things lost altogether," Cherry remembered.[45]

Once across the river, the emigrant wagon train, to the relief of Sully, left for the mining camps. The joy at the wagon train's departure was cut short when Sully realized that "quite a number of horses, mules and oxen turned up missing." Also stolen were pistols, rifles, and other army property. Troops were sent after the wagon train, which had scattered prior to the arrival of the patrol. One group of wagons was apprehended and nine oxen, six horses, and several rifles recovered. But making good their escape were sixty soldiers who had deserted from the 2nd Brigade.[46]

The column advanced downriver toward Fort Union, a trading post owned by the Northwestern Fur Company. Before their arrival at the post, the column had to cross the Missouri River, leading to further difficulties. The current was swift, and the men had to swim their horses across. Hodgson confessed, "This made many of the boys white about the gills. It was a rather dangerous undertaking for such as could not swim. They didn't have the courage to trust even the horses. Several hired the horses led over and crossed themselves in a canoe." A wise precaution, as six men drowned trying to cross the river.[47]

For a few days at Fort Union, the men relaxed and recovered, having spent weeks in the field. Each man took up his favorite pastime. Lewis Paxton took notes on a sermon delivered on August 21, on the topic of "Patience," with the text coming from Romans 5:3: "But we glory in tribulations also knowing that tribulation worketh patience." William Silvis, for his part, played poker for four straight days, winning fifty, then two hundred, dollars on the first two days and losing seventy-five and twenty dollars on the following days.[48]

On August 22 Sully left Fort Union and, heading homeward, marched to Fort Rice. The expedition moved down the Missouri River to the mouth of Snake Creek, then continued north to the Mouse River before heading southwest to Maison du Chien Butte and, finally, southward to Fort Rice. The march was an easy one, with men hunting buffalo, as "the Buffalo were so thick they could not be counted," according to Charles Hughes. One bull ran right into the camp, where he was shot, and Hughes thought "he was very good eating." Thomas Priestly enjoyed the peaceful evenings when he could be "listening to the howling of the wolves, beautiful serenading."[49]

On September 7 the column reached the site of Sibley's 1863 battles with the Sioux. An irritated Drips, still supporting a more complete punishment of the Sioux, proclaimed, "Here is where the General had a splendid chance to whip the Indians but failed to do so for reasons I suppose satisfactory to himself; if not the whole country." Earlier the grave of Lieutenant Frederick Beaver, lost along the bluffs of the Missouri River, had been located. The body was disinterred and later sent to his family in Wales.[50]

Beaver's was not the only burial site located. In a letter to his wife, Libbie, John Robinson related the discovery of a burial scaffold with the body of a five- to six-year-old child. "I could not help meditating upon the unhappy condition of the race and their superstitious ideas of religion," Robinson wrote, adding that he believed that if the Sioux had only been Christian, then the atrocities that occurred during the uprising would not have happened. To Robinson, "none but the most heathen and savage minds could have thought up such heart rending and soul sickening crimes as they perpetrated."[51]

Less than two months after Robinson wrote his wife came the massacre of a peaceful village of Cheyennes and Arapahos at

Sand Creek. Soldiers of the 3rd Colorado Cavalry, led by Colonel John Chivington—who had been a Methodist minister prior to joining the army—brutally slaughtered anywhere from 150 to 500 men, women, and children. Chivington ordered that no prisoners be taken, and an orgy of bloodletting followed, with pregnant women killed, their stomachs ripped open, and their unborn children pulled out; toddlers thrown into fields and used for target practice, and the dead scalped and mutilated, with soldiers taking body parts as trophies. The massacre set off a war across the Northern Plains, as the Cheyennes, Arapahos, and Lakotas sought revenge for the attack.

The Sioux had not completely forgotten about Sully's expedition. The army had been dogged by small raiding parties on the march to Fort Rice. One group attacked some men cutting hay for the horses. The hay cutters were being guarded by Company J, 6th Iowa Cavalry, who drove off the warriors after losing several horses to the raiders.[52] And then, having rid himself of one emigrant train, Sully now had to go to the aid of another, besieged by a much larger war party led by Sitting Bull.

James Fisk had ignored the warnings posted by Pope about traveling overland to the mining fields. With a wagon train of eighty-eight wagons, two hundred civilians, and a small military escort provided by the commander of Fort Rice, Fisk headed across the Dakota Territory. On September 2 his wagon train was discovered by a large force of Hunkpapas led by Sitting Bull that included Gall, another rising leader. Sitting Bull was still basking in the perceived victory over the army in the Badlands. "We routed the enemy and made it clear we wished to be left alone to live our lives in our own land," he later stated. Over the next few days the wagon train came under increasing attack, during which Sitting Bull was seriously wounded in the hip, before finally being surrounded. Hastily throwing up a fortification, Fisk sent for help from the army.[53]

Sully, close to arriving at Fort Rice, organized a relief force of troops from the fort and the column. Units from the 7th Iowa Cavalry, Brackett's Battalion, 30th Wisconsin Infantry, 2nd Minnesota Cavalry, and the 6th Iowa Cavalry, some nine hundred men, under the command of Fort Rice commander Colonel Daniel Dill, marched to the rescue of the trapped emigrants. Being so close to ending the campaign, the men who were forced to save the wagon train were not happy with this new adventure. The soldiers blamed Fisk and Dill for the situation.[54]

During the march, the Sioux struck the relief column at night, stealing a large number of horses and making the men even more irritated with the need to aid the emigrants. By the time the relief force arrived, after a nine-day journey, many of the Sioux, unable to penetrate the earthen fortifications established by the emigrants and soldiers and protected by an artillery piece, had departed. Harlen Bruch was impressed by the defensive position of the emigrants: "When we got there they had sod walls four feet thick and four feet high outside their wagon train, all the way around, and they had dug a underground trench to water 50 yards away." However, Hodgson was shocked by the vast amount of whiskey that was present in the camp: "It was one vast whiskey camp. It was a first-class fraud. The government had been bamboozled into aiding a grand scheme for shipping whiskey to Idaho, the men along were in a grand scheme for plunder." Fisk gave Dill an entire barrel of whiskey in gratitude for the rescue, but this gift was not extended to the soldiers. Having marched hundreds of miles to save the train, the troopers were charged $4.50 a canteen, which held three pints, for whiskey. The men were furious at being so treated, and Dill ordered the price lowered to 50 cents a canteen. Taking advantage of the reduced price for whiskey, Hodgson confessed that "there was one general unstinted, hilarious drunk" that night among the soldiers.[55]

Even after the expedition reached Fort Rice, the Sioux still made occasional raids. On September 21 Drips and his company, unarmed as usual, went out to care for their horses and happened upon a war party stealing horses. Giving the alarm, several men from Companies J and L, 6th Iowa Cavalry, armed themselves, mounted their horses, and pursued the raiders. The Sioux, practicing one of the oldest forms of American Indian warfare, allowed the soldiers to chase them for ten miles before leading them into an ambush. One private, named Hill, saw the Sioux closing in and yelled a warning that went unheeded. Hill broke free from the ambush and raced back to camp for assistance. Companies D and L of the same regiment went to aid their comrades and on their way found one man walking back to camp in his shirt, drawers, and socks, holding his pistol. He had escaped by hiding in some bushes. The disheveled soldier informed the patrol that the Sioux numbered more than forty warriors. Ten miles farther on, they found the body of a Sergeant Murphy. According to Drips, Murphy had been "literally cut to pieces, being mutilated in a horrible manner, stuck full of arrows, an awful gash from a tomahawk in his side, scalped and stripped and robbed of everything." One soldier, Thompson, had escaped by swimming the Missouri River and walking back to the fort. "He was pretty badly used up, being stiff from travelling and swimming the river," wrote Drips. When Brackett laid an ambush for the Sioux during the battle of Killdeer Mountain, Myers had found it amusing, but this attack struck him as just "one of the traps the red devils were always planning."[56]

The final action of the expedition occurred six days later near the Cannon Ball River. Company E, 6th Iowa Cavalry, was protecting a hay-cutting group hauling hay. The Sioux attacked, killing one soldier, wounding another, and taking several horses. One warrior was wounded.[57] Although these small raids did not change the larger outcome of the expedition, they were still considered successful victories by the Lakotas, for whom war was also a personal act.

With their campaign coming to a close, the soldiers became more concerned about the events of the larger conflict occurring in the South. Abner English reported the arrival of dispatches with "the gratifying intelligence that General Sherman had taken Atlanta, Georgia." When Albert Childs, 30th Wisconsin Infantry, learned his brother Ellsworth might be drafted, he encouraged Ellsworth to get out of it if he could. "You could claim an exemption on the grounds of being the only support of a widowed mother, and also over the grounds of being the support of a sister less than 16 years of age. Either one would clear you, as I read the law, if you would only stick for your rights," insisted Childs. As many soldiers were by that period of fighting, Childs was sick of the war and did not want to see another member of his family involved.[58]

Chelsey Pratt, 3rd Minnesota Artillery Battery, also yearned for home but still believed in the righteousness of the Union cause, having enlisted in the army in March 1864. A reflective man, Pratt wrote a poem expressing his views:

> At Midnight on my lonely beat
> When darkness veils the woods and lea;
> A visitor seems my view to greet
> Of one at home who prays for me
> She prays for me that's far away
> The soldier in his holy fight;
> And asks that God in mercy may
> Shield the loved one, and bless the right![59]

Sully's last march was to Fort Sully. With his arrival on October 7, the expedition officially came to an end. The units were sent into winter quarters at various locations, and in November some of the men of the 6th Iowa Cavalry were given their discharges, having served three years in the army. Wieneke, one of the lucky men, remarked, "Finally arriving at Sioux City where we recd our discharge and Quit." "Mustered out and started for home. Good time and happy as a clam," a pleased Amos Cherry wrote in his diary.[60]

CHAPTER 11

Aftermath

"THIS WHOLE THING IS ONE
CONFOUNDED HUMBUG"

With another expedition at an end, Sully, in his official report, professed his confidence in the success of the operation. "I think they never will again organize for resistance against a large body of troops," he wrote, adding, "I do not therefore think it will be necessary to have another expedition." Captain Leonard Aldrich, 8th Minnesota Infantry, did not support Sully's optimistic analysis of the 1864 expedition. Writing to his brother Joseph, Aldrich complained, "This whole thing is one confounded humbug. 1000 such expeditions would have no tendency to subdue those hostile Indians, we have only made them mad, like sticking a long stick into a hornets nest."[1]

The results of the campaign were not as positive as Sully supposed. In waging his war against the Sioux, Pope had pushed the frontier farther westward toward the Missouri River, protected by Forts Wadsworth, Sully, Rice, Berthold, and Union. Yet Sully had failed to establish posts at Devil's Lake or along the Yellowstone River. The Santees and Yanktonais desired peace, but the Lakotas remained unbowed in their determination to protect their lands. The punitive expeditions had only increased the tensions between them and the army, a fact that contributed—along with Sand Creek—to the massive war being fought out on the Northern Plains. That conflict occupied the Lakotas, preventing them from actively opposing any further operations planned by Pope.[2]

Sully's actions at Killdeer Mountain also drew criticism. Back East, newspapers and pro-Indian groups reported incidents of brutality and abuse. His use of artillery on women and children troubled civilians. Indian agents added their voices to those who found the army's campaigns against the Sioux obsessive. Wisconsin Senator James R. Doolittle, a supporter of American Indian rights, headed a congressional committee to investigate the treatment of the Western American Indian tribes by civil and military authorities.[3]

Called to testify before the committee, Sully stated his views on conditions in the West and the future of American Indians. He discussed the problems of venereal disease, alcoholism, and smallpox among the tribes, placing the blame on the close contact the tribes had with whites from whom came "all the vices and few of the virtues of the whites." The general was a strong advocate of assimilation, including forcing American Indian children to attend school, breaking up the tribes to create individualism, and "when they are fit," allowing American Indians to become citizens of the United States.[4]

With any criticism of his campaign behind him, Sully prepared to lead yet another expedition against the Sioux. By 1865 Pope's war with the Sioux had merged into the overall military conflict with the northern alliance of the Dakotas, Cheyennes, and Arapahos. As part of the army's operations on the Northern Plains, Sully was to once more advance into the Dakota Territory in search of hostile Sioux, even though finding any was highly unlikely. The Lakotas were fighting to the west, the Yanktonais wanted peace, and the Santees were, for the most part, a shattered and conquered people.

In 1865 there were a few raids into Minnesota by those small bands of Santees still willing to resist. Near Garden City, a farm family was killed and the cavalry patrol that pursued the raiders ambushed, resulting in the loss of one trooper. In May another raiding party led by John Campbell, a mixed-blood deserter from the army, struck close to Mankato, killing the five members of the A. J. Jewitt family. The war party was hunted down by local Sissetons scouting for the army. During the fighting, one scout, Two Stars, spotted his nephew, a member of the raiders. Two Stars aimed his rifle at his nephew and killed him with a single shot.[5]

With the exception of such minor raids, the Santees and Yanktonais overwhelmingly looked for peace. Conditions were worsening on the Crow Creek Reservation. In mid-July 1864 grasshoppers swarmed the area and destroyed what crops the Sioux had been able to plant in the difficult soil. Over time, large numbers of Dakotas succumbed to diarrhea, dysentery, whooping cough, exposure, and malnutrition. By fall of that year an estimated 25 percent of all Santees on the reservation would die.[6]

During the summer of 1864, those Santees who remained off the reservation gathered at Coteau des Prairies, a region west of Lake Traverse and Big Stone Lake. In July twenty-four chiefs announced their desire to surrender to Joseph Brown, their former Indian gent.[7] As Pope prepared for a third year of campaigning, the main issue was whether Sully would find any Sioux to fight.

Initially, Pope wanted to launch a multipronged offensive against the Lakotas and their allies into the Black Hills and Powder River country, where the main warfare with the Sioux was occurring. However, lack of cooperation from other departments, the waning morale of the volunteer soldiers as the Civil War ended, and unceasing pressure from Minnesota politicians and civilians for protection led Pope to scale down his plans.

Sully and a small force of fewer than nine hundred mounted troops from Iowa, Dakota, and Minnesota once more journeyed through the same region as that covered on the previous expeditions. Commencing in early June, the expedition encountered few Sioux, fought no engagements, and accomplished little more than "showing the flag" before ending the campaign in early August.[8]

Although Pope still believed the Sioux were a threat, forces beyond his control were pushing for a peaceful settlement to the conflict. Dakota Territory governor Newton Edmunds, who was also ex officio superintendent of Indian affairs for the territory, was behind the peace movement. Edmunds was opposed by the military and teamsters who were making a large profit from supplying the troops and the citizens of Sioux City, Iowa, and Yankton, Dakota Territory, whose cities served as military depots. The governor did have the support of President Lincoln and members of Congress. In the fall of 1865 Edmunds was appointed chair of the Northwest Indian Commission, and later that year at Fort Sully, before a gathering of 10,000 Sioux, the commission, including Henry Sibley, made nine separate treaties with the various Lakota and Yanktonais bands. But it was not until February 1867, at Fort Wadsworth, that the Santees finally achieved peace. The treaty ended the Dakota War of 1862, granting the Santees two reservations, one between Lake Traverse and Fort Wadsworth and the other at Devil's Lake. Earlier, the Crow Creek Reservation had been terminated and the 900 Dakotas moved to a better location near the mouth of the Niobrara River in Nebraska. Here they were joined by the 247 Sioux freed from their Davenport, Iowa, prison.[9]

Not all the Santees moved to the new reservations or settled in Canada: a small faction still resided in Minnesota. Some Sioux never left, others quietly returned, and a handful were Sioux who had never signed the 1853 treaties or lived on the reservation. They were joined by the 137 Sioux who had served as scouts for the army and their families. Having served against their kinsmen, the scouts could not join the other Sioux on their new reservations, so each was granted eighty acres of land in Minnesota. By 1866 374 Santees were living in the state. In 1884, the government created a reservation for them that gave them a permanent residence in Minnesota.[10]

After the war, Pope and Sully soon departed the area. For Pope the war proved a boon to his career. He had pushed a military solution to the conflict, and the results paid off for him. He could claim that his campaigns had been an operational success, pushing back the frontier, protecting the routes to the gold fields, and ending the Dakota War of 1862. In January 1865 he was given command of the Department of Missouri, and three months later he was promoted to the brevet rank of major general. He remained in the army for another twenty-one years, retiring in 1886 and considered an overall successful officer.[11]

The military career of Sully, on the other hand, lagged. He lost his brevet rank as general and returned to his regular rank of major. Serving in the West, he clashed with George Armstrong Custer—who, Sully felt, was arrogant and undisciplined—and was often transferred to various posts, eventually being promoted to lieutenant colonel. Over time Sully grew bitter, believing his accomplishments had been ignored, and suffering from declining health, he died in 1879. As for Sibley, in 1866 he mustered out of the army, and following his military career, he served on the commission that ended the war on the Northern Plains, held a number of business positions, and represented Minnesota in Congress.[12]

For the officers and men who served on the expeditions, the end of the Civil War saw them mustered out of service and returning to their civilian lives and families. Few forgot their experiences out West, and over time a fair number of them wrote memoirs, books, and articles about their adventures based on their experiences. Some wrote with great description and length, while others were more brief and factual in their accounts. Lewis

Paxton was one of the latter, a man of few words. Although brief, the July 22, 1865, entry in his diary dealing with arriving home after years of war would have found approval by his comrades. "I arrived in Lake City at 9:00. I went home with Will Townshend. Had a very pleasant time in the evening."[13] The soldiers had come home.

Over time, historians and other writers commenting on the expeditions have concluded that they were a militarily success for the U.S. Army. The questions of the necessity for the campaigns, the reasons why they were fought, and lessons learned are not quite so readily apparent. Following Sibley's creation of Camp Release there were still Dakotas, like Little Crow and Inkpaduta, who were willing to continue the struggle. However, most of the Santees wanted peace, and the expeditions mainly attacked those Sioux who either sought an end to hostilities or who had not yet participated in the conflict. The 1863 expedition clearly incited several bands of the Lakotas to take a warlike stance and oppose the following year's expedition. Pope's insistence that there be a military response and Sibley's failure to achieve a peaceful sur-render of the nonhostile Dakotas at Big Mound led to a series of battles that could have been avoided.

The high civilian losses when the Dakotas rose in Minnesota also contributed to the demand for expeditions. From the diaries and letters of the soldiers, it was plain that they saw all Sioux as guilty and wanted revenge and that there was little attempt to understand that a sizable portion of the Dakotas and nearly all of the Yanktonais had taken no part in the war: the Sioux had to be punished for what they had done. By 1864 Pope and other top leaders had found new reasons to continue the campaigns, but revenge still remained the main factor for the common soldier. Unfortunately, the revenge sought by the soldiers more often than not fell on those least responsible for the uprising.

Finally, the lessons learned from the expeditions were more immediate rather than long term. The campaigns were fought along the lines of other military operations in the Civil War. Offensives were launched against the enemy with a combined arms force of infantry, artillery, and cavalry, and the better armed infantry supported by artillery made success on the battlefield against the Sioux a near certainty. With the conclusion of the Civil War, however, any military lessons learned by the volunteer army during the expeditions were quickly forgotten as the approach to fighting American Indians changed. During the Indian Wars in the West, cavalry became the ultimate force used in fighting. Although infantry and artillery were used in campaigns at times, the old combined-arms approach of the Civil War fell into disuse.

The diverse and independent nature of the various villages and bands of the Lakotas made any long-term lessons learned by those who fought the army during the expeditions highly unlikely. Sitting Bull came away with a new understanding of how whites made war, and the firepower of the army perhaps caused the Sioux to realize that they must become better armed in future wars. More obvious is how quickly the Sioux learned to adapt during the 1863 and 1864 campaigns. Faced with the long-range and more effective firepower of the infantry and the army's use of cannons, the Sioux found ways to avoid the striking power of the artillery and minimize the long-range impact of the rifles.

It would also be a mistake to assume that the Sioux did not gain a certain level of success in the conflict. During the battle of Big Mound and the subsequent retreat to the Missouri River, Sioux warriors did a brilliant job of delaying the advance of Sibley's army and drawing attention to themselves and away from the noncombatants in the villages. The material loss was great, but the actions of the warriors kept human losses much lower than they could have been. The use of terrain and lack of water during the march through the Badlands displayed a high learning curve for the Sioux on neutralizing the advantages of the army while inflicting losses and lowering the morale of the soldiers. And finally, numerous accounts of warriors gaining individual honor and achievements are mentioned in the diaries and letters of the soldiers.

Whether viewed as an extension of the Civil War or part of the Western Indian Wars, the Punitive Expeditions of 1863 and 1864 impacted both the fighting of the Civil War and the Western frontier. For the Sioux nation, the Dakota War of 1862 and the following campaigns proved a disaster for the Santees and Yanktonais. To the soldiers, outside of a chance for supposed revenge against those who had murdered white civilians, they were seen as a wasteful diversion from the real reason they had enlisted, to fight against the Confederacy and save the Union. Conflicts with the Sioux would continue for the next decade or so, but they would be fought by the regular army. The volunteer soldiers returned to their civilian lives and reflected on their experiences in the West.

Notes

1. THE COMING OF WAR

1. Roy W. Meyer, *History of the Santee Sioux: United States Indian Policy on Trial* (Lincoln: University of Nebraska Press, 1967), 25–26.

2. Julian Rice, *Before the Great Spirit: The Many Faces of Sioux Spirituality* (Albuquerque: University of New Mexico Press, 1998), 7; Waziyatawin, *What Does Justice Look Like?: The Struggle for Liberation in Dakota Homeland* (St. Paul: Living Justice Press, 2008), 20.

3. Jessica Dawn Palmer, *The Dakota Peoples: A History of the Dakota, Lakota and Nakota through 1863* (Jefferson, N.C.: McFarland and Company, 2008), 41; Raymond J. DeMallie, "Sioux Until 1850," in *Handbook of the North American Indian*, ed. William C. Sturtevant (Washington, D.C.: Smithsonian Institution, 2001), vol. 13, pt. 2, 735, 750; Paul H. Carlson, *The Plains Indians* (College Station: Texas A & M University Press, 1998), 5; Amos E. Oneroad and Alanson B. Skinner, *Being Dakota: Tales and Traditions of the Sisseton and Wahpeton*, ed. Laura L. Anderson (St. Paul: Minnesota Historical Society, 2003), 5.

4. Rice, *Before the Great Spirit*, 43–44; DeMallie, "Sioux Until 1850," 718, 751, 752, 754; Patricia C. Albers, "Santee," in Sturtevant, *Handbook of the North American Indian*, vol. 13., pt. 2, 761; Raymond J. DeMallie, "Yankton and Yanktonai," in ibid., 777.

5. Carlson, *Plains Indians*, 34; Richard White, "The Winning of the West: The Expansion of the Western Sioux in the Eighteenth Century," in *Major Problems in American Indian History*, ed. Albert Hurtado and Peter Iverson (Lexington, Mass.: D. C. Heath and Company, 1994), 246; DeMallie, "Sioux Until 1850," 722, 727.

6. White, "Winning of the West," 244–45; Royal B. Hassrick, *The Sioux: Life and Customs of a Warrior Society* (Norman: University of Oklahoma Press, 1964), 65; Palmer, *The Dakota People*, 147.

7. White, "Winning of the West," 246–47.

8. Robert W. Galler, Jr., "Sustaining the Sioux Confederation: Yanktonai Initiatives and Influence on the North Plains, 1680–1880," *Western Historical Quarterly* 34, no. 4 (Winter 2008): 473, 476; Herbert Schell, *History of South Dakota* (Pierre: South Dakota State Historical Society Press, 2004), 21; Guy Gibbon, *The Sioux: The Dakota and Lakota Nations* (Malden, Mass.: Blackwell Publishers, 2003), 84.

9. Mark Diedrich, *The Odyssey of Chief Standing Buffalo* (Minneapolis: Coyote Books, 1988), 13; Galler, "Sustaining the Sioux Confederation," 469.

10. White, "Winning of the West," 248.

11. Robert Athearn, *Forts of the Upper Missouri* (Englewood Cliffs, N.J.: Prentice-Hall, 1967), 31.

12. For a more detailed account of the First Sioux War, please see R. Eli Paul, *Blue Water Creek and the First Sioux War, 1854–1856* (Norman: University of Oklahoma Press, 2004); and Paul N. Beck, *The First Sioux War: The Grattan Fight and Blue Water Creek, 1854–1856* (Lanham, Md.: University Press of America, 2004).

13. Robert Utley, *Frontiersmen in Blue* (Lincoln: University of Nebraska Press, 1967), 270–71; George Hyde, *Red Cloud's Folk* (Norman: University of Oklahoma Press, 1976), 82.

14. Max Swanholm, *Alexander Ramsey and the Politics of Survival* (St. Paul: Minnesota Historical Society Press, 1977), 7.

15. Edmond Jefferson Danziger, Jr., *Indians and Bureaucrats* (Urbana: University of Illinois Press, 1974), 98–99; Hank H. Cox, *Lincoln and the Sioux Uprising of 1862* (Nashville: Cumberland House Publishing, 2005), 18, 46; Swanholm, *Alexander Ramsey*, 10–11; Carlson, *The Plains Indians*, 149.

16. Don Diessner, *There Are No Indians Left but Me!: Sitting Bull's Story* (El Segundo, Calif.: Upton and Sons Publishers, 1993), 169; Swanholm, *Alexander Ramsey*, 18, 46.

17. Howard R. Lamar, *Dakota Territory, 1861–1889: A Study of Frontier Politics* (New Haven, Conn.: Yale University Press, 1956), 37–38; John R. Milton, *South Dakota: A History* (New York: W. W. Norton and Company, 1977), 70.

18. Galler, "Sustaining the Sioux Confederation," 481, 478–89; Palmer, *Dakota Peoples*, 43, 46–47; Meyer, *History of the Santee Sioux*, 105; Schell, *History of South Dakota*, 66–68.

19. Joseph Frazier Wall, *Iowa: A Bicentennial History* (New York: W. W. Norton and Company, 1976), 23, 25, 34, 38–39, 49.

20. For a more in-depth look at the massacre, see L. P. Lee, *History of the Spirit Lake Massacre* (Iowa City: State Historical Society of Iowa, 1918); and Paul N. Beck, *Inkpaduta: Dakota Leader* (Norman: University of Oklahoma Press, 2008).

21. Schell, *History of South Dakota*, 80, 85; Utley, *Frontiersmen in Blue*, 271.

22. Milton, *South Dakota*, 67, 71; David P. Robrock, "The Seventh Iowa Cavalry and the Plains Wars," *Montana* 39, no. 2 (Spring 1989): 4; Schell, *History of South Dakota*, 66.

23. Board of Commissioners, *Minnesota in the Civil and Indian Wars, 1861–1865*, vol. 1 (St. Paul: Pioneer Press Company, 1890), 2.

24. Judson W. Bishop, *The Story of a Regiment: Being a Narrative of the Service of the Second Regiment Minnesota Veteran Volunteer Infantry in the Civil War of 1861–1865*, ed. Newell L. Chester (St. Cloud, Minn.: North Star Press of St. Cloud, 2000), 64.

25. Board of Commissioners, *Minnesota in the Civil and Indian Wars*, vol. 1, 78, 147, 198, 243.

26. Ibid., 300.

27. Ibid.

28. Earl J. Hess, *Liberty, Virtue, and Progress: Northerners and Their War for the Union* (New York: New York University Press, 1988), 4–5, 18–19, 39, 131–32; Reid Mitchell, *The Vacant Chair: The Northern Soldier Leaves Home* (Oxford: Oxford University Press, 1993), 11–13; James M. McPherson, *For Cause and Comrades: Why Men Fought in the Civil War* (New York: Oxford University Press, 1997), 5, 18–20, 25–26, 83–84, 98–99, 131–34; Chandra Manning, "A 'Vexed Question': White Union Soldiers on Slavery and Race," in *The View from the Ground: Experiences of Civil War Soldiers*, ed. Aaron Sheehan-Dean (Lexington: University of Kentucky Press, 2007), 34, 39.

29. Charles Horton Papers, Minnesota Historical Society (hereinafter cited as MHS); Pehr Carlson to Wife, September 22, 1862, September

23, 1862, Pehr Carlson and Family Papers, MHS; George to Mariette Clapp, August 14, 1862, George C. Clapp and Family Papers, MHS; Board of Commissioners, *Minnesota in the Civil and Indian Wars*, vol. 1, 347; Robert S. Offenberg and Robert Rue Parsonage, eds. *The War Letters of Duren F. Kelley* (New York: Pageant Press, 1967), 14, 40.

30. Jacob Hamlin to Parents, April 6, 1862, Jacob Hamlin Papers, MHS.

31. Ruth-Ann M. Harris, "Civil War Soldier, Christopher Byrne, Writes Home" (paper delivered at the American Conference for Irish Studies, Minneapolis, June 2003); Thomas C. Hodgson, *Personal Recollections of the Sioux War with the Eighth Minnesota, Company F,* transcribed by Robert Olson (Roseville, Minn.: Park Genealogical Books, 1999), 1–2.

32. Mitchell, *The Vacant Chair*, 29–30; John to Marie Jones, July 10, 1863, John Jones Papers, MHS; Henry to Delia McConnell, October 5, 1862, Henry McConnell Papers, MHS.

33. George P. Belden, *The White Chief: or, Twelve Years among the Wild Indians of the Plains* (New York: C. F. Vent, 1870), 306–307.

34. Siegmund to Rosanah Rothammer, May 5, 1863, Siegmund Rothammer Papers, South Dakota Historical Society (hereinafter cited as SDHS).

35. Newcombe Kinney, "Reminiscences of the Sioux Indian and Civil Wars," 2, MHS; Amos E. Glanville, *I Saw the Ravages of an Indian War: A Diary by Amos E. Glanville Sr., Company F, 10th Minnesota Volunteers* (privately printed by John K. Glanville, 1988), 1; Frank Griswold to Parents, August 25, 1862, Frank Griswold Papers, MHS; Thomas Jefferson Hunt, "Observations of T. J. Hunt in the Sioux Indian and Civil Wars of 1862–1865," 1–2, MHS; Charles Watson to Unknown, November 4, 1862, Charles Watson Papers, MHS.

36. Robrock, "The Seventh Iowa Cavalry," 2, 4; Benjamin Stambaugh, ed., "Iowa Troops in the Sully Campaigns," *The Iowa Journal of History and Politics* 20, no. 3 (July 1922): 364, 374–75, 380–81, 389.

37. Stambaugh, "Iowa Troops," 407, 408.

38. Cox, *Lincoln and the Sioux Uprising of 1862*, 48; Gary Clayton Anderson and Alan R. Woolworth, *Through Dakota Eyes: Narrative Accounts of the Minnesota Indian War of 1862* (St. Paul: Minnesota Historical Society Press, 1988), 23; Diessner, *There Are No Indians Left but Me!*, 159.

39. Jerry Keenan, *The Great Sioux Uprising* (Cambridge, Mass.: Da Capo Press, 2003), 3; Anderson, *Through Dakota Eyes*, 24, 31–32; Oneroad and Skinner, *Being Dakota*, 7–8.

40. Anderson, *Through Dakota Eyes*, 26: Carlson, *The Plains Indians*, 149.

41. Cox, *Lincoln and the Sioux Uprising*, 21, 22.

42. Keenan, *The Great Sioux Uprising*, 26–28.

2. THE DAKOTA WAR OF 1862

1. U.S. War Department, *War of the Rebellion: A Compilation of the Official Records of the Union and Confederate Armies*, ser. 1, vol. 13, pt. 1 (Washington, D.C., 1880), 590.

2. Alvin M. Josephy, Jr., *Civil War in the American West* (New York: Alfred A. Knopf, 1991), 95; Peter Cozzens, *General John Pope: A Life for the Nation* (Urbana: University of Illinois Press, 2000), 200– 201; David A. Nichols, *Lincoln and the Indians: Civil War Policy and Politics* (Columbia: University of Missouri Press, 1978), 81; Richard Ellis, *General Pope and U.S. Indian Policy* (Albuquerque: University of New Mexico Press, 1970), 6.

3. Swanholm, *Alexander Ramsey and the Politics of Survival*, 12, 14; Diessner, *There Are No Indians Left but Me!*, 147, 153; Isaac V. D. Heard, *History of the Sioux War* (New York: Harper and Brothers Publishers, 1865), 335; Landon Sully, *No Tears for the General, Life of Alfred Sully* (Palo Alto, Calif.: American West Publishing Company, 1974), 166–67; William Watts Folwell, *A History of Minnesota* (St. Paul: Minnesota Historical Society Press, 1956), vol. 2, 53, 68.

4. Rhoda R. Gilman, *Henry Hastings Sibley: Divided Heart* (St. Paul: Minnesota Historical Society Press, 2004), 163–64; Diessner, *There Are No Indians Left but Me!*, 163, 168.

5. Alfred J. Hill, "History of Company E, of the Sixth Minnesota Regiment of Volunteer Infantry," published by Prof. T. H. Lewis (St. Paul: Pioneer Press Co., 1899), 1, 10; Board of Commissioners, *Minnesota in the Civil and Indian Wars*, vol. 1, 302.

6. Charles Horton Papers, MHS; John Pattee, "Reminiscences of John Pattee," *South Dakota Historical Collections* 5 (Pierre: State Publishing Company, 1910): 519; ibid., 273, 275–76, 283.

7. Board of Commissioners, *Minnesota in the Civil and Indian Wars*, vol. 1, 304; Diary, October 2, 1862, October 22, 1862, March 22, 1863, Charles Watson Papers, MHS.

8. Offenberg and Parsonage, *War Letters of Duren F. Kelley*, 19, 22, 29.

9. Leonard to Dr. Joseph Aldrich, 1862, Leonard Aldrich Papers, MHS; September 16, 1862, September 19, 1862, George Doud Diaries, MHS; William to Wife, December 12, 1862, William and Herbert Paist Papers, MHS; George to Abby Adams, October 22, 1862, George Adams Papers, MHS.

10. Cozzen, *General John Pope*, 200–201; Nichols, *Lincoln and the Indians*, 98; Gerald S. Hening, "A Neglected Cause of the Sioux Uprising," *Minnesota History* 45, issue 3 (1976): 109.

11. Cox, *Lincoln and the Sioux Uprising of 1862*, 108; Willoughby M. Babcock, "Minnesota's Frontier: A Neglected Sector of the Civil War," *Minnesota History* 38, issue 6 (1963): 274; Ellis, *General Pope and United States Indian Policy*, 6; *Mankato Semi-Weekly Record*, January, 24, 1863; Schell, *History of South Dakota*, 79.

12. Josephy, *Civil War in the American West*, 132; U.S. War Department, *War of the Rebellion*, ser. 1, vol. 13, 618, 642.

13. Offenberg and Parsonage, *War Letters of Duren F. Kelley*, 21, 29.

14. Cozzens, *General John Pope*, 208; Pope to Major General Henry Halleck, September 16, 1862, U.S. War Department, *War of the Rebellion*, ser. 1, vol. 13, 642; Marshall McKusick, *Iowa Northern Border Brigade* (Iowa City: University of Iowa Press, 1975), 137.

15. Pope to Colonel Henry Sibley, September 17, 1862, U.S. War Department, *War of the Rebellion*, ser. 1, vol. 13, 649; Richard Ellis, "The Humanitarian Generals," *Western Historical Quarterly* 3, no. 2 (April 1972): 178.

16. Brigadier General John Schoefiled to Halleck, September 18, 1862, U.S. War Department, *War of the Rebellion*, ser. 1. vol. 13, 649–50; Halleck to Pope, September 23, 1862, ibid., 663; Secretary of War Edwin Stanton to Pope, September 23, 1862, ibid., 662–63.

17. Meyer, *History of the Santee Sioux*, 118; The Sisseton and Wahpeton Bands of Sioux Indians v. The United States, original petition no. 22524, Court of Claims (Washington, D.C.: McGill and Wallace Law Printers, 1876–1906), 78; Stephen Riggs, ed., "The Narrative of Paul Mazakootermane," *Collections of the Minnesota Historical Society* 3 (St. Paul: Minnesota Historical Society Press, 1870–1880): 84.

18. Sisseton and Wahpeton Bands of Sioux Indians v. The United States, 79–80; Gary Clayton Anderson, *Kinsmen of Another Kind: Dakota-White Relations in the Upper Mississippi Valley, 1650–1862* (St. Paul: Minnesota Historical Society Press, 1997), 270–71.

19. Anderson, *Kinsmen of Another Kind*, 270; Oneroad and Skinner, *Being Dakota*, 9.

20. Anderson and Woolworth, *Through Dakota Eyes*, 23.

21. Offenberg and Parsonage, *War Letters of Duran F. Kelley*, 23; Andrea R. Forough, ed., *Go If You Think It Your Duty: A Minnesota Couple's Civil War Letters* (St. Paul: Minnesota Historical Society Press, 2008), 122.

22. Gabriel Renville, "A Sioux Narrative of the Outbreak in 1862, and of Sibley's Expedition in 1863," http://www.archive.org/stream /siouxnarrativeofoorenvrich/siouxnar.

23. Ibid.; Meyer, *History of the Santee Sioux*, 121–22.

24. Keenan, *Great Sioux Uprising*, 72–74; Anderson, *Kinsmen of Another Kind*, 273–74.

25. Riggs, "Narrative of Paul Mazakootermane," 87; Renville, "A Sioux Narrative."

26. Meyer, *History of the Santee Sioux*, 123; U.S. War Department, *War of the Rebellion*, ser. 1, vol. 13, 666–67; Renville, "A Sioux Narrative"; Riggs, "Narrative of Paul Mazkootermane," 87.

27. Charles Eastman, *Indian Boyhood* (Boston: Little, Brown and Company, 1926), 4, 13–14.

28. Forough, *Go If You Think It Your Duty*, 123; Meyer, *History of the Santee Sioux*, 127, 129.

29. Diary, December 26, 1862, Charles Watson Papers, MHS; Jacob Hamlin to Parents, November 12, 1862, Jacob Hamlin Papers, MHS.

30. Diessner, *There Are No Indians Left But Me!*, 187–88.

31. James H. Howard, *The Canadian Sioux* (Lincoln: University of Nebraska Press, 1984), 25; Anderson, *Kinsmen of Another Kind*, 278.

32. Celia M. Campbell, "Reminiscences," Celia Campbell Stay Papers, MHS; Robert Utley, *Frontiersmen in Blue* (Lincoln: University of Nebraska Press, 1967), 269; Gary Clayton Anderson, *Little Crow: Spokesman for the Sioux* (St. Paul: Minnesota Historical Society Press, 1986), 162.

33. Mark Diedrich, *The Odyssey of Chief Standing Buffalo* (Minneapolis: Coyote Books, 1988), 7, 16, 26, 31, 41–42; Anderson and Woolworth, *Through Dakota Eyes*, 293.

34. Diedrich, *Odyssey of Chief Standing Buffalo*, 41, 42–43; Sisseton and Wahpeton Bands of Sioux v. The United States, 96, 108; Anderson, *Little Crow*, 168.

35. Dierich, *Odyssey of Chief Standing Buffalo*, 41; Hassrick, *The Sioux*, 77.

36. Sibley to Standing Buffalo, Waawatan et al., October 3, 1862, U.S. War Department, *War of the Rebellion*, ser. 1, vol. 13, 708.

37. Pope to Sibley, September, 28, 1982, ibid., 686; Josephy, *Civil War in the American West*, 138.

38. Sibley to Pope, September 30, 1862, U.S. War Department, *War of the Rebellion*, ser. 1, vol. 13, 694; Sibley to Pope, October 3, 1862, ibid., 707–708; Sibley to Pope, October 5, 1862, ibid., 711.

39. Pope to Halleck, October 7, 1862, ibid., 716; Pope to Halleck, October 9, 1862, ibid., 722; Halleck to Pope, October 21, 1862, ibid., 755; Babcock, "Minnesota's Frontier: A Neglected Sector of the Civil War," 279.

40. *St. Paul Press*, October, 21, 1862; *St. Paul Pioneer*, October 23, 1862; Cozzens, *General John Pope*, 204–205.

41. Cozzens, *General John Pope*, 205; Ellis, *General Pope and U.S. Indian Policy*, 18; McKusick, *Iowa Northern Border Brigade*, 131, 135–36.

42. Utley, *Frontiersmen in Blue*, 271; Mildred Throne, ed., "Iowa Troops in Dakota Territory, 1861–1864, Based on the Diaries and Letters of Henry J. Wieneke," *Iowa Journal of History* 57, no. 2 (April 1959): 126–27; Diessner, *There Are No Indians left but Me!*, 35; W. A. Burleigh, Yankton Indian Agent, to William Dole, Commissioner of Indian Affairs, December 18, 1862, Letters Received and Sent, Office of Indian Affairs, Upper Missouri, Dakota Superintendency, RG 62, M-234, Roll 250; Ellis, *General Pope and U.S. Indian Policy*, 17.

43. Anderson, *Little Crow*, 169; Lamar, *Dakota Territory*, 89; Governor William Jayne to Commissioner of Indian Affairs William Dole, October 8, 1862, "Report of the Secretary of Interior," House Document 1, 37th Congress, 3rd Session, no. 35, 319–22; Burleigh to Dole, December 18, 1862, Letters Received and Sent, Upper Missouri, Dakota Superintendency, RG 62, M-234, Roll 250.

44. Anderson, *Kinsmen of Another Kind*, 278; Diedrich, *Odyssey of Chief Standing Buffalo*, 48–49; Peter Douglas Elias, *The Dakota of the Canadian Northwest* (Winnipeg: University of Manitoba Press, 1988), 17–21.

3. PREPARING FOR THE FIRST EXPEDITIONS

1. Cozzens, *General John Pope*, 228; A. P. Connolly, *A Thrilling Narrative of the Minnesota Massacre and the Sioux War of 1862–1863* (Chicago: A. P. Connolly, 1896), 211; Utley, *Frontiersmen in Blue*, 270; Josephy, *Civil War in the American West*, 139; Gibbon, *The Sioux*, 111; *St. Paul Pioneer and Democrat Weekly*, May 1, 1863; G. D. Hill to J. M. Edmund, June 11, 1863, Letters Received and Sent, Dakota Superintendency, RG 62, M-234, Roll 250.

2. "Sisseton and Wahpeton Bands of Sioux v. The United States," 184; Diedrich, *Odyssey of Chief Standing Buffalo*, 49; Meyer, *History of*

the Santee Sioux, 133; *St. Paul Pioneer and Democrat Weekly*, May 29, 1863.

3. Henry Reed to William Dole, Commissioner of Indian Affairs, January 14, 1863, Letters Received and Sent, Dakota Superintendency, RG 62, M-234, Roll 885.

4. Anderson, *Little Crow*, 172; Mark Diedrich, *Famous Chiefs of the Eastern Sioux* (Minneapolis: Coyote Books, 1987), 74

5. Elias, *Dakota of the Canadian Northwest*, 21; Anderson, *Little Crow*, 173; William Seward to J. P. Usher, Secretary of the Interior, January 12, 1863, Letters Received and Sent, Dakota Superintendency, RG 62, M-234, Roll 250.

6. Diedrich, *Odyssey of Chief Standing Buffalo*, 49–50; Anderson, *Little Crow*, 173.

7. Meyer, *History of the Santee Sioux*, 136–37, 140; Josephy, *Civil War in the American West*, 138.

8. Pope to J. C. Kelton, Assistant Adjunct General, U.S. War Department, *War of the Rebellion*, ser. 1, vol. 22, pt. 2, 305; Pope to Sibley, ibid., 115.

9. Pope to Sibley, ibid., 115; Geraldine Bean, "General Alfred Sully and the Northwest Indian Expedition," *North Dakota History* 33, no. 3 (Summer 1966): 245.

10. *Roster and Record of Iowa Soldiers in the War of the Rebellion*, vol. 4 (Des Moines: Emory English State Printer, 1910), 1115, 1117; Pattee, "Reminiscences of John Pattee," 291–92; J. H. Drips, *Three Years among the Indians in Dakota* (New York: Sol Lewis, 1974), 2.

11. Lurton Dunham Ingersoll, *Iowa and the Rebellion* (Philadelphia: J. B. Lippincott and Company, 1866), 690–91; *Roster and Record of Iowa Soldiers*, vol. 4, 1253; Stambaugh, "Iowa Troops," 364; Marshall McKusick, *The Iowa Northern Border Brigade* (Iowa City: University of Iowa, 1975), 5; David P. Robrock, "The Seventh Iowa Cavalry and the Plains Wars," *Montana* 39: no. 2 (Spring 1989): 8.

12. Board of Commissioners, *Minnesota in the Civil War and Indian Wars*, vol. 1, 519–20.

13. Mitchell, *Vacant Chair*, 26, 29.

14. George to Mariette, March 27, 1863, George C. Clapp and Family Papers, MHS; George to Abby, October 22, 1863, George Adams Papers, MHS; Henry to Maria, May 10, 1863, Henry J. Synder Papers, MHS; Philip to Wife, September 26, 1862, Philip Osborn Papers, Iowa State Historical Society (hereinafter cited as ISHS).

15. Henry to Delia, October 5, 1862, Henry McConnell Papers, MHS; George to Abby, October 22, 1863, George Adams Papers, MHS; May 5, 1863, Henry Hagadorn Diary, January 11–August 31, 1863, MHS.

16. May 15, 1863, Henry Hagadorn Diary, MHS; Philip to Wife, September 19, 1862, Philip Osborn Papers, ISHS.

17. John to Annie, February, 18, 1863, John B. Leo Letters, MHS; Thomas to Mary, September 16, 1862, Thomas Cheetham Letters, MHS.

18. James Marten, *Civil War America: Voices from the Home Front* (Santa Barbara, Calif.: ABC-CLIO, 2003), 125–26, 129.

19. Philip to Wife, October 30, 1862, Philip Osborn Papers, ISHS; George to Abby, April 24, 1862, George Adams Papers, MHS; William to Son, May 8, 1863, William and Herbert Paist Papers, MHS; Thomas to Mary, December 26, 1862, Thomas Cheetham Letters, MHS.

20. Offenberg and Parsonage, *War Letters of Duren F. Kelley*, 25, 33, 34.

21. John Smith and James R. Hart, *Tales of the Tenth Regiment, Minnesota Volunteers, 1862–1863* (Henderson, Minn.: Sibley County Historical Society, 1996), 9, 12.

22. Hamlin to Friends, February 15, 1863, Jacob Hamlin Papers, MHS.

23. Gibbon, *The Sioux*, 100; Ella Deloria, *Speaking of Indians* (Lincoln: University of Nebraska Press, 1998), 24–26.

24. Gibbon, *The Sioux*, 101; Hassick, *The Sioux*, 109–10.

25. Inez Hilgered, "The Narrative of Oscar One Bull," *Mid-America: An Historical Review* 28, no. 3 (July 1946): 156–57; Susan Bordeaux Bettelyoun and Josephine Waggoner, *With My Own Eyes: A Lakota Woman Tells Her People's History*, ed. Emily Levine (Lincoln: University of Nebraska Press, 1998), 9; Palmer, *Dakota Peoples*, 177, 181; Samuel W. Pond, *The Dakota or Sioux in Minnesota as They Were in 1863* (St. Paul: Minnesota Historical Society Press, 1986), 140.

26. Hilgered, "Narrative of Oscar One Bull," 156; Hassrick, *The Sioux*, 113–15; Pond, *Dakota or Sioux in Minnesota*, 142; Willard E. Rosenfelt, *The Last Buffalo: Cultural Views of the Plains Indians: The Sioux or Dakota Nation* (Minneapolis: T. S. Denison and Company, 1973), 44; Luther Standing Bear, *Land of the Spotted Eagle* (Boston: Houghton Mifflin Company, 1933), 10.

27. Pope to J. C. Kelton, Assistant Adjunct-General, U.S. War Department, *War of the Rebellion*, ser. 1, vol. 22, pt. 2, 304; Geraldine Bean, "General Alfred Sully and the Northwest Indian Expedition," *North Dakota History* 33, issue 3 (Summer 1966): 249.

28. Pattee, "Reminiscences," 289; William Eagan, "General Sully and That Other Seventh Cavalry," *True West* 37, issue 9 (September 1990): 30; Clair Jacobson, "The Battle of Whitestone Hill," *North Dakota History* 44, issue 3 (Summer 1972): 6; Cozzens, *General John Pope*, 229; Sully, *No Tears for the General*, 166.

29. Sully, ibid., 166; Bean, "General Alfred Sully," 243; Pope to Halleck, May 18, 1863, Halleck to Pope, May 19, 1863, Pope to Halleck, May 19, 1863, U.S. War Department, *War of the Rebellion*, ser. 1, vol. 22, pt. 2, 287–88.

30. Diessner, *There Are No Indians left but Me!,"* 195; Pope to Sibley, February 20, 1863, U.S. War Department, *War of the Rebellion*, ser. 1, vol. 22, pt. 2, 115.

31. Ellis, *General Pope and U.S. Indian Policy*, 19.

32. Halleck to Pope, April 28, 1863, U.S. War Department, *War of the Rebellion*, ser. 1, vol. 22, pt. 2, 260; Harry Reed to CIA William Dole, January 14, 1863, Letters Received and Sent, Upper Missouri, Dakota Superintendency, RG 62, M-234, Roll 885; J. M. Edmunds to William P. Delo, June 1863, Letters Received and Sent, Dakota Superintendency, RG 62, M-234, Roll 250; Lamar, *Dakota Territory, 1861–1889*, 101–102.

33. Ellis, *General Pope and U.S. Indian Policy*, 24–25.

34. Cozzens, *General John Pope*, 233; Nichols, *Lincoln and the Indians*, 66; Richard Ellis, "Political Pressures and Army Politics on the Northern Plains, 1862–1865," *Minnesota History* 42 (Summer 1970): 45.

35. Nathaniel West, *Ancestry, Life and Times of Hon. Henry Hastings Sibley* (St. Paul: Pioneer Press, 1889), 305; *St. Cloud Democrat*, May 28, 1863.

36. Secretary of War Annual Report, 1865, HED no. 83, 38th Congress, 2nd session, 1230.

37. Ellis, "Political Pressures and Army Politics," 46; Pope to Halleck, July 27, 1863, Pope to J. C. Kelton, U.S. War Department, *War of the Rebellion*, ser. 1, vol. 22, pt. 2, 304, 403–404.

38. Josephy, *Civil War in the American West*, 235.

39. James McPherson, *For Cause and Comrades*, 148; Reid Mitchell, *Civil War Soldiers* (New York: Viking Press, 1988), 24–25; Gerald F. Linderman, *Embattled Courage: The Experience of Combat in the American Civil War* (New York: Free Press, 1987), 65–67.

40. Ole Paulson, "General Sibley's Expedition," 7, MHS; May 10, 1863, Henry Hagadorn Diary, MHS; Ben Brunson, "Reminiscences," 10–11, MHS; A. P. Connolly, *A Thrilling Narrative*, 12.

41. Eli to Philena, June 3, 1863, Eli Pickett Correspondence, MHS; A. P. Connolly, *A Thrilling Narrative*, 199; Offenberg and Parsonage, *War Letters of Duren F. Kelley*, 59.

42. Offenberg and Parsonage, *War Letters of Duren F. Kelley*, 54; William to Henrietta, October 3, 1863, William and Herbert Paist Papers, MHS.

43. Henry to Delia, April 7, 1863, May 15, 1863, May 21, 1863, May 27, 1863, Henry McConnell Papers, MHS.

44. Merrill to Father, June 13, 1863, G. Merrill Dwelle Papers, MHS; Charles to Wife, November 4, 1862, Charles Watson Papers, MHS.

45. Offenberg and Parsonage, *War Letters of Duren F. Kelley*, 50–51; George to Mariette, March 27, 1863, April 24, 1863, George C. Clapp and Family Papers, MHS; Hart, Smith, *Tales of the Tenth Regiment*, 8.

46. Henry Hagadorn, Diary, May 1, 1863, MHS; Thomas to Parents, April 28, 1863, Thomas to Mother, May 23, 1863, Thomas Montgomery Letters, MHS.

47. Eli to Philena, June 3, 1863, Eli Pickett Correspondence, MHS; Hodgson, *Personal Recollections of the Sioux War*, 10; Henry to Marie, May 10, 1863, Henry J. Synder Papers, MHS; John to Annie, June 3, 1863, John B. Leo Letters, MHS.

48. John Nelson Papers, MHS.

49. *St. Paul Pioneer and Democrat Weekly*, April 24, 1863; Glanville, *I Saw the Ravages of an Indian War*, 87.

50. Edmund J. Danziger, Jr., "The Crow Creek Experiment: An Aftermath of the Sioux War of 1862," *North Dakota History* 37 (Spring 1970): 106–109, 114; Danziger, *Indians and Bureaucrats*, 95, 122.

51. Josephy, *The Civil War in the American West*, 139–40; Pope to Halleck, May 19, 1863, Sibley to Pope, May 19, 1863, Halleck to Pope, May 30, 1863, U.S. War Department, *War of the Rebellion*, ser. 1, vol. 22, pt. 2, 289, 306.

52. Henry Hagadorn Diary, May 9, 1863.

53. Ibid, May 10, 1863, May 11, 1863.

54. Ibid, May 13, 1863, May 14, 1863.

55. Ibid, May 30, 1863; George to Mariette, May 27, 1863, George C. Clapp and Family Papers, MHS.

56. Henry Hagadorn Diary, May 5, 1863; Thomas to Wife, May 23, 1863, Thomas James Cheetham Letters, MHS.

57. Charles to Father, June 7, 1863, Charles Watson Papers, MHS; Sibley to Captain E. A. Folsom, September 29, 1862, Letters Received, Fort

Ridgely, National Archives Record Group, 393; Henry Hagadorn Diary, June 2, 1863, MHS.

58. Connolly, *A Thrilling Narrative*, 200; Glanville, *I Saw the Ravages of an Indian War*, 110–11.

59. Henry Hagadorn Diary, June 4, 1863; Charles to Father, June 12, 1863, Charles Watson Papers, MHS; Thomas to Parents, June 2, 1863, Thomas Montgomery Letters, MHS; Offenberg and Parsonage, *War Letters of Duren F. Kelley*, 61; John to Annie, June 3, 1863, John B. Leo Letters, MHS.

60. Glanville, *I Saw the Ravages of an Indian War*, 111–12; Theodore Carter, "Reminiscences of the Sibley Expedition of 1863," Small Manuscript Collection, North Dakota Historical Society (hereinafter cited as NDHS), 17.

61. Charles to Father, June 12, 1863, Charles Watson Papers, MHS; Offenberg and Parsonage, *War Letters of Duren F. Kelley*, 59–60.

62. West, *Ancestry*, 303; James T. Ramer, Diary, June 9, 1862; Connolly, *A Thrilling Narrative*, 201.

63. West, *Ancestry*, 323.

64. Henry to Marie, [n.d.], Henry J. Synder Papers, MHS; John to Marie, June 12, 1863, John Jones Papers, MHS.

65. Thomas to Mother, June 15, 1863, Thomas Montgomery Letters, MHS; Charles Watson Diary, June 14, 1863, Charles Watson Papers, MHS; Offenberg and Parsonage, *War Letters of Duren F. Kelley*, 56, 60–61; Henry to Delia, June 14, 1863, Henry McConnell Papers, MHS.

66. Enoch Eastman, "Portions of the Diary of Enoch Eastman, Co. E Hatch's Battalion of Minnesota Volunteers, with Sibley's Expedition of 1863," *North Dakota Historical Quarterly* 1, issue 3 (April 1927): 41.

4. SIBLEY'S EXPEDITION DEPARTS

1. Carter, "Reminiscences," NDHS, 18; Eastman, "Portions of the Diary of Enoch Eastman," 41; Hermann Rothfuss, "German Witness of the Sioux Campaigns," *North Dakota History* 25, no. 4 (October, 1958): 124; Connolly, *A Thrilling Narrative*, 205; Thomas Jefferson Hunt, "Observations of T. J. Hunt in the Sioux Indian and Civil War: A Narrative of the Military Life of T. J. Hunt," 5, MHS.

2. West, *Ancestry*, 303; Connolly, *A Thrilling Narrative*, 205.

3. Rothfuss, "German Witness of the Sioux Campaign," 124; Eastman, "Portions of the Diary of Enoch Eastman," 41.

4. Eastman, "Portions of the Diary of Enoch Eastman," 41; Ransom Walters Diary, June 17, 1863, MHS.

5. Glanville, *I Saw the Ravages of an Indian War,* 113; Arthur Daniels, *Journal of Sibley's Indian Expedition during the Summer of 1863 and Record of the Troops Employed* (Minneapolis: James D. Thueson, 1980), 17; John to Marie, June 20, 1863, John Jones Papers, MHS.

6. Henry to Delia, June 21, 1863, Henry McConnell Papers, MHS; Offenberg and Parsonage, *War Letters of Duren Kelley,* 64–65.

7. Thomas to Mary, June 21, 1863, Thomas Cheetham Letters, MHS.

8. Daniels, *Journal of Sibley's Indian Expedition,* 19; Henry Hagadorn Diary, June 22, 1863, MHS.

9. Rothfuss, "German Witness of the Sioux Campaign," 125; Daniels, *Journal of Sibley's Expedition,* 19; Oscar Wall Diary, June 23, 1863, MHS.

10. Cozzens, *General John Pope,* 231–32; Board of Commissioners, *Minnesota in the Civil and Indian Wars,* vol. 1, 353, 520.

11. Rothfuss, "German Witnesses of the Sioux Campaign," 125; Glanville, *I Saw the Ravages of an Indian War,* 117.

12. Anonymous Diary, June 25, 1863, MHS; James Ramer Diary, June 25, 1863, MHS; Eastman, "Portions of the Diary of Enoch Eastman," 43.

13. Lewis Paxton, "Diary Kept by Lewis C. Paxton," *Collections of the State Historical Society of North Dakota* 2, issue pt. 2 (Minot: North Dakota Historical Society, 1908): 118.

14. John Pettibone Diary, June 26, 1863, MHS; Offenberg and Parsonage, *War Letters of Duren F. Kelley,* 66; Daniels, *Journal of Sibley's Indian Expedition,* 21; Granville, *I Saw the Ravages of an Indian War,* 118; John to Marie, August 5, 1863, John Jones Papers, MHS; Hunt, "Observations," 6; Eastman, "Portions of the Diary of Enoch Eastman," 127.

15. Daniels, *Journal of Sibley's Indian Expedition,* 21; West, *Ancestry,* 322; Jacob to Family, June 27, 1863, Jacob Hamlin Papers, MHS.

16. Anonymous Diary, June 29, 1863, MHS; Merrill to Carrie, May 29, 1863, G. Merrill Dwelle Papers, MHS; Eastman, "Portion of the Diary of Enoch Eastman," 43; James T. Ramer, Diary, June 28, 1863, MHS.

17. Daniels, *Journal of Sibley's Indian Expedition,* 21; Offenberg and Parsonage, *War Letters of Duren F. Kelley,* 66; Rothfuss, "German Witness of the Sioux Campaign," 125–26.

18. Daniels, *Journal of Sibley's Indian Expedition,* 21–22.

19. Ole Paulson, "General Sibley's Expedition," 4, MHS; Carter, "Reminiscences," NDHS, 18–19; Rothfuss, "German Witness of the Sioux Campaign," 126; Daniels, *Journal of Sibley's Indian Expedition*, 22.

20. Daniels, *Journal of Sibley's Indian Expedition*, 22; Connolly, *A Thrilling Narrative*, 209.

21. Rothfuss, "German Witness of the Sioux Campaign," 126; Glanville, *I Saw the Ravages of an Indian War*, 125–27.

22. Rothfuss, "German Witness of the Sioux Campaign," 126; Eastman, "Portion of the Diary of Enoch Eastman," 44; William Marshall Journal, July 3, 1863, NDHS.

23. Rothfuss, "German Witness of the Sioux Campaign," 126–27; Daniels, *Journal of Sibley's Indian Expedition*, 23.

24. Rothfuss, "German Witness of the Sioux Campaign," 127.

25. Eastman, "Portion of the Diary of Enoch Eastman," 44; James Ramer Diary, July 4, 1863; Charles to Father, July 4, 1863, Charles Watson Papers, MHS.

26. Paxton, "Diary Kept by Lewis C. Paxton," 119; Carter, "Reminiscences," 4, 10, 13.

27. Thomas to Parents, July 4, 1863, Thomas Montgomery Letters, MHS.

28. Rothfuss, "German Witness of the Sioux Campaign," 127; Hagadorn, Diary, July 4, 1863, MHS.

29. Diedrich, *Famous Chiefs of the Eastern Sioux*, 4; Major R. O. Selfridge to Sully, June 1, 1863, U.S. War Department, *War of the Rebellion*, ser. 1, vol. 22, pt. 2, 306.

30. Eastman, "Portions of the Diary of Enoch Eastman," 44; Hagadorn, Diary, July 5 and July 6, 1863, MHS; Hill, *History of Company E*, 21.

31. George to Mariette, July 9, 1863, George C. Clapp Family Papers, MHS; Daniels, *Journal of Sibley's Indian Expedition*, 25.

32. Thomas to Parents, July 10, 1863, Thomas Montgomery Letters, MHS; John to Marie, July 10, 1863, John Jones Papers, MHS; Diessner, *There Are No Indians Left but Me!*, 197.

33. Rothfuss, "German Witness of the Sioux Campaign," 128; West, *Ancestry*, 325; James King, ed., "The Civil War of Private Morton," *North Dakota History* 35, no. 1 (Winter 1968): 13.

34. Watson, Diary, July 20, 1863, Charles Watson Papers, MHS; Glanville, *I Saw the Ravages of an Indian War*, 138.

35. West, *Ancestry*, 307; Connolly, *A Thrilling Narrative*, 221.

36. Carter, "Reminiscences," NDHS, 16; Henry to Delia, July 4, 1863, Henry McConnell Papers, MHS; James Ramer Diary, July 19, 1863; Smith, *Tales of the Tenth Regiment*, 31; Daniels, *Journal of Sibley's Indian Expedition*, 31; Report, Colonel William Crooks to Captain R. C. Olin, August 5, 1863, U.S. War Department, *War of the Rebellion*, ser. 1, vol. 22, pt. 1, 361.

37. Connolly, *A Thrilling Narrative*, 202–203.

38. Oscar Wall Diary, July 18, 1863, MHS; Anonymous Diary, July 18, 1863, MHS; Thomas to Brothers, July 19, 1863, Thomas Montgomery Letters, MHS.

39. Diessner, *There Are No Indians Left but Me!*, 197; William to Henrietta, July 17, 1863, William and Herbert Paist Papers, MHS.

40. William to Henrietta, July 17, 1863, William and Herbert Paist Papers, MHS; Henry Hagadorn Diary, July 19, 1863, MHS; Charles to Father, July 21, 1863, Charles Watson Papers, MHS.

41. Connolly, *A Thrilling Narrative*, 221; Carter, "Reminiscence," NDHS, 18; William Marshall Journal, July 20, 1863, NDHS; George to Isadore, July 20, 1863, George C. Clapp Papers, MHS.

42. Daniels, *Journal of Sibley's Indian Expedition*, 31–32.

43. Sibley to J. F. Meline, August 23, 1863, U.S. War Department, *War of the Rebellion*, ser. 1, vol. 22, pt. 1, 908; King, "Civil War of Private Morton," 16; Charles Watson, Diary, July 21, 1863, Charles Watson Papers, MHS.

44. Daniels, *Journal of Sibley's Indian Expedition*, 33; Henry Hagadorn Diary, July 22, 1863, MHS; Thomas to Parents, July 21, 1863, Thomas Montgomery Letters, MHS.

5. THE BATTLES OF BIG MOUND, DEAD BUFFALO LAKE, AND STONY LAKE

1. Hilgered, "Narrative of Oscar One Bull," 169.

2. Iron Hoop Testimony, Sisseton and Wahpeton Bands of Sioux v. The United States, 211.

3. Daniel Paul Testimony, ibid., 236–37, 241–42; Doane Robinson, *A History of the Dakota or Sioux Indians* (Minneapolis: Ross and Haines, 1956), 318; Iron Hoop Testimony, Sisseton and Wahpeton Bands of Sioux v. The United States, 212.

4. Iron Hoop Testimony, Daniel Paul Testimony, Good Singer Testimony, Sisseton and Wahpeton Bands of Sioux v. The United States, 212, 233, 236; Diedrich, *Odyssey of Chief Standing Buffalo*, 51.

5. Iron Hoop Testimony, Daniel Paul Testimony, Sisseton and Wahpeton Bands of Sioux v. The United States, 212, 236.

6. Raymond J. DeMallie, "Lakota Belief and Ritual in the Nineteenth Century," in Raymond J. DeMallie and Douglas R. Parks, eds., *Sioux Indian Religion* (Norman: University of Oklahoma Press, 1987), 40–43.

7. Connolly, *A Thrilling* Narrative, 232; Glanville, *I Saw the Ravages of an Indian War,* 143; Daniels, *Journal of Sibley's Indian Expedition,* 34; Sibley's Report, in Board of Commissioners, *Minnesota in the Civil and Indian Wars,* vol. 2, 297–98; Hubert Eggleston Diary, July 24, 1863, Hubert Eggleston Papers, MHS; William Marshall to R. C. Olin, July 25, 1863, U.S. War Department, *War of the Rebellion,* ser. 1, vol. 22, pt. 1, 364.

8. Renville, "A Sioux Narrative of the Outbreak in 1862," n.p.; Anderson and Woolworth, *Through Dakota Eyes,* 288–89; Diedrich, *Odyssey of Chief Standing Buffalo,* 51.

9. Little Fish Testimony, Sisseton and Wahpeton Bands of Sioux v. The United States, 194; Smith and Hart, *Tales of the Tenth Regiment,* 31; Anonymous Diary, July 24, 1863, MHS; James Ramer Diary, July 24, 1863, MHS; Paulson, "General Sibley's Expedition," 7, MHS; King, "Civil War of Private Morton," 15; Oscar Wall Diary, July 24, 1863, MHS; Hunt, "Observations," MHS, 8.

10. Little Fish Testimony, Daniel Paul Testimony, Sisseton and Wahpeton Bands of Sioux v. The United States, 202, 237.

11. Paulson, "General Sibley's Expedition," MHS, 7; Diedrich, *Odyssey of Chief Standing Buffalo,* 51; Heard, *History of the Sioux War,* 322; John Danielson Diary, July 24, 1863, MHS; Robinson, *History of the Dakota,* 318.

12. Connolly, *A Thrilling Narrative,* 13, 232; Charles to Father, August 16, 1863, Charles Watson Papers, MHS; Carter, "Reminiscences," NDHS, 20.

13. Iron Hoop Testimony, Daniel Paul Testimony, "Sisseton and Wahpeton Bands of Sioux v. The United States," 212, 238.

14. Heard, *History of the Sioux War,* 321; Board of Commissioners, *Minnesota in the Civil and Indian Wars,* 311, 457.

15. Heard, *History of the Sioux War,* 322–23; Sibley to Major J. F. Meline, August 7, 1863, U.S. War Department, *War of the Rebellion,* ser. 1, vol. 22, pt. 1, 353; Sibley's Report, Board of Commissioners, *Minnesota in the Civil and Indian Wars,* vol. 2, 298; Glanville, *I Saw the Ravages of an Indian War,* 144; Paulson, "General Sibley's Expedition," MHS, 8.

16. William Marshall Journal, July 24, 1863, NDHS; Heard, *History of the Sioux War*, 323; George to Mariette, August 8, 1863, George C. Clapp and Family Papers, MHS; Thomas to Family, August 1863, Thomas Montgomery Letters, MHS.

17. Diedrich, *Odyssey of Chief Standing Buffalo*, 52; Newcombe Kinney, "Reminiscences of the Sioux Indian and Civil War," 4, MHS; Iron Hoop Testimony, "Sisseton and Wahpeton Bands," 213; Sibley to Meline, August 7, 1863, U.S. War Department, *War of the Rebellion*, ser. 1, vol. 22, pt. 1, 354.

18. Palmer, *Dakota Peoples*, 151–54, 176; Standing Bear, *Land of the Spotted Eagle*, 39; Howard, *Canadian Sioux*, 52–53.

19. Charles Bornarth Diary, July 24, 1863, MHS; Thomas to Family, August, 1863, Thomas Montgomery Letters, MHS; Diedrich, *Odyssey of Chief Standing Buffalo*, 51–52.

20. Crooks to Olin, August 5, 1863, U.S. War Department, *War of the Rebellion*, ser. 1, vol. 22, pt. 1, 361; Hill, "History of Company E," 19; Daniels, *Journal of Sibley's Indian Expedition*, 36.

21. William Marshall Journal, July 24, 1863, NDHS; George to Mariette, August 8, 1863, George C. Clapp and Family Papers, MHS; Thomas to Family, August, 1863, Thomas Montgomery Letters, MHS.

22. Carter, "Reminiscences," 20; Glanville, *A Thrilling Narrative*, 144; Heard, *History of the Sioux War*, 324–25; Diedrich, *The Odyssey of Chief Standing Buffalo*, 52.

23. Kinney, "Reminiscences of the Indian and Civil Wars," 4; McKusick, *The Iowa Northern Border Brigade*, 140; Watson, Diary, August 16, 1863, MHS; West, *Ancestry*, 309; Glanville, *A Thrilling Narrative*, 146–47.

24. Colonel James Baker to Captain R. C. Olin, August 5, 1863, U.S. War Department, *War of the Rebellion*, ser. 1, vol. 22, pt. 1, 370; Glanville, *I Saw the Ravages of an Indian War*, 145; Connolly, *A Thrilling Narrative*, 235; Hunt, "Observations," MHS, 7–8.

25. Sibley to Meline, August 7, 1863, U.S. War Department, *War of the Rebellion*, ser. 1, vol. 22, pt. 1, 354; Marshall to Olin, July 25, 1863, ibid., 364; John Daniels, Diary, July 24, 1863, MHS; George to Mariette, August 8, 1863, George C. Clapp and Family Papers, MHS; Anonymous, Diary, July 24, 1863, MHS; Carter, "Reminiscences," NDHS, 21.

26. Connolly, *A Thrilling Narrative*, 190, 194; Carter, "Reminiscences," NDHS, 20, 22.

27. August 6, 1863, Oscar Wall Diary, MHS; King, "Civil War of Private Morton," 16.

28. James Ramer Diary, July 24, 1863, MHS; Heard, *History of the Sioux War*, 324; Diedrich, *Odyssey of Chief Standing Buffalo*, 52; Daniel Paul Testimony, Sisseton and Wahpeton Bands of Sioux v. The United States, 241–42; Carter, "Reminiscences," NDHS, 22.

29. Hess, *The Union Soldier in Battle: Enduring the Ordeal of Combat in the Civil War* (Lawrence: University Press of Kansas, 1997), 6, 10, 19; McPherson, *For Cause and Comrades*, 33.

30. John to Marie, August 5, 1863, John Jones Papers, MHS; George to Mariette, August 8, 1863, George C. Clapp and Family Papers, MHS; George Clapp Diary, July 24, 1863, George C. Clapp and Family Papers, MHS.

31. Glanville, *I Saw the Ravages of an Indian War*, 145; Connolly, *A Thrilling Narrative*, 235.

32. James Ramer Diary, July 26, 1863, MHS; George to Mariette, August 8, 1863, George C. Clapp and Family Papers, MHS; Anonymous Diary, July 24, 1863, MHS; Connolly, *A Thrilling Narrative*, 236.

33. Paulson, "General Sibley's Expedition," MHS.

34. Connolly, *A Thrilling Narrative*, 235; Paulson, "General Sibley's Expedition," MHS, 9; John Pettibone Diary, July 24, 1863, MHS; Oscar Wall Diary, July 24, 1863, MHS.

35. Palmer, *Dakota Peoples*, 213–14; Diedrich, *Odyssey of Chief Standing Buffalo*, 21–22.

36. West, *Ancestry*, 312; Little Fish Testimony, Iron Hoop Testimony, Sisseton and Wahpeton Bands of Sioux v. The United States, 194–95, 212–13; Eastman, *Indian Boyhood*, 15.

37. Daniels, *Journal of Sibley's Indian Expedition*, 38; Connolly, *A Thrilling Narrative*, 238; Edwin Patch Diary, July 26, 1863, MHS; James Ramer Diary, July 26, 1863, MHS.

38. Heard, *History of the Sioux War*, 327; Glanville, *I Saw the Ravages of an Indian War*, 147; Connolly, *A Thrilling Narrative*, 237; Hunt, "Observations," MHS, 8.

39. Sibley's Report, in Board of Commissioners, *Minnesota in the Indian and Civil Wars*, vol. 2, 299–300; Richard D. Rowen, ed., "The Second Nebraska's Campaign against the Sioux," *Nebraska History* 44 (March 1963): 45; Heard, *History of the Sioux War*, 327–28; Daniels, *Journal of Sibley's Indian Expedition*, 38–39.

40. Heard, *History of the Sioux War*, 328; Danielson Diary, July 26, 1863, MHS; William Marshall Journal, July 26, 1863, NDHS; *Minnesota*

in the Indian and Civil Wars, vol. 2, 522; Connolly, *A Thrilling Narrative,* 238; George to Mariette, August 8, 1863, George C. Clapp and Family Papers, MHS.

41. Connolly, *A Thrilling Narrative,* 237; Daniels, *Journal of Sibley's Indian Expedition,* 40; Carter, "Reminiscence," NDHS, 23; West, *Ancestry,* 311; Pettibone Diary, July 26, 1863, MHS.

42. Daniels, *Journal of Sibley's Indian Expedition,* 40–41; Heard, *History of the Sioux War,* 329; Hill, "History of Company E," 20.

43. July 28, 1863, Oscar Wall Diary, MHS; Carter, "Reminiscences," 24; Daniels, *Journal of Sibley's Indian Expedition,* 41.

44. Colonel James Baker, 10th Minnesota, to R. C. Olin, August 5, 1863, U.S. War Department, *War of the Rebellion,* ser. 1, vol. 22, pt. 1, 370; Glanville, *I Saw the Ravages of an Indian War,* 148; West, *Ancestry,* 313; Paulson, "General Sibley's Expedition," 11; Kinney, "Reminiscences," MHS, 4; George to Mariette, August 8, 1863, George C. Clapp and Family Papers, MHS.

45. Sibley to Meline, August 7, 1863, U.S. War Department, *War of the Rebellion,* ser. 1, vol. 22, pt. 1, 355; Carter, "Reminiscences," NDHS, 24; July 28, 1863, Oscar Wall Diary, MHS; James Cornell, "Reminiscences of the Sibley Expedition, 1863," July 28, 1863, Small Manuscripts Collection, NDHS.

46. Heard, *History of the Sioux War,* 330; Glanville, *I Saw the Ravages of an Indian War,* 149.

47. Board of Commissioners, *Minnesota in the Indian and Civil Wars,* vol. 2, 522; Baker to Olin, August 5, 1863, U.S. War Department, *War of the Rebellion,* ser. 1, vol. 22, pt. 1, 370; Glanville, *I Saw the Ravages of an Indian War,* 155.

48. Sibley's Report, in Board of Commissioners, *Minnesota in the Indian and Civil Wars,* vol. 2, 300–301; Connolly, *A Thrilling Narrative,* 241.

49. Sibley to Meline, August 7, 1863, U.S. War Department, *War of the Rebellion,* ser. 1, vol. 22, pt. 1, 355; Carter, "Reminiscences," NDHS, 24–25; Pettibone Diary, July 28, 1863, MHS; James Ramer Diary, July 28, 1863, MHS; Heard, *History of the Sioux War,* 330–31; Anonymous Diary, July 28, 1863, MHS.

50. Connolly, *A Thrilling Narrative,* 242–46.

51. Carter, "Reminiscences," NDHS, 26.

52. Eastman, *Indian Boyhood,* 13–15; Anderson and Woolworth, *Through Dakota Eyes,* 270.

53. Diessner, *There Are No Indians Left but Me!*, 36–37; Kurt D. Bergemann, *Brackett's Battalion: Minnesota Cavalry in the Civil War and Dakota War* (St. Paul: Borealis Books, 2004), 110.

54. Daniels, *Journal of Sibley's Indian Expedition*, 42; John Smith and James R. Hart, *Tales of the Tenth Regiment, Minnesota Volunteers, 1862–1863* (n.p.: Joseph R. Brown Heritage Society, 1996), 10.

55. Crooks to Olin, August 5, 1863, U.S. War Department, *War of the Rebellion*, ser. 1, vol. 22, pt. 1, 363; Daniels, *Journal of Sibley's Indian Expedition*, 43–44; Pettibone Diary, July 29, 1863, MHS; Hill, "History of Company E," 20; Edwin Patch Diary, July 29, 1863, MHS; Kinney, "Reminiscences," MHS, 5.

56. Carter, "Reminiscences," NDHS, 26; Connolly, *A Thrilling Narrative*, 247; Offenburg and Parsonage, *The War Letters of Duren F. Kelley*, 151; Charles to Father, August 16, 1863, Charles Watson Papers, MHS.

57. Loren Collins, "Memorandum of the Sibley Expedition," July 29, 1863, MHS; Connolly, *A Thrilling Narrative*, 247–48, 251; James Ramer, Diary, July 30, 1863, MHS; Cornell, "Reminiscences of the Sibley Expedition, 1863," NDHS; Heard, *History of the Sioux War*, 331.

58. Sibley to Meline, August 7, 1863, U.S. War Department, *War of the Rebellion*, ser. 1, vol. 22, pt. 1, 357; Heard, *History of the Sioux War*, 332–34.

59. Heard, *History of the Sioux War*, 332; August 1, 1863, Oscar Wall Diary, MHS; Daniels, *Journal of Sibley's Indian Expedition*, 46, 49; Carter, "Reminiscences," NDHS, 28; Charles to Father, August 16, 1863, Charles Watson Papers, MHS.

60. Carter, "Reminiscences," NDHS, 28; Daniels, *Journal of Sibley's Indian Expedition*, 49–50; Connolly, *A Thrilling Narrative*, 252–53.

61. Patch Diary, August 2 and 3, 1863, MHS; Carter, "Reminiscences," NDHS, 27; Connolly, *A Thrilling Narrative*, 190.

6. SULLY'S 1863 EXPEDITION

1. Ingersoll, *Iowa and the Rebellion*, 680–81; Eagan, "General Sully," 31; Rowen, "Second Nebraska's Campaign," 3–4; Pattee, "Reminiscences," 291–92; Clair Jacobson, "The Battle of Whitestone Hill," *North Dakota History* 44, no. 3 (Summer 1972): 6.

2. Kim Allen Scott and Ken Kempcke, "A Journey to the Heart of Darkness: John W. Wright and the War against the Sioux, 1863–1865,"

Montana: The Magazine of Western History 50, no. 4 (Winter 2000): 3–4; Drips, *Three Years among the Indians in Dakota,* 2; Frank Myers, *Soldering in Dakota, Among the Indians; in 1863–4–5* (Huron, N. Dak.: Huronite Printing House, 1888), 4; Throne, "Iowa Troops," 135.

3. Scott and Kempcke, "Journey to the Heart of Darkness," 5; Throne, "Iowa Troops," 138, 157; Drips, *Three Years among the Indians,* 2.

4. Siegmund to Rosanah, May 24, May 27, June 7, 1863, Siegmund Rothammer Papers, SDHS.

5. Stambaugh, "Iowa Troops," 413–15; Throne, "Iowa Troops," 136, 139, 147.

6. Schell, *History of South Dakota,* 79; Bean, "General Alfred Sully," 242; George W. Kingsnorth, "The Sully Expedition," Western History Collections, University of Oklahoma Library (hereinafter cited as UOL).

7. Siegmund to Rosanah, April 18, May 5, 1863, Siegmund Rothammer Papers, SDHS; David Wilson to Wife Henrietta, April 10, 1863, ISHS.

8. Stambaugh, "Iowa Troops," 416.

9. Throne, "Iowa Troops," 155–56.

10. Abner English, "Dakota's First Soldiers," *South Dakota Historical Collections* 9 (Pierre: South Dakota Historical Society, 1918): 265; Drips, *Three Years among the Indians,* 33; Goodwin, "Letters of Private Milton Spencer," 248; Siegmund to Rosanah, June 20, 1863, Siegmund Rothammer Papers, SDHS; Pattee, "Reminiscences," 293.

11. English, "Dakota's First Soldiers," 265; Drips, *Three Years among the Indians,* 33; Throne, "Iowa Troops," 157; Goodwin, "Letters of Private Milton Spencer," 245; Pattee, "Reminiscences," 293; Siegmund to Rosanah, June 20, 1863, Siegmund Rothammer Papers, SDHS.

12. Siegmund to Rosanah, June 20, 1863, Siegmund Rothammer Papers, SDHS; Throne, "Iowa Troops," 158.

13. Siegmund to Rosanah, May 27, 1863, Siegmund Rothammer Papers, SDHS; Rowen, "The Second Nebraska's Campaign," 15–16, 29; English, "Dakota's First Soldiers," 244; Drips, *Three Years among the Indians,* 26.

14. Sully, *No Tears for the General,* 129–30, 193–94, 234; Josephy, *Civil War in the West,* 141.

15. Throne, "Iowa Troops," 159; Goodwin, "Letters of Private Milton Spencer," 245; Siegmund to Rosanah, July 4, 1863, Siegmund Rothammer Papers, SDHS.

16. Siegmund to Rosanah, July 12, 1863, Siegmund Rothammer Papers, SDHS; Rowen, "Second Nebraska's Campaign," 29; Albert to Ellsworth, July 18, 1863, Albert Childs Letters, Wisconsin Historical Society (hereinafter cited as WHS).

17. Carol G. Goodwin, ed., "The Letters of Private Milton Spencer, 1862–1865: A Soldier's View of Military Life on the Northern Plains," *North Dakota History* 37, no. 4 (Fall 1970): 242; Siegmund to Rosanah, June 5, June 8, 1863, Siegmund Rothammer Papers, SDHS; Rowen, "Second Nebraska's Campaign," 10, 27.

18. Siegmund to Rosanah, June 7, 1863, Siegmund Rothammer Papers, SDHS; Goodwin, "Letters of Private Milton Spencer," 244.

19. Hassrick, *The Sioux*, 174–75; Gibbon, *The Sioux*, 84.

20. Hassrick, *The Sioux*, 279, 281; John G. Neihardt, trans., *Black Elk Speaks: Being the Life of a Holy Man of the Oglala Sioux* (Lincoln: University of Nebraska Press, 1988), 97–98; Pond, *Dakota or Sioux in Minnesota*, 102; Throne, "Iowa Troops," 154.

21. Siegmund to Rosanah, June 7, 1863, Siegmund Rothammer Papers, MHS.

22. *Yankton Weekly Dakotan*, July 28, 1863; Throne, "Iowa Troops," 162; Newton Edmunds to William P. Dole, September 20, 1864, *Report of the Commissioner of Indian Affairs for 1863*, Annual Reports of the Commissioner of Indian Affairs, 1830–1870.

23. Albert to Ellsworth, August 25, 1863, Albert Childs Letters, WHS; Rowen, "The Second Nebraska's Campaign," 37.

24. Pope to Sully, August 5, August 25, August 31, 1863, U.S. War Department, *War of the Rebellion*, ser. 1, vol. 22, pt. 2, 434, 496, 503.

25. Bean, "General Alfred Sully," 251; Sully to Meline, September 11, 1863, U.S. War Department, *War of the Rebellion*, ser. 1, vol. 22, pt. 1, 555; Drips, *Three Years among the Indians*, 37; Rowen, "Second Nebraska's Campaign," 7, 38–39.

26. Drips, *Three Years among the Indians*, 37–38.

27. Ibid., 38; Rowen, "Second Nebraska's Campaign," 20; Goodwin, "Letters of Private Milton Spencer," 249.

28. James Thomson Diary, August 20, 1863, NDHS; Drips, *Three Years among the Indians*, 39.

29. Throne, "Iowa Troops," 165.

30. Ibid., 166; Rowen, "Second Nebraska's Campaign," 21; English, "Dakota's First Soldiers," 266; Drips, *Three Years among the Indians*, 41.

31. Throne, "Iowa Troops," 166; Rowen, "Second Nebraska's Campaign," 21, 43; Sully to Meline, August 26, 1863, U.S. War Department, *War of the Rebellion*, ser. 1, vol. 22, pt. 1, 556.

32. Palmer, *Dakota People*, 101; DeMallie, "Lakota Belief and Ritual in the Nineteenth Century," 31–32; Gibbon, *The Sioux*, 84; Diedrich, *The Odyssey of Chief Standing Buffalo*, 16.

33. Palmer, *Dakota People*, 96; Hassrick, *The Sioux*, 198–99; Rosenfelt, *The Last Buffalo*, 27; Neihardt, *Black Elk Speaks*, 53.

34. Neihardt, *Black Elk Speaks*, 56–57; Palmer, *Dakota People*, 98; Hilger, "Narrative of Oscar One Bull," 167.

35. Hilger, "Narrative of Oscar One Bull," 167; Hassrick, *The Sioux*, 201; Neihardt, *Black Elk Speaks*, 58–59.

36. Sully to Meline, September 11, 1863, U.S. War Department, *War of the Rebellion*, ser. 1, vol. 22, pt. 1, 556–57; Rowen, "Second Nebraska's Campaign," 22–23, 44–45; Belden, *The White Chief: Or, Twelve Years among the Wild Indians of the Plains* (New York: C. F. Vent, 1870), 357; Hassrick, *The Sioux*, 112–13.

37. John to Marie, August 5, 1863, John Jones Papers, MHS; Offenburg and Parsonage, *War Letters of Duren F. Kelley*, 67.

38. Eli to Philena, August 7, 1863, Eli Pickett Correspondence, MHS.

39. Henry Hagadorn Diary, August 9, 1863, MHS; George to Mariette, August 14, 1863, George C. Clapp and Family Papers, MHS.

40. Daniels, *Journal of Sibley's Indian Expedition*, 53, 55, 58–59, 64; Henry Hagadorn Diary, August 21, 1863, MHS.

41. Myers, *Soldiering in Dakota*, 7; Jacobson, "Battle of Whitestone Hill," 7.

7. WHITESTONE HILL

1. Throne, "Iowa Troops," 167; Drips, *Three Years among the Indians*, 53; Rowen, "Second Nebraska's Campaign," 23.

2. Drips, *Three Years among the Indians*, 53; J. C. Luse, "The Battle of Whitestone Hill," *South Dakota Historical Collections* 5 (Pierre: South Dakota Historical Society, 1910), 417; Jacobson, "Battle of Whitestone Hill," 7.

3. Luse, "Battle of Whitestone Hill," 417–18; Bean, "General Alfred Sully," 241; Jacobson, "Battle of White Stone Hill," 7; Author interview

with La Donna Allard, Yanktonai tribal genealogist, February 11, 2009; James Thomson Diary, September 3, 1863, NDHS.

4. Jacobson, "The Battle of Whitestone Hill," 11–12; Report of Major Albert House, September 3, 1963, U.S. War Department, *War of the Rebellion*, ser. 1, vol. 22, pt. 1, 564; Diedrich, *Odyssey of Standing Buffalo*, 54, 62; Galler, "Sustaining the Sioux Confederation," 484.

5. Aaron McGaffey Beede, *Heart-in-the-Lodge: All a Mistake*, 3, 7–8, 13, 20, Aaron McGaffey Beede and Ralph Gordon Beede Papers, University of North Dakota Library.

6. Doane Robinson, *A History of the Dakota or Sioux Indians* (Minneapolis: Ross and Haines, 1956), 327; Bean, "Battle of Whitestone Hill," 253; Cozzens, *General John Pope*, 234.

7. Author interview with La Donna Allard, April 27, 2007; author interview with Ambrose Little Ghost, May 2, 2007.

8. Luse, "Battle of Whitestone Hill," 417–18; Drips, *Three Years among the Indians*, 54; House Report, September 3, 1863, U.S. War Department, *War of the Rebellion*, ser. 1, vol. 22, pt. 1, 564; Kingsnorth, "Sully Expedition," UOL, 17–18.

9. Sully, *No Tears for the General*, 173–74; Throne, "Iowa Troops," 168; James Thomson Diary, September 3, 1863, NDHS; Rowen, "Second Nebraska's Campaign," 46.

10. Throne, "Iowa Troops," 167–69; Siegmund to Rosanah, November 13, 1863, Siegmund Rothammer Papers, SDHS.

11. Sully, *No Tears for the General*, 174; Joseph S. Phebus to Orin Grant Libby, December 6, 1915, Orin Grant Libby Papers, NDHS.

12. Drips, *Three Years among the Indians*, 55; Throne, "Iowa Troops," 170–72, Luse, "Battle of Whitestone Hill," 418.

13. Throne, "Iowa Troops," 169, 170; Sully to Meline, September 3, 1863, U.S. War Department, *War of the Rebellion*, ser. 1, vol. 22, pt. 1, 558; Sully, *No Tears for the General*, 174; Myers, *Soldiering in Dakota*, 8.

14. Drips, *Three Years among the Sioux*, 56; Ruth Landes, "Dakota Warfare," *Journal of Anthropological Research* 44, no. 3 (Autumn 1986): 47; Palmer, *Dakota People*, 156; Sully, *No Tears for the General*, 175.

15. Belden, *White Chief*, 359–60; Rowen, "Second Nebraska's Campaign," 46; Jacobson, "Battle of Whitestone Hill," 9.

16. Goodwin, "Letters of Private Milton Spencer," 251; Throne, "Iowa Troops," 170, 173; Scott and Kempcke, "Journey to the Heart of Darkness," 7; Rowen, "Second Nebraska's Campaign," 46–47.

17. Luse, "Battle of Whitestone Hill," 419; Goodwin, "Letters of Private Milton Spencer," 251; Throne, "Iowa Troops," 170–71; Belden, *White Chief*, 360; Rowen, "Second Nebraska's Campaign," 47; author interview with La Donna Allard, February 11, 2009.

18. Report of Colonel David Wilson, in U.S. War Department, *War of the Rebellion*, ser. 1, vol. 22, pt. 1, 562; Drips, *Three Years among the Indians*, 46; Report of Colonel Robert Furnas, in U.S. War Department, *War of the Rebellion*, ser. 1, vol. 22, pt. 1, 565.

19. McKusick, *Iowa Northern Border Brigade*, 138; Drips, *Three Years among the Indians*, 45; Sully to Meline, September 3, 1863, U.S. War Department, *War of the Rebellion*, ser. 1, vol. 22, pt. 1, 559–60; Beede, *Heart-in-the-Lodge*, 28; author interview with La Donna Allard, February 11, 2009.

20. Drips, *Three Years among the Indians*, 45; Rowen, "Second Nebraska's Campaign," 48; Siegmund to Rosanah, November 13, 1863, Siegmund Rothammer Papers, SDHS; Sully to Meline, September 3, 1863, U.S. War Department, *War of the Rebellion*, ser. 1, vol. 22, pt. 1, 559; Phebus to Libby, December 6, 1915, Orin Grant Libby Papers, NDHS; McKusick, *Iowa Northern Brigade*, 138.

21. Sully to Meline, September 3, 1863, U.S. War Department, *War of the Rebellion*, ser. 1, vol. 22, pt. 1, 557; Luse, "Battle of Whitestone Hill," 417.

22. Drips, *Three Years among the Indians*, 45; Rowen, "Second Nebraska's Campaign," 47; Throne, "Iowa Troops," 170–71; Belden, *White Chief*, 360–61.

23. Rowen, "Second Nebraska's Campaign," 24, 47; Throne, "Iowa Troops," 171.

24. Throne, "Iowa Troops," 171; Phebus to Libby, December 6, 1915, Orin Grant Libby Papers, NDHS.

25. Rowen, "Second Nebraska's Campaign," 49; Jacobson, "Battle of Whitestone Hill," 10; Belden, *White Chief*, 366.

26. Rowen, "Second Nebraska's Campaign," 171.

27. Drips, *Three Years among the Indians*, 46; Sully to Meline, September 3, 1863, U.S. War Department, *War of the Rebellion*, ser. 1, vol. 22, pt. 1, 559; Standing Bear, *Land of the Spotted Eagle*, 84.

28. Sully, *No Tears for the General*, 175; Rowen, "Second Nebraska's Campaign," 24, 48; Kingsnorth, "Sully Expedition," UOL, 17–18; Belden, *White Chief*, 367–68.

29. Luse, "Battle of Whitestone Hill," 419; Drips, *Three Years among the Indians*, 49, 51.

30. Kingsnorth, "Sully Expedition," UOL, 18; Bean, "General Alfred Sully," 254; Josephy, *Civil War in the American West*, 146; Danziger, "Crow Creek Experiment," 110–11.

31. Diedrich, *Odyssey of Chief Standing Buffalo*, 56; Elias, *Dakota of the Canadian Northwest*, 22; Eastman, *Indian Boyhood*, 15–16; Diessner, *There are no Indians left but Me!*, 202.

32. Sully, *No Tears for the General*, 178; Pope to Halleck, August 20, 1863, U.S. War Department, *War of the Rebellion*, ser. 1, vol. 22, pt. 1, 463; Ellis, *General Pope and US Indian Policy*, 29.

33. Albert to Ellsworth, August 25, 1863, Albert Childs, Letters, WHS; King, "Civil War of Private Milton Spencer," 17; Daniels, Journal of Sibley's Indian Expedition, 33, MHS; Hunt, "The Observations of T. J. Hunt," 9.

34. Diessner, *There Are No Indians Left but Me!*, 200–201; *Minneapolis State Atlas*, September 23, 1863; *Yankton Dakotian*, October 13, 1863; *St. Paul Weekly Press*, November 19, 1863.

35. Cozzens, *General John Pope*, 235–36; Pope to Sibley, August 29, 1863, U.S. War Department, *War of the Rebellion*, ser. 1, vol. 22, pt. 1, 498.

36. *Mankato Semi-Weekly Record*; Robert Perry to William Rice, August 18, 1863, MHS.

37. Siegmund to Rosanah, October 10, 1863, Siegmund Rothammer Papers, SDHS; Mother to Hubert, August 28, 1863, Hubert Eggleston Papers, MHS.

38. J. B. Hoffman to N. Edmunds, August 20, 1864, *Report of the Commissioner of Indian Affairs for 1863*; Goodwin, "Letters of Private Milton Spencer," 256.

8. SULLY'S 1864 EXPEDITION

1. Halleck to Pope, January 17, 1864, U.S. War Department, *War of the Rebellion*, ser. 1, vol. 34, pt. 2, 100.

2. Pope to Sibley, January 18, 1864, ibid., 109; Pope to Sully, January 18, 1864, ibid., 110; Josephy, *Civil War in the American West*, 147; Ellis, *General Pope and U.S. Indian Policy*, 52–53.

3. Halleck to Pope, February 14, 1864, U.S. War Department, ser. 1, vol. 34, pt. 2, 330.

4. Sibley to Editors of Pioneer and Editors of Press, March 9, 1864, ibid., 541; Utley, *Frontiersmen in Blue*, 214, 274; Diessner, *There Are No Indians Left but Me!*, 192.

5. Sibley to Pope, April 26, 1864, U.S. War Department, ser. 1, vol. 34, pt. 2, 306; Sibley to Pope, March 23, 1864, ibid., 712; Sully to Sibley, April 28, 1864, ibid., 330; Pope to Sully, ibid., 219–20.

6. R. C. Olin to E. A. C. Hatch, March 9, 1864, ibid., 540; Pope to Halleck, May 4, 1864, ibid., 447; Pope to Edmunds, ibid.

7. Myers, *Soldering in Dakota among the Indians*, 9; David Kingsbury, "Sully's Expedition against the Sioux in 1864," *Collections of the Minnesota Historical Society*, vol. 8, (St. Paul: Minnesota Historical Society Press, 1898), 449; Nicholas Hilger, "General Alfred Sully's Expedition of 1864" *Contributions to the Historical Society of Montana*, vol. 2 (Helena: Rocky Mountain Publishing Company, 1907), 322; Heard, *History of the Sioux War*, 337.

8. Kurt D. Bergemann, *Bracket's Battalion*, 9, 101; Goodwin, "Letters of Private Milton Spencer," 254, 256.

9. Albert to Ellsworth, [n.d.], Albert Childs Letters, WHS; James Thomson Diary, April 27, 1864, NDSH.

10. Kingsbury, "Sully's Expedition," 450; John to Libbie, October 11, 1864, John Robinson Letter, MHS; English, "Dakota's First Soldiers," 273.

11. Sibley to Pope, March 23, 1864, U.S. War Department, *War of the Rebellion*, ser. 1, vol. 34, pt. 2, 712; Lieutenant Colonel Edward Barlett, February 6, 22, 1864, Fort Sully, Letters Sent, RG 98, National Archives; Anderson and Woolworth, *Through Dakota Eyes*, 278; Diedrich, *Odyssey of Chief Standing Buffalo*, 60.

12. Diedrich, *Odyssey of Chief Standing Buffalo*, 59; Anderson and Woolworth, *Through Dakota Eyes*, 271.

13. Howard, *Canadian Sioux*, 28; Elias, *Dakota of the Canadian Northwest*, 23; Sibley to Pope, March 15, 1864, U.S. War Department, *War of the Rebellion*, ser. 1, vol. 34, pt. 2, 625.

14. Board of Commissioners, *Minnesota in the Civil and Indian Wars*, vol. 1, 386–87; William Love, *Wisconsin in the War of the Rebellion* (Chicago: Church and Goodman Publishers, 1866), 833–35; Pope to Sully, May 3, 1864, U.S. War Department, *War of the Rebellion*, ser. 1, vol. 34, pt. 2, 427; Bergemann, *Brackett's Battalion*, 12–16, 89–90.

15. Halleck to Pope, February 8, 1864, U.S. War Department, *War of the Rebellion*, ser. 1, vol. 34, pt. 2, 275; Curtis to Pope, March, 1864, ibid., 652; Pope to Halleck, April 5, 1864, ibid., pt. 3, 56; Pope to Halleck, March 30, 1864, ibid., pt. 2, 792–93; Halleck to Pope, April 3, 1864, ibid., pt. 3, 33; Halleck to Pope, May 25, 1864, ibid., pt. 4, 40.

16. Ellis, *General Pope and U.S. Indian Policy*, 56–58.

17. Sibley to Pope, February 11, 1864, U.S. War Department, *War of the Rebellion*, ser. 1, vol. 34, pt. 2, 303; Pope to Sibley, February 11, 1864, ibid., 303–304.

18. Sibley to Pope, April 9, 1864, ibid., pt. 3, 113–14; Sibley to Pope, June 9, 1984, ibid., pt. 4, 288–89.

19. Sibley to Pope, May 20, 1864, ibid., pt. 3, 694; Pope to Sibley, May 21, 1864, ibid., 712; *Mankato Record Weekly*, May 7, 1864.

20. A. N. Judd, *Campaigning against the Sioux* (New York: Sol Lewis, 1974), 12, 13, 16; John to Libbie, October 11, 1864, John Robinson Letter, MHS.

21. Goodwin, "Letters of Private Milton Spencer," 252; Connelly, *A Thrilling Narrative*, 260; George Doud Diaries, July 17, 1864, MHS; Merrill to Carrie, September 25, 1864, G. Merrill Dwelle Papers, MHS.

22. Albert to Ellsworth, March 27, 1864, Albert Childs Letters, WHS; Robrock, "Seventh Iowa Cavalry," 8; Throne, "Iowa Troops," 177.

23. Board of Commissioners, *Minnesota in the Civil and Indian Wars*, vol. 1, 389; Kingsbury, "Sully's Expedition," 451.

24. Olin to Colonel M. T. Thomas, May 25, 1864, U.S. War Department, *War of the Rebellion*, ser. 1, vol. 34, pt. 4, 41; Robert McLaren Diary, June 6, 1864, Robert McLaren Papers, MHS; Charles Hughes Diary, [n.d.], MHS.

25. Ebenezer Rice Diary, June 6, 1864, MHS; George Doud Diaries, June 6, June 7, June 9, 1864, MHS; Paxton, "Diary kept by Lewis C. Paxton," 137.

26. Sibley to Jennings, March 10, 1864, U.S. War Department, *War of the Rebellion*, ser. 1, vol. 34, pt. 2, 560; "Notice to Emigrants by way of the Missouri River and Upper Plains to the Idaho Mines," ibid., 608–609; Sully, *No Tears for the General*, 181; Bergemann, *Brackett's Battalion*, 103.

27. Robert McLaren Diary, June, 1864, Robert McLaren Papers, MHS; Connelly, *A Thrilling Narrative*, 258.

28. Kingsbury, "Sully's Expedition," 453; John to Libbie, October 11, 1864, John Robinson Letter, MHS; George Doud Diaries, June 15, 1864, MHS; Hodgson, *Personal Recollections of the Sioux War*, 27; John to Libbie, October 11, 1864, John Robinson Letter, MHS.

29. Charles Hughes Diary, June 25, 1864, MHS; Kingsbury, "Sully's Expedition," 451.

30. Kingsbury, "Sully's Expedition," 452; Robert McLaren Diary, June 29, June 30, 1864, Robert McLaren Papers, MHS; David Jenkins Diary, June 30, 1864, David Jenkins Papers, MHS.

31. Drips, *Three Years among the Indians*, 67; Myers, *Soldering in Dakota*, 26; Sully to Pope, June 21, 1864, U.S. War Department, *War of the Rebellion*, ser. 1, vol. 34, pt. 4, 497.

32. Pattee, "Reminiscences," 303; Pope to Fielner, April 15, 1864, U.S. War Department, *War of the Rebellion*, ser. 1, vol. 34, pt. 3, 169.

33. Pattee, "Reminiscences," 303; English, "Dakota's First Soldiers," 274; Myers, *Soldiering in Dakota*, 10; Siegmund Rothammer Diary, June 29, 1864, Siegmund Rothammer Papers, SDHS.

34. Sylvester Sterling Campbell Diaries, June 28, 1864, NDHS; James Thomson Diary, June 28, 1864, NDHS; Throne, "Iowa Troops," 182.

35. Pattee, "Reminiscences," 284; Ole Oland Diary, June 28, 1864, NDHS; English, "Dakota's First Soldiers," 276.

36. Judd, *Campaigning against the Sioux*, 3.

37. Drips, *Three Years among the Indians*, 69; English, "Dakota's First Soldiers," 278; Bergemann, *Brackett's Battalion*, 102.

38. Drips, *Three Years among the Sioux*, 70; Sully to Pope, September 9, 1864, U.S. War Department, *War of the Rebellion*, ser. 1, vol. 34, pt. 1, 151.

39. Abner English Diary, July 3, 1864, SDHS; Eli Williamson Diary, July 2, July 4, 1864, MHS; Drips. *Three Years among the Sioux*, 71; Ole Oland Diary, July 4, 1864, NDHS.

40. Hodgson, *Personal Recollections of the Sioux War*, 28.

41. Siegmund Rothammer Diary, July 5, 1864, Siegmund Rothammer Papers, SDHS.

42. George Doud Diary, July 6, 1864, George Doud Diaries, MHS; Siegmund Rothammer Diary, July 7, 1864, Siegmund Rothammer Papers, SDHS, English, "Dakota's First Soldiers," 280.

43. Paxton, "Diary Kept by Lewis C. Paxton," 140; Bergemann, *Brackett's Battalion*, 104; Pattee, "Reminiscences," 306.

44. David Jenkins Diary, July 10, July 22, 1864, David Jenkins Papers, MHS; George Doud Diaries, July 16, 1864, MHS; John Henry Strong, "A Journal of the Northwestern Indian Expedition under General Sully," July 10, 1864, MHS; Leonard to Joseph, July 10, 1864, Leonard Aldrich Papers, MHS.

45. David Jenkins, Dairy, July 17, 1864, David Jenkins Papers, MHS; Eli Williamson Diary, July 17, 1864, MHS; Pattee, "Reminiscences," 306; Judd, *Campaigning against the Sioux*, 7.

46. Myers, *Soldiering in Dakota*, 12.

47. Ole Oland Diary, July 21, 1864, MHS; William Silvas Diary, January 1–November 4, 1864, July 21, 1864, MHS; Robert McLaren Diary, July 22, 1864, Robert McLaren Papers, MHS; Paxton, "Diary Kept by Lewis C. Paxton," 141.

48. Robert McLaren Diary, July 24, 1864, Robert McLaren Papers, MHS; Myers, *Soldiering in Dakota*, 13.

49. Alfred Sully Report, July 31, 1864, U.S. War Department, *War of the Rebellion*, ser. 1, vol. 41, pt. 1, 142.

50. George Doud Diaries, July 26, 1864, MHS; Scott and Kempcke, "Journey to the Heart of Darkness," 9; Judd, *Campaigning against the Sioux*, 9; Drips, *Three Years among the Indians in Dakota*, 76; Robert McLaren Diary, July 26, 1864, Robert McLaren Papers, MHS; Stambaugh, "Iowa Troops," 422; Pattee, "Reminiscences," 306.

51. Board of Commissioners, *Minnesota in the Civil and Indian Wars*, vol. 1, 544; James Thomson Diary, July 27, 1864, NDHS; Alfred Sully Report, July 31, 1864, U.S. War Department, *War of the Rebellion*, ser. 1, vol. 34, pt. 1, 142.

9. THE BATTLE OF KILLDEER MOUNTAIN

1. George Doud Diaries, July 28, 1864, MHS; English, "Dakota's First Soldiers," 281; Myers, *Soldiering in Dakota*, 14.

2. Drips, *Three Years among the Indians*, 77; Myers, *Soldiering in Dakota*, 14; John to Libbie, October 11, 1864, John Robinson Letter, MHS; Bergemann, *Brackett's Battalion*, 107–108; Scott and Kempcke, "Journey to the Heart of Darkness," 9; Board of Commissioners, *Minnesota in the Civil and Indian Wars*, vol. 1, 672.

3. Pattee, "Reminiscences," 308; Kingsbury, "Sully's Expedition," 454.

4. Pattee, "Reminiscences," 307; English, "Dakota's First Soldiers," 282; Samuel Pollock Report, in U.S. War Department, *War of the Rebellion*, ser. 1, vol. 41, pt. 1, 157; Kingsbury, "Sully's Expedition," 454; Kingsnorth, "Sully Expedition," 21.

5. Bergemann, *Brackett's Battalion*, 110; author's correspondence with Ernie LaPointe, November 12, 2008; Robert W. Larson, *Gall: Lakota War Chief* (Norman: University of Oklahoma Press, 2007), 45; Diessner, *There Are No Indians Left but Me!*, 43.

6. Walter Camp Collection, Box 105, Notebook 24, 1–2, Western History Collections, UOL.

7. Sully Report, July 31, 1864, U.S. War Department, *War of the Rebellion*, ser. 1, vol. 41, pt. 1, 142–43; Pattee, "Reminiscences," 307; Robert McLaren Diary, July 28, 1864, Robert McLaren Papers, MHS; English, "Dakota's First Soldiers," 282; Drips, *Three Years among the Sioux*, 77; Bergemann, *Brackett's Battalion*, 108.

8. Stambaugh, "Iowa Troops," 370; Throne, "Iowa Troops," 184–85; Andrew Fisk Diary, July 28, 1864, James Liberty Fisk Family Papers, MHS; Harlen Page Bruch, "Army Services of Harlen Page Bruch: Adventurer, Soldier and Settler of Pioneer Days," 2, NDHS.

9. Judd, *Campaigning against the Sioux*, 9; Sully Report, July 31, 1864, U.S. War Department, *War of the Rebellion*, ser. 1, vol. 41, pt. 1, 142; Throne, "Iowa Troops," 186; Kingsnorth, "Sully Expedition," 21.

10. Hassrick, *The Sioux*, 99; Gibbon, *The Sioux*, 72; Walter Camp Collection, Box 105, Notebook 24, 2, Western History Collections, UOL; Bergemann, *Brackett's Battalion*, 111.

11. Ben Brunson, "Reminiscences," 5, MHS; Pattee, "Reminiscences," 308.

12. Hodgson, "Personal Recollections of the Sioux War," 29; Oneroad and Skinner, *Being Dakota*, 65; Hilger, "General Alfred Sully's Expedition," 323; George Doud Diaries, July 28, MHS.

13. Andrew Fisk Diary, July 28, 1864, James Liberty Fisk Papers, MHS; Kingsbury, "Sully's Expedition," 456; Bruch, "Army Services of Harlan Page Bruch," 2.

14. John Henry Strong, "A Journal of the Northwestern Indian Expedition under General Sully," July 24, 1864, MHS; Diessner, *There Are No Indians Left but Me!*, 43; Bergemann, *Brackett's Battalion*, 111; Kingsbury, "Sully's Expedition," 454; John to Libbie, October 11, 1864, John Robinson Letter, MHS; Abner English Diary, July 28, 1864, SDHS.

15. Walter Camp Collection, Box 105, Notebook 24, 4, Western History Collections, UOL.

16. Ibid., 5–6; Bergemann, *Brackett's Battalion*, 112.

17. Myers, *Soldiering in Dakota*, 14; John to Libbie, October 11, 1864, John Robinson Letter, MHS.

18. David Jenkins Diary, July 28, 1864, David Jenkins Papers, MHS; Robert McLaren Diary, July 28, 1864, Robert McLaren Papers, MHS; Ebenezer Rice Diary, July 28, 1864, MHS; Scott and Kempcke, "Journey to the Heart of Darkness," 6.

19. John Barsness and William Dickinson, "The Sully Expedition of 1864," *Western History* 33, no. 3 (July 1966): 24; Kingsnorth, "Sully

Expedition," 21; Sully, *No Tears for the General*," 187; Kingsbury, "Sully's Expedition," 454; Bergemann, *Brackett's Battalion*, 111; Hodgson, "Personal Recollections of the Sioux War," 30.

20. Judd, *Campaigning against the Sioux*, 9; Myers, *Soldiering in Dakota*, 15; Hilger, "General Alfred Sully's Expedition," 323.

21. English, "Dakota's First Soldiers," 281–82; Sylvester Sterling Campbell Dairy, July 28, 1864, MHS; Myers, *Soldiering in Dakota*, 15; Report of Captain Nelson Minor, August 2, 1864, U.S. War Department, *War of the Rebellion*, ser. 1, vol. 41, pt. 1, 162.

22. Drips, *Three Years among the Sioux*, 78; Throne, "Iowa Troops," 188; Goodwin, "Letters of Private Milton Spencer," 261.

23. Kingsbury, "Sully's Expedition," 454; Myers, *Soldiering in Dakota*, 16; Report of Major Alfred Brackett, U.S. War Department, *War of the Rebellion*, ser. 1, vol. 41, pt. 1, 161; Board of Commissioners, *Minnesota in the Civil and Indian Wars*, vol. 1, 581.

24. Bergemann, *Brackett's Battalion*, 112–13, 115; Judd, *Campaigning against the Sioux*, 9.

25. Drips, *Three Years among the Indians*, 78–79; Strong, "Journal of the Northwestern Indian Expedition," July 24, 1864, MHS; Report of Major Alfred Brackett, August 1, 1864, U.S. War Department, *War of the Rebellion*, ser. 1, vol. 41, pt. 1, 161.

26. Bergemann, *Brackett's Battalion*, 115; Strong, "Journal of the Northwestern Indian Expedition," July 24, 1864, MHS.

27. Walter Camp Collection, Box 105, Notebook 24, 4, Western History Collections, UOL.

28. Hodgson, "Personal Recollections of the Sioux War," 30–31; Report of Captain Stufft, August 2, 1864, U.S. War Department, *War of the Rebellion*, ser. 1, vol. 41, pt. 1, 163.

29. Myers, *Soldiering in Dakota*, 16; Kingsbury, "Sully's Expedition," 455.

30. Stambaugh, "Iowa Troops," 423; Kingsbury, "Sully's Expedition," 456; English, "Dakota's First Soldiers," 283; Judd, *Campaigning against the Sioux*, 12; Stambaugh, "Iowa Troops," 371; Brunson, "Reminiscences," MHS, 7; Kingsbury, "Sully's Expedition," 456; Scott and Kempcke, "Journey to the Heart of Darkness," 7; Myers, *Soldiering in Dakota*, 16.

31. English, "Dakota's First Soldiers," 283; Throne, "Iowa Troops," 188.

32. Myers, *Soldiering in Dakota*, 17; Sully, *No Tears for the General*, 188.

33. David Jenkins Diary, July 29, 1864, David Jenkins Papers, MHS; English, "Dakota's First Soldiers," 283; Myers, *Soldiering in Dakota*, 17; Report of Robert McLaren, July 29, 1864, U.S. War Department, *War of the Rebellion*, ser. 1, vol. 41, pt. 1, 173.

34. Robert McLaren Diary, July 29, 1864, Robert McLaren Papers, MHS; English, "Dakota's First Soldiers," 283; Stambaugh, "Iowa Troops," 423; Hodgson, "Personal Recollections of the Sioux War," 31; Kingsbury, "Sully's Expedition," 456.

35. Throne, "Iowa Troops," 185; Myers, *Soldiering in Dakota*, 17; Merrill to Carrie, September 25, 1864, G. Merrill Dwelle Papers, MHS.

36. Throne, "Iowa Troops," 185; Drips, *Three Years among the Indians*, 79; Myers, *Soldiering in Dakota*, 17; Board of Commissioners, *Minnesota in the Civil and Indian Wars*, vol. 1, 546.

37. Throne, "Iowa Troops," 185; George Doud Diaries, July 30, 1864, MHS; Kingsbury, "Sully's Expedition," 455; Hodgson, "Personal Recollections of the Sioux War," 34; Hilger, "General Alfred Sully's Expedition," 324.

38. David Jenkins Diary, July 31, 1864, David Jenkins Papers, MHS.

10. THE FIGHT IN THE BADLANDS

1. Sully, *No Tears for the General*, 188–89; Board of Commissioners, *Minnesota in the Civil and Indian Wars* vol. 1, 547; Stambaugh, "Iowa Troops," 424.

2. Stambaugh, "Iowa Troops," 371, 424; Robert McLaren Diary, August 5, 1864, Robert McLaren Papers, MHS; Scott and Kempcke, "Journey to the Heart of Darkness," 13; Hilger, "General Alfred Sully's Expedition," 315.

3. Report of Alfred Sully, August 13, 1864, U.S. War Department, *War of the Rebellion*, ser. 1, vol. 41, pt. 1, 144; Hilger, "General Alfred Sully's Expedition," 315; Judd, *Campaigning against the Sioux*, 12.

4. Bergemann, *Brackett's Battalion*, 122; Palmer, *Dakota People*, 152; Barsness and Dickinson, "Sully Expedition of 1864," 29.

5. Diessner, *There Are No Indians Left but Me!*, 44.

6. Report of Alfred Sully, U.S. War Department, *War of the Rebellion*, ser. 1, vol. 41, pt. 1, 147.

7. Connolly, *A Thrilling Narrative*, 264–65; Judd, *Campaigning against the Sioux*, 12; English, "Dakota's First Soldiers," 284; Kingsbury, "Sully's Expedition," 457.

8. English, "Dakota's First Soldiers," 285; Report of Alfred Sully, August 13, 1864, U.S. War Department, *War of the Rebellion,* ser. 1, vol. 41, pt. 1, 145; Sully, *No Tears for the General*, 189; Pattee, "Reminiscences," 311; Hilger, "General Alfred Sully's Expedition," 316; Drips, *Three Years among the Indians*, 81.

9. Bergemann, *Brackett's Battalion*, 121; Hilger, "General Alfred Sully's Expedition," 317.

10. Pattee, "Reminiscences," 311; Report of Alfred Sully, August 13, 1864, U.S. War Department, *War of the Rebellion,* ser. 1, vol. 41, pt. 1, 145.

11. Report of Alfred Sully, August 13, 1864, U.S. War Department, *War of the Rebellion,* ser. 1, vol. 41, pt. 1, 145; Judd, *Campaigning against the Sioux*, 12.

12. Pattee, "Reminiscences," 311.

13. Hilger, "General Alfred Sully's Expedition," 317, 319; Sully, *No Tears for the General*, 189.

14. Hilger, "General Alfred Sully's Expedition," 317; Judd, *Campaigning against the Sioux*, 13.

15. English, "Dakota's First Soldiers," 285.

16. Myers, *Soldiering in Dakota*, 19; Stambaugh, "Iowa Troops," 372.

17. Goodwin, "Letters of Private Milton Spencer," 261; Hilger, "General Alfred Sully's Expedition," 316; Report of Alfred Sully, August 13, 1864, U.S. War Department, *War of the Rebellion,* ser. 1, vol. 41, pt. 1, 146; Scott and Kempcke, "Journey to the Heart of Darkness," 13; Charles Hughes Diary, August 7, 1864, MHS.

18. Stambaugh, "Iowa Troops," 372; English, "Dakota's First Soldiers," 285; David Jenkins Diary, August 7, 1864, David Jenkins Papers, MHS.

19. Sully, *No Tears for the General*, 190; Hilger, "General Alfred Sully's Expedition of 1864," 318; Eli Williamson Diary, August 7, 1864, MHS.

20. English, "Dakota's First Soldiers," 285; Judd, *Campaigning against the Sioux*, 15.

21. Hilger, "General Alfred Sully's Expedition," 318.

22. Stambaugh, "Iowa Troops," 372; Pattee, "Reminiscences," 312.

23. Myers, *Soldiering in Dakota*, 20; Barsness and Dickinson, "Sully Expedition of 1864," 28, Robert McLaren Diary, August 8, 1864, MHS.

24. Strong, "Journal of the Northwestern Indian Expedition," August 8, 1864, MHS; Report of Minor Thomas, August 13, 1864, U.S. War Department, *War of the Rebellion*, ser. 1, vol. 41, pt. 1, 167; Hilger, "General Alfred Sully's Expedition of 1864," 325; Drips, *Three Years among the Indians*, 83.

25. Sully, *No Tears for the General*, 190–91; Myers, *Soldiering in Dakota*, 21; Strong, "Journal of the Northwestern Indian Expedition," August 8, 1864, MHS; Hilger, "General Alfred Sully's Expedition of 1864," 325; Drips, *Three Years among the Indians*, 83.

26. Judd, *Campaigning against the Sioux*, 13.

27. Ibid., 14; English, "Dakota's First Soldiers," 286.

28. George Campbell, "Reminiscence," 25, George T. Campbell and Family Papers, MHS; Judd, *Campaigning against the Sioux* 13; Drips, *Three Years among the Indians*," 82–83.

29. English, "Dakota's First Soldiers," 287–88.

30. Rothfuss, "German Witness of the Sioux Campaigns," 131–32; Robert McLaren Diary, August 8, 1864, Robert McLaren Papers, MHS.

31. Pattee, "Reminiscences," 313; Myers, *Soldiering in Dakota*, 21; English, "Dakota's First Soldiers," 288.

32. Walter Camp Collection, Box 105, Notebook 24, 8, Western Historical Collections, UOL.

33. Ibid, 9–10.

34. George Doud Diaries, August 8, 1864, MHS; Hodgson, "Personal Recollections of the Sioux War," 35.

35. Judd, *Campaigning against the Sioux*, 18; Hilger, "General Alfred Sully's Expedition," 325; David Jenkins Diary, August 8, 1864, David Jenkins Papers, MHS; Stambaugh, "Iowa Troops," 425; Hodgson, "Personal Recollections of the Sioux War," 34.

36. Hilger, "General Sully's Expedition of 1864," 319; Myers, *Soldiering in Dakota*, 21–22.

37. James Liberty Fisk Diary, August 8, 1864, James Liberty Fisk Family Papers, MHS; Judd, *Campaigning against the Sioux*, 15.

38. Stambaugh, "Iowa Troops," 373; Drips, *Three Years among the Indians*, 84.

39. Drips, *Three Years among the Indians*, 84; Bergemann, *Brackett's Battalion*, 124.

40. English, "Dakota's First Soldiers," 289; Stambaugh, "Iowa Troops," 373, 425.

41. Scott and Kempcke, "Journey to the Heart of Darkness," 14; Sully, *No Tears for the General*, 196; Myers, *Soldering in Dakota*, 23; Stambaugh, "Iowa Troops," 425.

42. Drips, *Three Years among the Indians*, 85; George Doud Diaries, August 11, 1864, MHS.

43. Myers, *Soldiering in the Dakotas*, 24; English, "Dakota's First Soldiers," 290; Kingsbury, "Sully's Expedition," 459.

44. Bruch, "Army Services of Harlen Page Bruch," NDHS, 3; Stambaugh, "Iowa Troops," 373; Strong, "Journal of the Northwestern Indian Expedition," August 12, 1864, MHS.

45. Charles Hughes Diary, August 14, 1864, MHS; Paxton, "Diary kept by Lewis C. Paxton," 142; Stambaugh, "Iowa Troops," 426.

46. Kingsbury, "Sully's Expedition," 460; Report of Alfred Sully, August 18, 1864, U.S. War Department, *War of the Rebellion*, ser. 1, vol. 41, pt. 1, 148; James Thomson Diary, August 17, 1864, NDHS.

47. Hodgson, "Personal Recollections of the Sioux War," 35; Paxton, "Diary kept by Lewis C. Paxton," 142.

48. Paxton, "Diary kept by Lewis C. Paxton," 143; William Silvis Diary, August 20–23, 1864, MHS.

49. Abner English Diary, September 5, 1864, SDHS; Charles Hughes Diary, September 5, 1864, MHS; Thomas Priestly Diary, September 7, 1864, MHS.

50. Drips, *Three Years among the Indians*, 91; Pattee, "Reminiscences," 316–17.

51. John to Libbie, October 11, 1864, John Robinson Letter, MHS.

52. Drips, *Three Years among the Indians*, 93.

53. Ibid., 92; Diessner, *There Are No Indians Left but Me!*, 45; Larson, *Gall: Lakota War Chief*, 50.

54. Drips, *Three Years among the Indians*, 92; Love, *Wisconsin in the War of the Rebellion*, 835–36; Report of Alfred Sully, September 11, 1864, U.S. War Department, *War of the Rebellion*, ser. 1, vol. 41, pt. 1, 152.

55. Bruch, "Army Services of Harlen Page Bruch," 4, NDHS; Hodgson, "Personal Recollections of the Sioux War," 36–37.

56. Drips, *Three Years among the Indians*, 93–94; Myers, *Soldiering in the Dakotas*, 31.

57. Drips, *Three Years among the Indians*, 95.

58. Abner English Diary, September 19, 1864, SDHS; Albert to Ellsworth, August 1, 1864, Albert Childs Letters, WHS.

59. Chelsey Pratt Poem, Chelsey Pratt Family Papers, MHS.

60. Myers, *Soldiering in Dakota*, 31; Drips, *Three Years among the Indians*, 96–97; Stambaugh, "Iowa Troops," 374, 439.

11. AFTERMATH

1. Report of Alfred Sully, September 11, 1864, U.S. War Department, *War of the Rebellion*, ser. 1, vol. 41, pt. 1, 154–55; Leonard to Joseph, September 16, 1864, Leonard Aldrich Papers, MHS.

2. Utley, *Frontiersmen in Blue*, 280; Josephy, *Civil War in the American West*, 152–53.

3. Sully, *No Tears for the General*, 200.

4. Ibid.

5. *Mankato Semi-Weekly Record*, May 6, 1865; Diedrich, *Odyssey of Chief Standing Buffalo*, 67.

6. Danziger, "Crow Creek Experiment," 112–13, 137.

7. Diedrich, *Odyssey of Chief Standing Buffalo*, 61; Meyer, *History of the Santee Sioux*, 198.

8. Ellis, "Political Pressures and Army Politics on the Northern Plains, 1862–1865," 43; Elias, *Dakota of the Canadian Northwest*, 26.

9. Lamar, *Dakota Territory*, 105; Bean, "General Alfred Sully," 255; Schell, *History of South Dakota*, 86–87; Meyer, *History of the Santee Sioux*, 198; Danziger, "Crow Creek Experiment," 121.

10. Meyer, *History of the Santee Sioux*, 258–60, 264–65.

11. Ezra J. Warner, *Generals in Blue: Lives of the Union Commanders* (Baton Rouge: University of Louisiana Press, 1964), 377, 445–46;

12. Sully, *No Tears for the General*, 217, 219, 233.

13. Paxton, "Diary kept by Lewis C. Paxton," 163.

Bibliography

PRIMARY RECORDS

GOVERNMENT RECORDS

Annual Reports of the Commissioner of Indian Affairs, 1830–1870. Report of 1863.

Dakota Superintendency. Office of Indian Affairs. Letters Received and Sent. Record Group 62. National Archives. Washington, D.C.

Fort Ridgely. Letters Received. Record Group 393. National Archives. Washington, D.C.

Fort Sully, Letters Sent. Record Group 89. National Archives. Washington, D.C.

Roster and Record of Iowa Soldiers in the War of the Rebellion. 6 vols. Des Moines: Emory English State Printers, 1910.

The Sisseton and Wahpeton Bands of Sioux Indians v. The United States. Original Petition no. 22524, Court of Claims. Washington, D.C.: McGill and Wallace Law Printers, 1876–1906.

U.S. Congress. House. *Annual Report, Secretary of War*. H Doc. 83, 38th Congress, 2nd Session, 1865.

U.S. Congress. House. *Report of the Secretary of Interior*. H Doc. 1, 37th Congress, 3rd Session, 1862.

U.S. War Department. *The War of the Rebellion: A Compilation of the Official Records of the Union and Confederate Armies*. 128 vols. Washington, D.C.: Government Printing Office, 1891–95.

MANUSCRIPT COLLECTIONS

Iowa State Historical Society
Osborn, Philip. Papers.
Wilson, David. Letters.

Minnesota Historical Society
Adams, George. Papers.
Aldrich, Leonard. Papers.
Anonymous. Diary.
Bornarth, Charles. Diary.
Brunson, Ben. "Reminiscences."
Campbell, George T., and Family. Papers.
Carlson, Pehr, and Family. Papers.
Cheetham, Thomas James. Letters.
Clapp, George C., and Family. Papers.
Collins, Loren. "Memorandum of the Sibley Expedition."
Danielson, John. Diary.
Doud, George. Diaries.
Dwelle, G. Merrill. Papers.
Eggleston, Hubert. Papers.
Fisk, James Liberty, Family. Papers.
Griswold, Frank. Papers.
Hagadorn, Henry. Diary.
Hamlin, Jacob. Papers.
Horton, Charles. Papers.
Hughes, Charles. Diary.
Hunt, Thomas Jefferson. "Observations of T. J. Hunt in the Sioux Indian and Civil Wars of 1862–1865: A Narrative in the Military Life of T. J. Hunt."
Jenkins, David. Papers.
Jones, John. Papers.
Kinney, Newcombe. "Reminiscences of the Sioux Indian and Civil Wars."

Leo, John. Letters.
McConnell, Henry. Papers.
McLaren, Robert. Papers.
Montgomery, Thomas. Letters.
Paist, William and Herbert. Papers.
Patch, Edwin. Diary.
Paulson, Ole. "General Sibley's Expedition."
Perry, Robert. Letter.
Pettibone, John. Diary.
Pickett, Eli. Correspondence.
Pratt, Chelsey. Papers.
Priestly, Thomas. Diary.
Ramer, James. Diary.
Rice, Ebenezer. Diary.
Robinson, John. Letter.
Silvas, William. Diary.
Stay, Celia Campbell. Papers.
Strong, John Henry. "A Journal of the Northwest Indian Expedition under General Sully."
Synder, Henry J. Papers.
Wal, Oscar. Diary.
Walters, Ransom. Diary.
Watson, Charles. Papers.
Williamson, Eli. Diary.

North Dakota Historical Society

Bruch, Harlen Page. "Army Services of Harlen Page Bruch: Adventurer, Soldier and Settler of Pioneer Days."
Campbell, Sylvester Sterling. Diaries.
Carter, Theodore. "Reminiscences of the Sibley Expedition of 1863."
Cornell, James. "Reminiscences of the Sibley Expedition, 1863."
Libby, Orin Grant. Papers.
Marshall, William. Journal.
Oland, Ole. Diary.
Thomson, James. Diary.

South Dakota Historical Society

English, Abner. Diary.
Rothammer, Siegmund. Papers

University of North Dakota Library

Beede, Aaron McGaffey. *Heart-in-the-Lode: All a Mistake.* Aaron Mc-Gaffey Beede and Ralph Gordon Beede Papers.

University of Oklahoma Library

Camp, Walter. Collection. Western History Collections.

Kingsnorth, George W. "The Sully Expedition." Western History Collections.

Wisconsin Historical Society

Childs, Albert. Letters.

BOOKS AND ARTICLES

Anderson, Gary Clayton, and Alan R. Woolworth. *Through Dakota Eyes: Narrative Accounts of the Minnesota Indian War of 1862.* St. Paul: Minnesota Historical Society Press, 1988.

Belden, George P. *The White Chief: Or, Twelve Years among the Wild Indians of the Plains.* New York: C. F. Vent, 1870.

Bettelyoun, Susan Bordeaux, and Josephine Waggoner. *With My Own Eyes: A Lakota Woman Tells Her People's History,* edited by Emily Levine. Lincoln: University of Nebraska Press, 1998.

Bishop, Judson W. *The Story of a Regiment: Being a Narrative of the Service of the Second Regiment Minnesota Veteran Volunteer Infantry in the Civil War of 1861–1865,* edited by Newell Chester. St. Cloud, Minn.: North Star Press of St. Cloud, 2000.

Board of Commissioners. *Minnesota in the Civil and Indian Wars, 1861–1865.* 2 vols. St. Paul: Pioneer Press, 1890.

Connelly, A. P. *A Thrilling Narrative of the Minnesota Massacre and the Sioux War of 1862–1863.* Chicago: A. P. Connelly, 1896.

Daniels, Arthur, *Journal of Sibley's Indian Expedition during the summer of 1863 and Record of the Troops Employed.* Minneapolis: James D. Thueson, 1980.

Drips, J. H. *Three Years among the Indians in Dakota.* New York: Sol Lewis, 1974.

Eastman, Charles. *Indian Boyhood.* Boston: Little, Brown and Company, 1926.

Eastman, Enoch. "Portions of the Diary of Enoch Eastman, Co. E Hatch's Battalion of Minnesota Volunteers, with Sibley's Expedition of 1863."

North Dakota Historical Quarterly 1, no. 3 (April 1927): 41–45; ibid., no. 4 (July 1927): 12–13; ibid., no. 2 (January 1928): 126–27.

English, Abner. "Dakota's First Soldiers." *South Dakota Historical Collections* 9:241–307. Pierre: South Dakota Historical Society, 1918.

Forough, Andrea R., ed. *Go If You Think It Your Duty: A Minnesota Couple's Civil War Letters.* St. Paul: Minnesota Historical Society Press, 2008.

Glanville, Amos E. *I Saw the Ravages of an Indian War: A Diary by Amos Glanville Sr. Company F, 10th Minnesota Volunteers.* John K. Glanville, privately published, 1988.

Goodwin, Carol G., ed. "The Letters of Private Milton Spencer, 1862–1865: A Soldier's View of Military Life on the Northern Plains." *North Dakota History* 37, no. 4 (Fall 1970): 232–69.

Harris, Ruth-Ann M. "Civil War Soldier, Christopher Byrne, Writes Home." Paper delivered at the American Conference for Irish Studies, Minneapolis, June 2003.

Hilger, Nicholas. "General Alfred Sully's Expedition of 1864." *Contributions to the Historical Society of Montana*, vol. 2. Helena: Rocky Mountain Publishing Company, 1907.

Hilgered, Inez. "The Narrative of Oscar One Bull." *Mid-America: An Historical Review* 28, no. 3 (July 1946): 147–72.

Hill, Alfred J. "History of Company E. of the Sixth Minnesota Regiment of Volunteer Infantry." Published by Prof. T. H. Lewis. St. Paul: Pioneer Press, 1899.

Hodgson, Thomas C. *Personal Recollections of the Sioux War: With the Eighth Minnesota, Company F.* Transcribed by Robert Olson. Roseville, Minn.: Park Genealogical Books, 1999.

Ingersoll, Lurton Dunham. *Iowa and the Rebellion.* Philadelphia: J. B. Lippincott and Co., 1866.

Judd, A. N. *Campaigning against the Sioux.* New York: Sol Lewis, 1974.

King, James, ed. "The Civil War of Private Morton" *North Dakota History* 35, no. 1 (Winter 1968): 232–69.

Kingsbury, David. "Sully's Expedition against the Sioux in 1864." *Collections of the Minnesota Historical Society*, vol. 8. St. Paul: Minnesota Historical Society, 1898.

Meyers, Frank. *Soldiering in Dakota, Among the Indians; in 1863–4–5.* Huron, S. Dak.: Huronite Printing House, 1888.

Neihardt, John G., trans. *Black Elk Speaks: Being the Life of a Holy Man of the Oglala Sioux.* Lincoln: University of Nebraska Press, 1988.

Offenberg, Robert S., and Robert Rue Parsonage, eds. *The War Letters of Duren F. Kelley.* New York: Pageant Press, 1967.

Oneroad, Amos A, and Alanson B. Skinner. *Being Dakota: Tales and Traditions of the Sisseton and Wahpeton,* edited by Laura L. Anderson. St. Paul: Minnesota Historical Society, 2003.

Pattee, John. "Reminiscences of John Pattee." *South Dakota Historical Collections* 5: 275–350. Pierre: State Publishing Company, 1910.

Paxton, Lewis C. "Diary Kept by Lewis C. Paxton." *Collections of the State Historical Society of North Dakota* 2, issue pt. 2: 102–63. Minot: North Dakota Historical Society, 1908.

Pond, Samuel W. *The Dakota or Sioux in Minnesota as They Were in 1863.* St. Paul: Minnesota Historical Society Press, 1986.

Renville, Gabriel. "A Sioux Narrative of the Outbreak in 1862, and of Sibley's Expedition in 1863." http://www.archive.org/stream/siouxnarrativeofoorenvrich/siouxnar.

Riggs, Stephen, ed. "The Narrative of Paul Mazakootermane." *Collections of the Minnesota Historical Society* 3:82–90. St. Paul: Minnesota Historical Society Press, 1870–1880.

Rothfuss, Hermann. "German Witness of the Sioux Campaign." *North Dakota History* 25, no. 4 (October 1958): 123–33.

Rowen, Richard D., ed. "The Second Nebraska's Campaign against the Sioux." *Nebraska History* 44 (March 1963): 3–53.

Scott, Kim Allen, and Ken Kempcke. "A Journey to the Heart of Darkness: John W. Wright and the War against the Sioux, 1863–1865." *Montana: Magazine of Western History* 50, no. 4 (Winter 2000): 2–17.

Smith, John, and James R. Hart. *Tales of the Tenth Regiment, Minnesota Volunteers, 1862–1863.* Henderson, Minn.: Sibley County Historical Society, 1996.

Stambaugh, Benjamin, ed. "Iowa Troops in the Sully Campaigns." *The Iowa Journal of History and Politics* 20, no. 3 (July 1922): 364–443.

Standing Bear, Luther. *Land of the Spotted Eagle.* Boston: Houghton Mifflin Company, 1933.

Throne, Mildred, ed. "Iowa Troops in Dakota Territory, 1861–1865: Based on the Diaries and Letters of Henry J. Wieneke." *Iowa Journal of History* 57, no. 2 (April 1959): 97–190.

INTERVIEWS

Ambrose Little Ghost, May 2, 2007
Ernie LaPointe, November 12, 2008
La Donna Allard, Yanktonai tribal genealogist, April 27, 2007, February 11, 2009,

NEWSPAPERS

Mankato Semi-Weekly Record
Mankato Weekly Record
Minneapolis State Atlas
St. Paul Pioneer and Democratic Weekly
St. Paul Press
St. Paul Weekly Press
Yankton Weekly Dakotian

SECONDARY SOURCES

BOOKS AND ARTICLES

Anderson, Gary Clayton. *Kinsmen of Another Kind: Dakota-White Relations in the Upper Mississippi Valley, 1650–1862.* St. Paul: Minnesota Historical Society Press, 1997.

———. *Little Crow: Spokesman for the Sioux.* St. Paul: Minnesota Historical Society Press, 1986.

Athearn, Robert. *Forts of the Upper Missouri.* Englewood Cliffs, N.J.: Prentice-Hall, 1967.

Babcock, Willoughby M. "Minnesota's Frontier: A Neglected Sector of the Civil War." *Minnesota History* 38, no. 6 (1963): 274–86.

Barsness, John, and William Dickinson. "The Sully Expedition of 1864." *Western History* 33, no. 3 (July 1966): 23–29.

Bean, Geraldine. "General Alfred Sully and the Northwest Indian Expedition." *North Dakota History* 33, no. 3 (Summer 1966): 240–59.

Beck, Paul N. *The First Sioux War: The Grattan Fight and Blue Water Creek, 1854–1856.* Lanham, Md.: University Press of America, 2004.

———. *Inkpaduta: Dakota Leader.* Norman: University of Oklahoma Press, 2008.

Bergemann, Kurt D. *Brackett's Battalion: Minnesota Cavalry in the Civil War and Dakota War*. St. Paul: Borealis Books, 2004.

Carlson, Paul H. *The Plains Indians*. College Station, Texas: A and M University Press, 1998.

Cox, Hank H. *Lincoln and the Sioux Uprising of 1862*. Nashville: Cumberland House Publishing, 2005.

Cozzens, Peter. *General John Pope: A Life for the Nation*. Urbana and Chicago: University of Illinois Press, 2000.

Danziger, Edmond Jefferson, Jr. *Indians and Bureaucrats*. Urbana: University of Illinois Press, 1974.

———. "The Crow Creek Experiment: An Aftermath of the Sioux War of 1862." *North Dakota History* 37 (Spring 1970): 104–23.

Deloria, Ella. *Speaking of Indians*. Lincoln: University of Nebraska Press, 1998.

DeMallie, Ramond J. "Lakota Belief and Ritual in the Nineteenth Century." In *Sioux Indian Religion*, edited by Douglas R Parks and Ramond J. DeMallie. Norman: University of Oklahoma Press, 1987.

Diedrich, Mark. *Famous Chiefs of the Eastern Sioux*. Minneapolis: Coyote Books, 1987.

———. *The Odyssey of Chief Standing Buffalo*. Minneapolis: Coyote Books, 1988.

Diessner, Don. *There Are No Indians Left but Me!: Sitting Bull's Story*. El Sequndo, Calif.: Upton and Sons Publishers, 1993.

Eagan, William. "General Sully and That Other Seventh Cavalry." *True West* 37, no. 9 (September 1990): 30–34.

Elias, Peter Douglas. *The Dakota of the Canadian Northwest*. Winnipeg: University of Manitoba Press, 1988.

Ellis, Richard. *General Pope and U.S. Indian Policy*. Albuquerque: University of New Mexico Press, 1970.

———. "The Humanitarian Generals." *Western Historical Quarterly* 3, no. 2 (April 1972): 169–78.

———. "Political Pressures and Army Politics on the Northern Plains, 1862–1865." *Minnesota History* 42 (Summer 1970): 43–53.

Folwell, William W. *A History of Minnesota*. 4 vols. St. Paul: Minnesota Historical Society, 1956.

Galler, Robert W., Jr. "Sustaining the Sioux Confederation: Yanktonai Initiatives and Influences on the North Plains, 1690–1880." *Western Historical Quarterly* 34, no. 4 (Winter 2008): 467–90.

Gibbon, Guy. *The Sioux: The Dakota and Lakota Nations.* Malden, Mass.: Blackwell Publishers, 2003.

Gilman, Rhoda R. *Henry Hastings Sibley: Divided Heart.* St. Paul: Minnesota Historical Society Press, 2004.

Hassrick, Royal B. *The Sioux: Life and Customs of a Warrior Society.* Norman: University of Oklahoma Press, 1964.

Heard, Isaac V. D. *History of the Sioux War.* New York: Harper and Brothers Publishers, 1865.

Hening, Gerald S. "A Neglected Cause of the Sioux Uprising." *Minnesota History* 45, no. 3 (1976): 107–10.

Hess, Earl. *Liberty, Virtue, and Progress: Northerners and Their War for the Union.* New York: New York University Press, 1988.

————. *The Union Soldier in Battle: Enduring the Ordeal of Combat in the Civil War.* Lawrence: University Press of Kansas, 1997.

Howard, James H. *The Canadian Sioux.* Lincoln: University of Nebraska Press, 1984.

Hyde, George. *Red Cloud's Folk.* Norman: University of Oklahoma Press, 1976.

Jacobson, Clair. "The Battle of Whitestone Hill." *North Dakota History* 44, no. 3 (Summer 1972): 4–14.

Josephy, Alvin M., Jr. *The Civil War in the American West.* New York: Alfred A. Knopf, 1991.

Keenan, Jerry. *The Great Sioux Uprising.* Cambridge, Mass.: Da Capo Press, 2003.

Lamar, Howard L. *Dakota Territory, 1861–1889: A Study in Frontier Politics.* New Haven, Conn.: Yale University Press, 1956.

Landes, Ruth. "Dakota Warfare." *Journal of Anthropological Research* 44, no. 3 (Autumn 1986): 239–48.

Larson, Robert. *Gall: Lakota War Chief.* Norman: University of Oklahoma Press, 2007.

Lee, L. P. *History of the Spirit Lake Massacre.* Iowa City: State Historical Society of Iowa, 1918.

Linderman, Gerald F. *Embattled Courage: The Experience of Combat in the American Civil War.* New York: Free Press, 1987.

Love, William. *Wisconsin in the War of the Rebellion.* Chicago: Church and Goodman Publishers, 1866.

Luse, J. C. "The Battle of Whitestone Hill." *South Dakota Historical Collections* 5:417–19. Pierre: South Dakota Historical Society, 1910.

Manning, Chandra. "A 'Vexed Question': White Union Soldiers on Slavery and Race." In *The View from the Ground: Experiences of Civil War Soldiers*, edited by Aaron Sheedan-Dean. Lexington: University of Kentucky Press, 2007.

Martin, James. *Civil War America: Voices from the Home Front.* Santa Barbara, Calif.: ABC-CLIO, 2003.

McKusick, Marshall. *The Iowa Northern Border Brigade.* Iowa City: University of Iowa Press, 1975.

McPherson, James M. *For Cause and Comrades: Why Men Fought in the Civil War.* New York: Oxford University Press, 1997.

Meyer, Roy W. *History of the Santee Sioux: United States Indian Policy on Trial.* Lincoln: University of Nebraska Press, 1967.

Milton, John R. *South Dakota: A History.* New York: W. W. Norton and Company, 1977.

Mitchell, Reid. *Civil War Soldiers.* New York: Viking Press, 1988.

———. *The Vacant Chair: The Northern Soldier Leaves Home.* Oxford: Oxford University Press, 1993.

Nicholas, David A. *Lincoln and the Indians: Civil War Policy and Politics.* Columbus: University of Missouri Press, 1978.

Palmer, Jessica Palmer. *The Dakota Peoples: A History of the Dakota, Lakota and Nakota through 1863.* Jefferson, N.C.: McFarland and Company, 2008.

Paul, R. Eli. *Blue Water Creek and the First Sioux War, 1854–1856.* Norman: University of Oklahoma Press, 2004.

Rice, Julian. *Before the Great Spirit: The Many Faces of Sioux Spirituality.* Albuquerque: University of New Mexico Press, 1998.

Robinson, Doane. *A History of the Dakota or Sioux Indians.* Minneapolis: Ross and Haines, 1956.

Robrock, David P. "The Seventh Iowa Cavalry and the Plains Wars." *Montana* 39, no. 2 (Spring 1989): 2–17.

Rosenfelt, Willard E. *The Last Buffalo: Cultural Views of the Plains Indians: The Sioux or Dakota Nation.* Minneapolis: T. S. Denison and Company, 1973.

Schell, Herbert. *History of South Dakota.* Pierre: South Dakota Historical Society Press, 2004.

Smith, John, and James R. Hart. *Tales of the Tenth Regiment, Minnesota Volunteers, 1862–1863.* N.p.: Joseph R. Brown Heritage Society, 1996.

Sturtevant, William C. *Handbook of North American Indians.* 17 vols. Washington, D.C.: Smithsonian Institution, 2001.

Sully, Landon. *No Tears for the General: The Life of Alfred Sully*. Palo Alto, Calif.: American West Publishing Company, 1974.

Swanholm, Max. *Alexander Ramsey and the Politics of Survival*. St. Paul: Minnesota Historical Society Press, 1977.

Utley, Robert. *Frontiersmen in Blue*. Lincoln: University of Nebraska Press, 1967.

Wall, Joseph Frazier. *Iowa: A Bicentennial History*. New York: W. W. Norton and Company, 1976.

Warner, Ezra J. *Generals in Blue: Lives of the Union Commanders*. Baton Rouge: University of Louisiana Press, 1964.

Waziyatawin. *What Does Justice Look Like?: The Struggle for Liberation in Dakota Homeland*. St. Paul. Living Justice Press, 2008.

West, Nathaniel. *Ancestry, Life and Times of Hon. Henry Hasting Sibley*. St. Paul: Pioneer Press, 1889.

White, Richard, "The Winning of the West: The Expansion of the Western Sioux in the Eighteenth Century." In *Major Problems in American Indian History*, edited by Alberto Hurtado and Peter Iverson, 243–57. Lexington, Mass.: D. C. Heath and Company, 1994.

Index